POWER
SHARING

Oxford Studies in Anthropological Linguistics
William Bright, General Editor

Recent Volumes Published:

POWER SHARING

Language, Rank,
Gender, and
Social Space in
Pohnpei, Micronesia

Elizabeth Keating

New York   Oxford
Oxford University Press
1998

Oxford University Press

Oxford   New York

Athens   Auckland   Bangkok   Bogotá   Bombay   Buenos Aires   Calcutta
Cape Town   Chennai   Dar es Salaam   Delhi   Florence   Hong Kong   Istanbul
Karachi   Kuala Lumpur   Madrid   Melbourne   Mexico City   Mumbai
Nairobi   Paris   São Paulo   Singapore   Taipei   Tokyo   Toronto   Warsaw

and associated companies in
Berlin   Ibadan

Copyright © 1998 by Elizabeth Keating

Published by Oxford University Press, Inc.
198 Madison Avenue, New York, New York 10016

Oxford is a registered trademark of Oxford University Press, Inc.

Library of Congress Cataloging-in-Publication Data
Keating, Elizabeth Lillian.
Power sharing : language, rank, gender, and social space in
Pohnpei, Micronesia / Elizabeth Keating.
p. cm. — (Oxford studies in anthropological linguistics : 23)
Includes bibliographical references and index.
ISBN 0-19-511197-4
1. Chiefdoms—Micronesia (Federated States)—Madolenihmw District
(Pohnpei)   2. Power (Social sciences)—Micronesia (Federated
States)—Madolenihmw District (Pohnpei)   3. Sex role—Micronesia
(Federated States)—Madolenihmw District (Pohnpei)   4. Language and
culture—Micronesia (Federated States)—Madolenihmw District
(Pohnpei)   5. Micronesian languages—Honorific.   6. Micronesian
languages—Sex differences.   7. Madolenihmw District (Pohnpei,
Micronesia)—Social life and customs.   I. Title.   II. Series.
GN671.C3K43 1998
306.44'09966—dc21   98-36857

1   3   5   7   9   8   6   4   2

Printed in the United States of America
on acid-free paper

To my parents

Preface

Whenhen I first arrived on the island of Pohnpei in 1990, I went to the district of Madolenihmw, in the southeast part of the island, because I had introduction credentials to the people of that community through my family. I was very fortunate that once it was understood that I wanted to study the language and the daily life, the secondary chief and chieftess of Madolenihmw invited me to stay at their residence. Later I found this to be a most appropriate choice as traditionally the secondary chief and chieftess interfaced with outsiders and the paramount chief and chieftess remained more secluded.

Although the secondary chief was well into his seventies by then, he had an appreciation for the power of videotape and he enthusiastically encouraged the videorecording of daily and ceremonial practices. I was fortunate to have such support, as well as a never-ending supply of tolerance for my naive behaviors. The secondary chieftess became one of my most important consultants.

During other field trips to Madolenihmw, including my extended visit in 1992–93, I was fortunate to also stay for a time with the paramount chief and chieftess. This gave me a wider perspective on the Pohnpeian chiefly system and the use of honorifics in daily life. The paramount chieftess and secondary chieftess were gracious and helpful, and anxious to fatten me up to meet expectations about women's beauty (this was a perennial goal of my island hostesses), and to present the proper image of a woman of authority.

I had the help of many Pohnpeian consultants, including the Nanmwarki (paramount chief) of Madolenihmw, Likend (paramount chieftess), Nahnken (secondary chief), and Nahnken Iei (secondary chieftess). I would especially like to thank the current Likend (the former Nahnken Iei) for her expert care and guidance and her wisdom in helping me navigate between two cultures. Soulik en Peinyap (Adolihno David) and Nalik (Bernet Silbanuz) watched videotapes with me and explained many details. Alicy Poll Ehtse clarified many points. Mindy Smith and Maria Spegal spent long hours transcribing and translating, and I am very grateful to them. Mammer Perin gave me insights from her experience as an "outer islander" living in Pohnpei. I would like to gratefully acknowledge the help and support of all these people, as well as especially Father Cavanagh and staff members at the Pohnpeian Agriculture and Trade School and also Fran Hezel, S.J. and Greg Mulhaupt, S.J. Sister Dasco and Sister Maria Pz-Caballero assisted me in innumerable ways during my field stays in Pohnpei, sustaining me both intellectually and nutritionally. Very special thanks is due to the many Pohnpeians who generously consented to be videotaped and were so kind and helpful during my fieldwork.

In California I had the help of several Pohnpeians in transcribing and translating and in clarifying ethnographic and language details: Marianne Ladore, who also assisted me in Pohnpei in 1995, the Walters family, and Tony Oliver.

This book would not have been possible without the support and guidance of Alessandro Duranti, who introduced me to the exciting field of linguistic anthropology and whose work and dedication are always an inspiration to me. I would also like to thank Tim Earle, Manny Schegloff, Asif Ahga, and Marcyliena Morgan for their expert help on earlier versions of this work. Others whose reading of drafts helped clarify and enrich this work include Candy Goodwin, Maria Egbert, Karen Nero, Joel Sherzer, and Ward Keeler. I would also like to acknowledge my debt to former colleagues at the Max Planck Institute for Psycholinguistics, including Shanley Allen, Melissa Bowerman, Penny Brown, Martha Crago, Eve Danziger, Susan Duncan, James Essegbey, Claus Heeschen, Henriette Hendriks, Kyoko Inoue, Sotaro Kita, Steve Levinson, Eric Pederson, Eva Schultze-Berndt, Gunter Senft, Christel Stolz, David Wilkins, and Roberto Zavala, for many stimulating and inspiring discussions about language during my term as a research fellow there. I would also like to thank Ann Walters of UCLA and Edith Sjoerdsma of the Max Planck Institute for providing generous, warm, and skillful help in institutional navigation. I also wish to express my thanks to my editors Bill Bright and Peter Ohlin.

Any mistakes and omissions of course are my own responsibility.

I would like to thank my family for their encouragement and support, particularly my parents. I am indebted to my aunt and uncle George and Barbara Peabody for providing me with an introduction to the chiefs and chieftesses of Madolenihmw through their long and generous efforts helping to establish and sustain the Pohnpeian Agriculture and Trade School first envisaged by Father Hugh Costigan.

I gratefully acknowledge support from the National Science Foundation (# 9120466) and the International Institute for Education (Fulbright) for the long-term field research in 1992–93 that led to this book. I also received support from the Anthropology Department at the University of California, Los Angeles for research in 1991, and from the Max Planck Institute, Nijmegen, The Netherlands for two research trips to Pohnpei in 1995. The University of Texas at Austin provided writing support during the completion of this book.

Without the cooperation and generosity of the people of Pohnpei this work would not have been possible, and I sincerely thank them.

Contents

Introduction   3

1. The Ethnographic Setting   18

2. What Are Honorifics?   37

3. Paths and Regions in Honorific Speech: Hierarchy of
   Place and Access to Status   68

4. Honorific Possession: Grammatical Relations of
   Control and Permanence   99

5. Women's Power Etiquette: Relationships between
   Gender and Honorifics   122

6. Positioned Knowledge: Constructing Asymmetrical
   Epistemologies   155

7. Valuing Stratification: Honor in Oratory and
   Feasting Practices   178

   Conclusion   195

   Bibliography   199

   Index   211

POWER
SHARING

Introduction

My main interest in this book is to look at how power and status relations are created and negotiated through language among the Pohnpeian people of Micronesia. My goal is to show how closely examining particular social interactions between people at a "micro" level (focusing on small details) can explicate the nature and constitution of what are usually understood as "macro" (larger) social processes, such as power and status relations. Because I subscribe to the view that culture and society are constituted through activity involving social actors in particular contexts, the study of language in interaction is crucial for understanding how relations of domination are established and maintained by particular strategies that must be "endlessly renewed" (Bourdieu 1977:183). Pohnpeian interactional data provide an ideal corpus for examining how power and status inequalities are constituted and negotiated moment by moment, given the grammatical features used by the Pohnpeian language to explicitly indicate relative status among participants: honorific speech. In concert with grammar, an elaborate visual map of ranked social space is encoded onto the physical environment.

This study combines ethnography with a number of other methods, including linguistic analysis at the phrase and morpheme level, the analysis of naturally occurring talk developed by conversation analysts[1] and discourse analysts, ethnographies of speaking,[2] and work by linguists on cognition and metaphor.[3] Studying language as social action[4] and examining specific utterances in specific ethnographic contexts reveal how stratification is organized through language in interaction and how linguistic forms contribute to the naturalization of hierarchical relationships and the collaborative construction of meaning.

POHNPEI

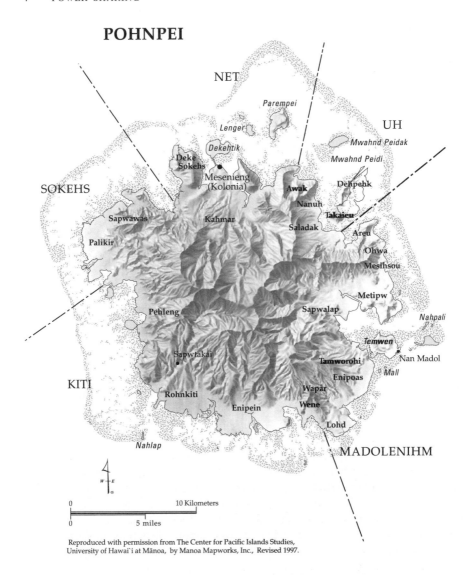

Reproduced with permission from The Center for Pacific Islands Studies,
University of Hawai`i at Mānoa, by Manoa Mapworks, Inc., Revised 1997.

This study shows how the analysis of sequential interactional data informed by ethnographic detail can challenge widely held theories on the nature of social stratification and power relationships, including women's roles in the constitution of hierarchy. Power relations are often represented as categories of powerful versus powerless, but close analysis of interactional data reveals an ongoing, active negotiation about power and status relationships among peers as well as among subordinates and superordinates. Power is shared among members of this community, and it is through power sharing that hierarchical relations are negotiated; gender is one variable that can be constituted within these negotiations.

In addition to questioning notions of power as a "top-down" phenomenon and recognizing the importance of lower-status members' role in the construction of inequality, this book engages a number of other theoretical viewpoints. First, in contrast to a number of authors working on the topic of honorifics, I focus quite a bit of attention on what has been termed "humiliative," or low-status, marking. I contend that high and low status are not just different "levels" of the same phenomenon, that is, high status and low status are not just constituted as polarities but as states with differing degrees of agency and/or causality. There is a greater reduction in the range of vocabulary items to index those terms that refer to low-status individuals and groups than to those that refer to high-status individuals and groups (this is also found in other honorific systems), and high-status markers are used invariantly in Pohnpei, whereas low-status markers vary according to topic, context, and other pragmatic considerations.

Second, there is a relationship between the rule-governedness of honorific use and particular social contexts, that is, not all contexts are relevant for status marking. The Pohnpeian use of honorific forms is not as regularized as native speakers imply or as theories would predict. This suggests that asymmetries of status may be context specific in ways not revealed by generalized descriptions of a society's social organization. Situational and contextual factors, as well as topic and stance (e.g., confrontational and epistemic), can influence choice of honorific register, and participant identity or role is not always a reliable guide.

Third, I question the conventional notions of power and solidarity and argue that these are far more intertwined than social theorists have proposed. In Pohnpei, the two ideas can have a sequential relation, that is, among the same participants, markers of solidarity precede the construction of the rank hierarchy through language. I suggest that honorifics are used to structure intimacy, either by, for example, providing a means to issue a directive to a high-status person or by creating a context in which a high-status person is vulnerable to dependencies from low-status individuals (cf. Duranti 1992; Goody 1972; Irvine 1974). Hierarchical relations on Pohnpei are constructed in culturally specific ways, that is, hierarchical relations constitute not only relations of power and status but also relations of dependence. Although in some languages there is a direct relation between high-status marking and morphemes (units of meaning) indicating distance, the distance relation has obscured the role of "microinteractions" in negotiating relative status. Pohnpeian honorific speech in interaction shows how lower-status individuals gain symbolic power through proximity and linguistic sharing of verbal symbols of status, for example, through dynamic uses of inclusive and exclusive pronouns in oratory.

Fourth, I examine the role of nonverbal signs as they co-produce and mediate status relations. They differ in important ways to the construction of hierarchy in language. Often studies of language practices do not also include a description of other communicative resources speakers regularly use. In Pohnpei the spatial hierarchy can more finely discern each person's status relationship so that whereas language can only differentiate between two statuses, or at most three, and children are grouped with titled men and women using the same low-status verb, the spatial map of status in Pohnpei can communicate that one is higher on the rank hierarchy than another. However, through language, a participant's activities can be constituted to have two different status levels by different speakers. Spatial signs do not show this flexibility, indicating the importance of language as well as the contestable nature of status in language.

Finally, I propose that the practice of honor in Pohnpei (and perhaps elsewhere) fundamentally and essentially organizes positive embodied attitudes (including affective displays) about individual social difference, particularly (1) positively valuing and rationalizing acts of self- and other-subordination (part of this practice involves discursively construing literal subordination/depletion/humiliation as its opposite, i.e., symbolic elevation), and (2) positively valuing structural hierarchy, including gender hierarchies. Linguistic forms and feasting practices contribute to the creation of a homology[5] between getting honor and giving honor, between honor and humiliation/abasement.

The notion of power sharing is used here to describe the process I observe in Pohnpeian interactions whereby lower-status persons are empowered through honorific speech forms to construct their own and others' status relationships. These relationships built through language in interaction can have far-reaching consequences for the constitution, reproduction, and naturalization of asymmetry across events, across space, and across time.

Each member of Pohnpeian society has the power, through language, to construct not only his or her own relative status but the status of every other member of the community, and this power is exercised every day through the use of status-marked speech (the focus of this book), terms of address, body posture, amount of food, and sequential order of food serving. Interestingly, the only persons who do *not* have the power to socially divide those of high status from those of low status are the highest-ranking members of the society, for example, the paramount chiefs. Thus the Pohnpeian social structure, where no two members have equal status, and indeed where it is an insult to say to someone *ke parakieng aramas koaros*, or "you are equal to everyone else," is built from the bottom up.

To characterize the complex dynamics of this process of building and celebrating asymmetry, I investigate videotaped interactions and show how members of the community participate in creating and maintaining social hierarchy through language and nonverbal sign systems. I look at the set of symbolic resources used to build hierarchy in Pohnpei, through particular ways of constituting society and recursively individual representations of social reality.

An anthropologically informed look
at communicative practice

This book takes as its primary focus specific language forms called "honorifics" by scholars in linguistics and linguistic anthropology. These language forms mark social features of a situation, most significantly the social status relationships among members of a community. Status relationships may be invoked through the use of whole words or portions of words, such as affixes (a general category covering prefixes, infixes, and suffixes), and are discussed in more detail in chapter 2 (in this volume).

Language in this study is assumed to be not only a rule-governed system with its own internal logic (learned by every child in the community) but a system of tools for the constitution of social life. This system includes language structure, language practice, visual codes, the interface between verbal and visual codes, and relationships to habitual modes of thought. Whereas linguists are often more interested in the meaningful relationship between components of a language system, for example, how parts of speech work together, linguistic anthropologists are primarily interested in the relationship between linguistic components and the lived in world. In this study I examine communicative acts between people where honorifics are used as I videotaped them in various contexts of "everyday" life. Particularly, I look at the relationship between the words and grammatical particles that encode status and how these particles are employed by speakers in their "mundane" everyday conversations, as well as in the more structured linguistic practice of oratory.

Language as social action

This book, although it will take advantage of (and is indebted to) much of the traditional work in linguistics, such as the identification and organization of grammatical categories, notions of basic meaningful units, analysis of word structure, semantic properties, and theories of grammaticalization (the development of language forms), is also influenced by the idea of language as principally *action.*

One of the most influential proponents of the notion of language as action was John Austin, who developed speech act theory (1962). Language is seen not as a tool for reference or description but as a way of doing things in the world. Austin identified language as a force and delineated several different ways language could influence the social world. He identified (1) the act of making the utterance itself (locutionary force), (2) the conventional effect of the utterance in interaction (illocutionary force), and (3) the more far-reaching effects of utterances, side effects or consequences, which can be triggered by accident, irrespective of the speaker's intentions (perlocutionary force). Austin argued that from the perspective of ordinary language, speech is not reducible to logic or "truth conditions" (as linguists and philosophers had argued). In this perspective, as expanded by Searle (1969) into a general theory of human communication, "speech acts . . . are the basic or minimal units of linguistic communication" (16). In the production of an utterance, a speaker performs an action. That this "action" then makes relevant some next action is the great contribution of those who have analyzed and described the structures of conversational interaction (e.g., Sacks, Schegloff and Jefferson 1974; Schegloff, Jefferson, and Sacks 1977; Pomerantz 1978, 1984; Schenkein 1978; C. Goodwin 1981; Atkinson and Heritage 1984; and others) and expanded Austin's notion of action beyond the single individual.

Austin's understanding of the importance of acts embedded in other acts and his discussion of conventionalized meaning focuses attention not on the referential or descriptive content of an utterance but on what is accomplished through language (reminding, denying, criticizing, accusing, pledging, swearing, urging, demanding, nominating, apologizing, greeting, complimenting, etc.). In this book, I focus principally on what honorifics *do* in interaction, that is, raise or lower participants' status, not on the referential properties of these forms.

Austin's view of language as action enriches our understanding of communication and lays the groundwork for using language as a tool for investigating human actions (including building the social order) and how speakers indicate their understandings and interpretations of such behaviors, as well as how meanings are negotiated and conventionalized. The critiques of speech act theory, including its disattention to the importance of the context of utterance and certain Eurocentric assumptions about the person (Rosaldo 1982), have also been taken into account in this study. Ethnographic accounts of communicative events cross-culturally have shown the importance of context in understanding language practices (see, e.g., Hymes 1962, 1974; Gumperz and Hymes 1972; Bauman and Sherzer 1974). Utterances and actions are both context shaped and context renewing (Heritage 1984; Duranti 1992). Certain features of language invoke contextual assumptions (Gumperz 1982; Hoem 1993). Work in conversation analysis has shown conclusively that talk is designed and interpreted as meaningful in relation to particular sequences and contexts (Schegloff 1984). A certain linguistic expression can perform an action (e.g., a request, offer, or apology) only to the extent to which there is a system of dispositions already shared in the community (Bourdieu 1984:133). Even within a community, the act of "complimenting" can have very different interactional achievements depending on context and the relationships among participants.

Based on her ethnographic studies among the Ilongot of the Philippines, Rosaldo (1982) argues persuasively that not only is language action (as proposed by Austin) but it is used to display and negotiate particular shared understandings. Speakers themselves organize speech acts into sets of practices that instantiate the social order.[6] As argued by Wittgenstein (1958), "meaning is use" (paragraph 43), and utterances are only understandable in relation to activities. As has been shown, understanding speakers' intentions, which forms an important part of interpreting acts in some cultures, is relatively unimportant in others (see Duranti 1988). Those working in the "ethnography of speaking" tradition have demonstrated the importance of describing language in its social setting, focusing on units larger than the individual sentence or utterance, understanding the range of language activities within a society, and the importance of looking at how language is actually performed, as well as the importance of the role of the hearer(s) (Bauman and Sherzer 1974; Gumperz and Hymes 1972; Sherzer 1983).

Language as a tool: Mediated activity

In addition to taking into account the importance of context, a notion of activity as a unit of analysis in the study of "talk in interaction" follows from the work of Vygotsky, who along with Luria and Leont'ev, argued for an activity-oriented investigation of mental processes, including the role of language.

Vygotsky conceived of the individual and the social as mutually constitutive elements of a single interacting system, an approach he and his students called "sociocultural" or "sociohistorical" (Cole 1985:148). Higher psychological function appears first between people as an interpsychological category and then within the individual child as an intrapsychological category (Vygotsky 1978:57). Language is an important tool or mediating device in this process, while at the same time activity mediates linguistic and sociocultural knowledge.

This study takes as its premise that the relationships between "culture" and social interactions between members of a culture are mutually constitutive, that is, they shape each other: "[C]ulture emerges through social interaction and at the same time organizes social interaction" (Ochs 1988:7). As Geertz describes: "[C]ulture . . . is public . . . it does not exist in someone's head" (Geertz 1973:51). Structures are at the same time sources and products of social activity, and there is a relationship between structure and personal agency or autonomy (Giddens 1984). Members of a group share a system of dispositions, "a past which survives in the present and tends to perpetuate itself into the future by making itself present in practices structured according to its principles" (Bourdieu 1977:82). The role of language in this recursive process of mediation between structure and social action is extremely important. Children develop concepts of a "socioculturally structured universe" through their participation in language activities and acquisition of language (Ochs 1988:14). "To speak is to take up a position in a social field in which all positions are moving and defined relative to one another" (Hanks 1996:201). Using the grammatical feature of Pohnpeian that marks relative social status is an opportunity to investigate how processes of social differentiation emerge and are negotiated in interaction.

Indexicality

In looking at status-marked language, this book is concerned with the language phenomenon called "indexicality" or "deixis" by linguists. The term is borrowed from the Greek word for pointing or indicating as these linguistic items "call upon the hearer to use his powers of observation, and establish a real connection between his mind and the object" (Peirce 1940:110).

Some very common types of deictics are person markers, such as "I" and "you," place markers, such as "here" and "there," and time indicators, such as "now" and "then." These terms have no meaning apart from the context in which they are uttered. I or you can refer to the same person or another person at different points in a stretch of talk. The meanings of here or there or now must be ascertained from contextual cues (i.e., the physical position in space of the speaker or the time of the utterance). Following is an example of problems in interpretation when deictic meanings are underspecified (from Levinson 1983:54). Suppose we are walking along the beach and find a bottle which has washed up on shore with a message in it: "Meet me here a week from now with a stick about this big." There is no way to interpret who to meet, where or when, or the size of the stick required.

Discourse deixis and social deixis have recently been added to the traditional categories of deixis—person, place, and time (Lyons 1968, 1977; Fillmore 1971, 1975). Discourse deixis refers to the use of deictic particles which refer to previous discourse, that is, topic (e.g., *that* was the funniest joke I've heard in a long time), and social deixis concerns the encoding of social distinctions that are relative to the social relationship between participants in an interaction. The latter is the focus of this book. Within sociolinguistics and linguistic anthropology, indices and indexical relations have become an important area of research. Deixis is a critical point at which languages mediate important features of context. The interpretation of deictics depends a great deal on social and cultural aspects of meaning, and analysis can elucidate relationships between language and the constitution of social life. In some languages, social deixis is more prominently marked than others. "Scarcely a single sentence of, for example, Japanese, Javanese or Korean can be properly described from a strictly linguistic point of view without an analysis of social deixis" (Levinson 1983:94).

One of the most well-known forms of social deixis is the "T/V" distinction. This term refers to alternations in the use between the second person singular and plural pronouns in some European languages, for example, *tu* and *vous* in French, *du* and *Sie* in German, *ty* and *vy* in Russian. A lower-status person uses *vous* to refer to a higher-status person, whereas a superior uses *tu* to refer to an inferior in French. This alternation has consequences for indicating status relations. Through an examination of interactional data I show how social deixis works in Pohnpei, and how this indexing in turn constructs asymmetrical social relations in interactions and even inscribes them on the landscape.

Specialized registers

Honorific speech can be described as a "register" of Pohnpeian speech, and readers will encounter the term "register" used throughout this book. "Register" is a term widely used in sociolinguistics to mean varieties of the same language that are appropriate in different contexts. Examples are the sometimes formal language used in American business letter writing (e.g., "enclosed please find the following"), which we recognize as different from personal letter writing, and which indicates and constructs a certain set of relationships between participants. Registers are often related to technical contexts, for example, scientific discourse, the legal profession, or sportscasting (Ferguson 1983) and can also be related to participants, such as with baby talk (Ferguson 1964). Some register shifts are accompanied by shifts in prosody like intonation, volume, or speed. In Pohnpeian it is certainly possible to carry on a conversation entirely in what I call in this book "common speech," that is, unmarked for status. In certain contexts, and to construct certain contexts, speakers shift into honorific register, meaning that certain word forms are used particular to status relationships. As noted previously, shifts in register are by no means uniform among participants and among speech acts.

Gender

Previous studies of the relationship between language and power in the Pacific focused on events that are male dominated (see, e.g., Watson-Gegeo and White 1990; Brenneis and Myers 1984), resulting in a heavy emphasis on male language strategies. Men more often have public speech roles (though the Western[7] dichotomy between public and private can prove problematic when applied cross-culturally). Rosaldo and Lamphere (1974) suggest that analysis of women's strategies can demonstrate that women have significant power: "[A]lthough the formal authority structure of a society may declare that women are impotent and irrelevant, close attention to women's strategies and motives . . . indicates that even in situations of overt sex role asymmetry women have a good deal more power than conventional theorists have assumed" (Rosaldo and Lamphere 1974:9).

Reliance on consultants' idealizations about honor in previous studies has over-emphasized the male role in constituting honor practices at the expense of women's roles. The Pohnpeian interactions show that women play a significant role in constructing and maintaining status asymmetries through honorific speech. Hierarchical relations are negotiated, and gender is one variable that can be constituted within these negotiations.

Pohnpei's matrilineality "gives mothers and sisters a primary place of value" in the society (Kihleng 1996:386), especially with regard to the legitimacy of rank claims. Women ultimately determine the ascribed status and political ranking of their male kinsmen, and social differentiation between chiefs and commoners is more salient than gender in matters of status and dominance (Kihleng 1996:3, 58). The paramount chieftess, for example, outranks many of the men in the chiefdom. Pohnpeian women "maintain their power and efficacy" through their central involvement in feasting and exchange (Kihleng 1996:ix), which are important sites for the reproduction of hierarchy and are discussed in more detail in chapter 7 (in this volume). The issue of gender and the reproduction of hierarchy are discussed in more detail in chapter 5 (in this volume).

Power

Western ethnographers have been criticized for unquestioningly applying a simplified Western model of power as "unidirectional and nonreciprocal" (Wetzel 1993:389) to analyses of other than Western social systems and for failing to note differences cross-culturally in the expression or constraint of the exhibition of power (S. Errington 1990:5). Wetzel (1993) calls for a reconsideration of the term "power" in discussions of the encoding of vertical relationships by linguistic means, based on differences between "Eastern" and "Western" construals of "domination." Power is a concept "essentially contested" in scholarship, and use of the term is "inextricably tied to a given set of (probably unacknowledged) value-assumptions which predetermine the range of empirical application" (Lukes 1974:26). Ideas about power almost universally undervalue the part subordinate groups play in constructing power relations.

Rethinking conflicting models of what power is, or what is meant by the term, is of course a key theme in Foucault's work, specifically the relation between power and knowledge (*pouvoir/savoir*), the history of power, and the idea of power as having positive as well as negative effects.

> [P]ower would be a fragile thing if its only function were to repress, if it worked only through the mode of censorship, exclusion, blockage and repression, in the manner of a great Superego, exercising itself only in a negative way. . . . Far from preventing knowledge, power produces it. . . . The fact that power is so deeply rooted and the difficulty of eluding its embrace are effects of all these connections. That is why the notion of repression which mechanisms of power are generally reduced to strikes me as very inadequate and possibly dangerous. (Foucault 1980a:59)

Whether power is tied to human agency or to structure seems to be a key point in debates about the nature of power. Foucault claims that there is no power without agents, that power is something that is exercised rather than possessed, and only local exercises of power are real. There is no binary and all-encompassing opposition between rulers and ruled at the root of power relations (1980b:94), and the traditional notion of power as one group exercising sovereign control over another should be set aside.

I follow Foucault (1972, 1979) in assuming that power does not exist outside social relationships but, rather, is a product of them, and that Pohnpeians negotiate this "product" (or, rather, process) in part through the construction of dominant and subordinate social relationships in honorific speech. Hierarchy, like other "traditional explainers of social action," is not a thing but a process "manipulated or composed during the course of interaction" (Moerman 1988:2). Like the Pohnpeian idea of *manaman* ("sacred power"), power is positive and productive (manaman is discussed in more detail in chapter 1 in this volume).

Turn-by-turn, and word-by-word analysis of Pohnpeian social interactions reveals a process I term "power sharing," by which agents organize and incorporate power. Lower-status individuals construct the very character of their own status and that of others through honorific language, that is, their society's hierarchy of status asymmetry. This is a complex process, a multiplication of layers of "symbolic and cultural capital" (Bourdieu 1977), invoked and contested in interaction. Chiefs and chieftesses evidence strategies of collaboration with lower-status members in this process and thus *share power* with subordinates. One of the ways I develop this idea is through a discussion of food-sharing practices and the complex metaphorical relationships between food and low-status indexing speech and land and high-status indexing speech (discussed in greater detail in chapter 4, in this volume). Power sharing, though not without risk, secures the collaboration of all members of the community in the construction of symbolic inequalities.

In Pohnpeian, speakers can lower their own or others' status or raise another's status by choosing specific honorific vocabulary. A single utterance can index two separate levels of status aimed at two separate individuals. Contrary to what previous ethnographers reported, *honorific speech is not used in all chiefly interactions*. Rather, a cluster of features, including a certain degree of formality, co-occurs with a speaker's choice to use this register. In addition, not all topic domains are significant factors. Instead, *honorific vocabulary clusters around the domains of body location in space, possession, knowledge, food, and references to speech itself*. These domains are significantly tied to elaborated areas of power transfer in Pohnpei. Honorific speech, an etiquette of power relations, allows agents to transform and channel power to negotiate a status hierarchy. Linking honorifics with appropriate social behavior links them with shared values (and solidarity building), which interactional data show is an important component in constructing systems of social inequality and resolving contradictions within such systems. Conventionalized, these vocabulary terms can have great force in creating systems of synchronized inequality.

Although the term "power" is often appropriate in discussions of honorific language use, the complexities of power relationships in honorific speech are better addressed by a concept such as "power sharing." This term better describes the reciprocal and synergistic constitution and negotiation of power in interactions. Pohnpeians, similar to the Japanese described by Wetzel (1993) and Dunn (1996), construe the natural way of the world as hierarchical, but this should not lead *us* to conclude that hierarchy does not entail some members of society dominating over others, even if the control of those in power in the "East" is often reported as more paternalistic than the model in the "West" (Kondo 1990). As others have pointed out, even so-called egalitarian societies still hierarchize certain relationships (Sahlins 1958; Brenneis and Myers 1984), most notably within the family regarding women and men and in broader family models of hierarchy.

In studies of honorific languages, some researchers take the position that such speech is not an indication of real power relations but rather an indication of respect or deference. Wetzel (1993) and Agha (1993) focus on the idea of the deference due to a particular role relation, as a measure of a legitimate, balanced order rather than with contested and negotiated power relationships. Showing such deference is considered part of an individual's demonstration of a knowledge of appropriate and conventional speech and societal norms. This demonstration of esteem, however, I feel does have implications for the exercise of power relations because, for example, this showing of deference can take the form of deferring to another's wishes or letting their judgments stand uncontested, and in the construction of a particular hierarchical order.

The strong connection between manaman (sacred power), honorific speech, and spatial symbolism of hierarchy in Pohnpei, together with cultural prescriptions such as those that indicate that the paramount chief's desires (always expressed in honorific speech) must be obeyed without question, indicates that honorifics do not merely index role relations but power relationships too. There is no appropriate (i.e., honorific) form of a negative answer to a chief's request, for example.

Information management is linked to issues of status and power sharing, and is an important domain for status marking in Pohnpei (this is discussed in detail in chapter 6, in this volume). Sharing knowledge decreases power (manaman) and information is organized to conserve power. In casual speech, this is done through strategies of epistemic uncertainty; in oratory by framing all speech under the power of the chief. Pohnpeians constitute positioned knowledges, and the source location of knowledge is tied to legitimacy. Metapragmatic verbs of speaking (i.e., speaking about speech) are also status-marked. Speaking publically can force high-status persons to risk power, yet at the same time, as noted by Brenneis and Meyers (1984:24), "maintaining a polity requires linguistic work."

Hierarchical sharing of resources: Honorific speech
and food exchange

Several authors link the asymmetrical "exchange" of honorifics (e.g., the T/V pronouns) to other asymmetrical exchanges in the same society, such as those concerning food. Haviland (1979), for example, notes that in Australia in former times in addition to language restraints "there were also severe restrictions on the sharing of food and possessions between a man and his parents-in-law" (223). In India hierarchical rules underlie Hindu food and service transfers. Levinson (1982) finds a "parallelism" between the "giving" of "intimate" pronoun (solidarity) and food, and the giving of "distant" pronoun and services. In food providing the giver is higher than the receiver, in service the opposite. Food sharing is classed as intimate behavior (121).

The Pohnpeian system of unequal food sharing is specifically indexed in honorific speech by the use of special terms for high-status food, and for high-status "leftovers," as well as by a direct synonymous link between the humiliative expression for eating and the humiliative expression for all possession (these topics are discussed in detail in chapter 4, in this volume). The idea that power sharing in society may be modeled on food sharing is an intriguing one. A Pohnpeian title is in fact a food-sharing title because it specifically entitles one to a certain share of the food and produce distributed at feasts and funerals. Titles are called out in descending order at these events, as the choicest portions are divided up (see chapter 7, in this volume). The entire community keeps a mental tally of the significance of each portion, and these details are retold over the next few days with commentary and discussion. Modjeska (1982) observes for the Duna of New Guinea that in a similar public sharing of pork, the apportionment of shares was to be "straight" and equal, not based on any system of inequality. A Duna consultant described such a distribution as "that of the mother, exactly dividing morsels" (Modjeska 1982:85). This description suggests that food sharing is highly symbolic of underlying principles of equality or inequality in Pacific societies. It may further suggest that hierarchy is based on a repudiation or reversal of the model of the mother. The link between status and food is important in understanding contexts of honorific use on Pohnpei. For example, at an event discussed in chapter 2 (in this volume), a switch to honorific register occurs at the beginning of the *sakau*[8] ceremony (the verb "eat" is always used in reference to sakau).

The outline of the book

Chapter 1 introduces the ethnographic setting. This includes a discussion of the Pohnpeian rank structure as well as a broader discussion of Oceanic chiefdom organization. I discuss the importance of the concept of manaman (sacred power), as well as the hierarchical spatial symbolism of the feasthouse and its relation to social rank. The ritual beverage (*kava* or sakau) made from the pounded roots of the pepper plant is described, as several of the interactions detailed in the book take place within the context of sakau preparation and consumption. Aspects of the Pohnpeian language relative to the issues raised in this study are discussed, and a description of methodologies given. Chapter 2 introduces honorifics as a cross-cultural language phenomenon. This chapter also discusses specifics of Pohnpeian status marked speech, including its polysemous nature. The conventional idea of solidarity as the polar opposite of hierarchy is discussed in light of interactional data that suggest these two concepts are far more intertwined than previous theories suggest. The chapters following chapter 2 deal with specific domains of status marking in Pohnpei. In chapter 3, I discuss status marking and verbs denoting location in space, as well as the relationship of status marking in language to nonverbal symbols of spatial hierarchy in an interaction with the secondary chief. In chapter 4, I analyze possessive constructions in both common speech and honorific speech and discuss the important differences between these two speech levels, as well as metaphorical connections between honorific possessive classifiers and other aspects of Pohnpeian cognitive organization schemes. In chapter 5 I examine relationships between honorific speech and gender in Pohnpeian society, especially women's roles in constituting hierarchy. In chapter 6 I discuss how knowledge and acts of speaking are expressed in honorific speech, that is, how hierarchies of meaning are constructed and how this affects the organization of information and a stratified ideology of authorship. In chapter 7 I analyze the cultural concept of honor, as it is constituted in oratory, and competitive prestige or honor events.

One of the principal aims of this book is to understand how social inequality is built in particular interactions between particular members of society, and how building social inequality is a collaborative process. I examine how specific practices, namely, language practices and other symbolic systems of communication and reproduction, construct maintain, and challenge status differences. In Pohnpei, as in many societies, hierarchy is socially valued and viewed as a "natural" and productive way of ordering social life.

To be a linguistic anthropologist is to be interested in the role of language in the construction of culture and society. Language is not only a mode of thinking but, above all, a cultural practice, that is, "a form of action that both presupposes and at the same time brings about ways of being in the world" (Duranti 1997:2). Languages mark stances and attitudes and signal changes in context and interpretive frame through small morphemic insertions or alternations. In this study I look at language as social action (e.g., Austin 1962; Searle 1969); therefore, I focus on what honorifics *do* in interaction (i.e., raise or lower status) rather than exclusively at their referential properties.

Notes

1. See, for example, Schegloff 1968; Sacks, Schegloff and Jefferson 1974; Schegloff, Jefferson and Sacks 1977; Pomerantz 1978, 1984; Schenkein 1978; C. Goodwin 1981; Atkinson and Heritage 1984.

2. See, for example, Hymes 1962, 1974; Gumperz and Hymes 1972; Bauman and Sherzer 1974.

3. See, for example, G. Lakoff 1987; G. Lakoff and Johnson 1980; Sweetser 1990.

4. For example, Austin 1962; Searle 1969; Gumperz and Hymes 1972.

5. I am indebted to Eve Danziger for suggesting this term.

6. Hymes 1962, 1974; Gumperz and Hymes 1972; Bauman and Sherzer 1974.

7. I am aware that "Western" is a problematic term, but here I mean a body of literature that reflects a sense of hegemony that the term assumes.

8. Chapter 1 explains the practice of *sakau*.

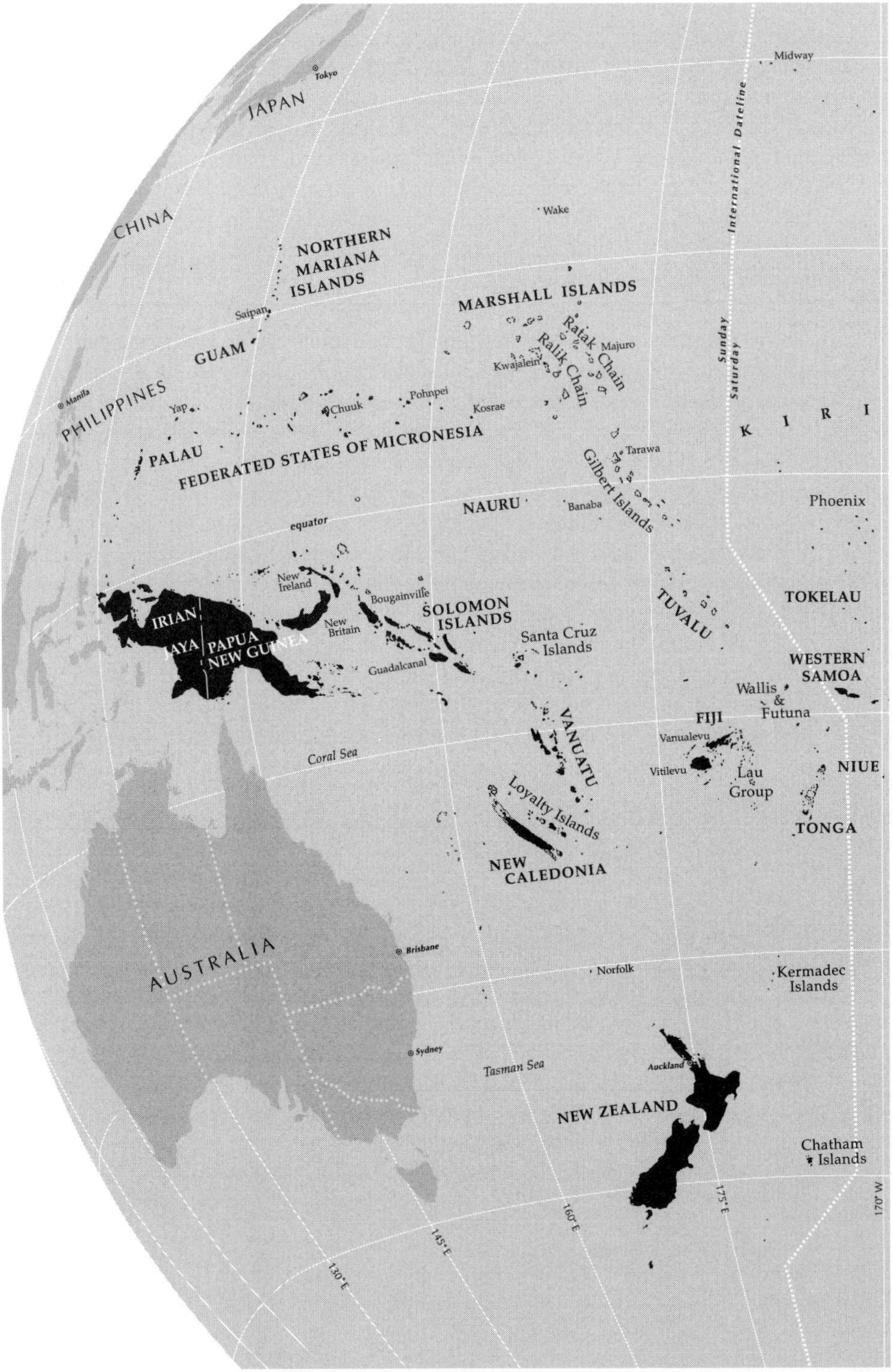
Midway
Tokyo
JAPAN
International Dateline
Wake
CHINA
NORTHERN
MARIANA
ISLANDS
MARSHALL ISLANDS
Saipan
Ratak Chain
Ralik Chain
Majuro
Kwajalein
GUAM
Sunday
Saturday
Manila
PHILIPPINES
Yap
Chuuk
Pohnpei
Kosrae
K I R I
PALAU
FEDERATED STATES OF MICRONESIA
Tarawa
Gilbert Islands
NAURU
Banaba
Phoenix
equator
New
Ireland
Bougainville
SOLOMON
ISLANDS
TUVALU
TOKELAU
IRIAN
JAYA
PAPUA
NEW GUINEA
New
Britain
Guadalcanal
Santa Cruz
Islands
WESTERN
SAMOA
Wallis
&
Futuna
FIJI
VANUATU
Vanualevu
Vitilevu
Lau
Group
NIUE
Coral Sea
Loyalty Islands
TONGA
NEW
CALEDONIA
AUSTRALIA
Brisbane
Norfolk
Kermadec
Islands
Sydney
Tasman Sea
Auckland
NEW ZEALAND
Chatham
Islands
130°E
145°E
160°E
175°E
170°W

UNITED STATES

30°N

Los Angeles ©

MEXICO

Oahu

Hawaii

HAWAII

Johnston

15°N

Mexico City ©

North Pacific Ocean

Clipperton .

B   A   T   I

Kiritimati

Line Islands

Islands

0 °

equator

C
O
O
K

Marquesas
Islands

F
R
E
N
C
H

P
O
L
Y
N
E
S
I
A

I
S
L
A
N
D
S

Tuamotu Archipélago

AMERICAN
SAMOA

15°S

Tahiti

Society Islands

Rarotonga .

Austral Islands

Gambier Islands

Pitcairn
Islands

South Pacific Ocean

30 °S

Easter .

THE PACIFIC ISLANDS

Reproduced with permission from the Center for Pacific Islands Studies
University of Hawai`i at Manoa
by Manoa Mapworks, Inc.
Revised 1997.

135°W

140°W

N

W   E

S

125°W

45 °S

110°W

Chapter 1

The Ethnographic Setting

Pohnpei is one of the widely scattered Caroline Islands, small and limited points in a seemingly unlimited ocean and sky. The island is roughly sixteen kilometers wide and circular in shape. It is just above the equator, north of New Guinea and east of the Philippines (7 degrees north latitude, 158 degrees east longitude). On this island, whose name is literally translated as "upon a stone altar," live approximately 30,000 Pohnpeians and a smaller fraction of settlers from outlying atolls to the east and south. Thick jungle growth covers the now inactive volcano that once rose straight from the ocean floor. Almost all the shore of the island is protected from eroding ocean waves by a dense mangrove swamp and an outer coral reef. Rainfall can be as high as 400 inches per year in the interior and is commonly around 200 inches in other areas. Temperatures range between 80 and 90 degrees Fahrenheit with very high humidity.

Linguistic evidence and reconstructions of Proto-Austronesian and Proto-Oceanic languages suggest that the people who now speak Pohnpeian are descendants of a group which first left what is called Island Southeast Asia (Indonesia, Malaysia, the Philippines, and Taiwan) 3,000 to 5,000 years ago. The structure of the Oceanic family tree has been interpreted as "indicating a rapid dispersal of Oceanic-speaking peoples from northwestern Melanesia across southern Melanesia and into the Central Pacific" (Pawley and Ross 1993:441). Estimates are that by 1000 B.C. people who spoke Proto-Micronesian arrived in Kosrae and Pohnpei (Rehg 1981) by way of the Marshall and Gilbert Islands and before that the northern New Hebrides. Pohnpeian oral history describes it thus: *wahr oapwoat pwilisang sekeren wai keilahn aio*, "one canoe left from a foreign shore the other side of yesterday (long ago)." Whether the first

Pohnpeians brought honorific or status-marked language with them is not known, although Kosrae (about 320 kilometers miles east of Pohnpei) seems to have had a well-developed "respect vocabulary" at one time (Fischer 1969). Rehg (ms) argues, based on linguistic evidence, that Western Polynesians, apparently Samoans, voyaged more than once to Pohnpei, and that this contact played a role in shaping Pohnpeian culture.

Pohnpeian is a member of the Oceanic group of the Austronesian language family. About one sixth of the world's languages are Austronesian, and Austronesian has been described as "the world's largest well-established language family" (Pawley and Ross 1993:429). The cultural diversity of the populations of this group and their island or insular habitats have made them of great interest to anthropologists (Pawley and Ross 1993:425).

In contrast to the many coral atolls of the Pacific, Pohnpei is a "high island" with central peaks rising to 750 meters. As is typical of high island people, in contrast to atoll dwellers, the settlers found enough sustenance and raw material on their island and therefore did not develop extensive trading relationships with other islands. The skills in long-distance ocean voyaging that brought them to the island fell into disuse. Although scholars had at first supposed that Oceania might be a natural laboratory for observing stages along the way to the evolution of "complex society," Kirch (1984) notes that archaeological and linguistic evidence suggests the colonizers most certainly brought with them pyramidal social structures, the tradition of first fruits and tribute, and the notion of chiefs as representatives of deities (281). The term for chief, for example, *'ariki*, has been reconstructed for Proto-Oceanic and can be found in the Pohnpeian term for the paramount chief *Nanmwarki*. This indicates that a system of hereditary rank was found in the society whose language was ancestral to all the Austronesian languages of Melanesia, Polynesia, and Nuclear Micronesia (Pawley and Ross 1993:444). The organizational basis of early Polynesian societies was the conical clan, in which distinctions among clan members were made on the basis of genealogical distance from the founding ancestor: "The conical clan is, at every level, a ranked structure. Older and younger siblings, chiefs and commoners, higher and lesser ramages—all are positioned on a continuous scale with the fundamental criterion of seniority of descent. This principle of genealogical seniority may be viewed as a set of structural equivalents: father:son::older brother:younger brother::chief: commoner" (Kirch 1984:34). Women are similarly included in this rank structure. Daughters are subordinate to mothers, younger sister to older sister, male or female "commoner" to chieftess. Whereas in some Polynesian societies the line of succession is patrilineal, descent in Micronesian societies such as Pohnpei is matrilineal, although it is men who claim the highest rank, and titles (with a female counterpart title) are most often given to men.

At this point I would like to mention that the classifying schemas that have been developed for Oceania (i.e., Melanesia, Polynesia, and Micronesia) are somewhat artificial constructs, based partly on geography and on what have been perceived as different physical characteristics of the populations. This poses some problems, as, for example, Belau and Yap, classified as islands of Micronesia, are not considered part of the Nuclear subgroup of Micronesian languages (Pawley and Ross 1993). In the case of Pohnpei, many features of the social structure resemble quite closely features of Polynesian social structure and practices (e.g., the ranked structure of the conical clan). Pohnpei alone in Micronesia practices the kava (sakau) ceremony (discussed later) as a central symbol in the construction of community and hierarchy, a widespread practice throughout Polynesia. A full discussion of these issues as well as a full portrayal of Pohnpeian society is beyond the scope of this work; however, some background is provided below to situate the study, and more ethnographic detail will be provided in following chapters.[1] Today, Pohnpei is the administrative center for the four Federated States of Micronesia, all of which have a form of democratic government. The democratic-style government, based on the American model (Pohnpei was part of the U.S. Trust Territory from 1947 to 1983), coexists with the traditional ranked chiefly structure (see Pinsker 1997). The focus of this book is interactions involving chiefs and chieftesses and necessarily centers around the traditional hierarchical organization and daily practices.

The Pohnpeian rank structure

Pohnpei has historically been divided into five independent chiefdoms, called *wehi*, each with a paramount chief (Nanmwarki) and chieftess (*Likend*) and a secondary chief *Nahnken* and secondary chieftess *Nahnken Iai*. Although today the island is united under a form of democratic government, the wehi organization is vital and remains an important organizing principle in the practices of the island. Pohnpeians think of the five chiefdoms as quite separate. A person's identity is partly defined by his or her chiefdom of birth; the customary differences between them are well-known and often verbalized in a joking way if a person visits another chiefdom. The chiefdom or wehi in which I did my fieldwork is Madolenihmw. Madolenihmw traditionally is thought of as the highest-ranking chiefdom; that is, if all the chiefs and chieftesses come together for an important funeral or other occasion, the chief and chieftess of Madolenihmw occupy the symbolically highest places in the feast house. This ranking of subgroups is a principle common to Polynesian societies, a result of fissioning of initial founding groups into subgroups or ramages (Firth 1936; Kirch 1984:31; Earle 1987), a process discussed in Pohnpeian oral histories (see Mauricio 1993 for an excellent historical account of these records together with archaeological data). Each chiefdom is further divided into sections or *pwihn* and into neighborhood communities or *kousapw*. The kousapw in which I lived is called Enipoas, meaning "the dancing place of spirits." This is where the Nahnken, or second-ranking chief of Madolenihmw, lived until his death in 1992. The highest-ranking chief, the Nanmwarki, lives in the kousapw of Temwen, a few miles away. Most of my work centered in these two kousapws, which were in Sections Five (*Pwihn Kelimau*) and Six (*Pwihn Kewenou*), as well as some videotaping done in Section One (*Pwihn Keiehu*).

Pohnpeians do not live in villages but on their separate farms or plantations on the flatter lands near the shoreline. The port town of Kolonia, however, first built by Spanish colonizers, is organized according to Western ideas of space and townships. Because the islanders live in widely scattered homesteads, often obscured from sight by dense jungle growth, the customary practice of neighbors joining together in the late afternoons to share sakau (a drink made from water and the pounded root of the pepper plant *piper methysticum*) is an important setting for the creation and maintenance of community relationships including the constitution of relative hierarchy. The hierarchical symbols inherent in the preparation of sakau are discussed shortly.

Pohnpeian society was organized into more than twenty matrilineal, totemic, and exogamous clans at the time of the first written records (Hanlon 1988; Riesenberg 1968). Today, eighteen clans are still in existence (Kihleng 1996:88). Status within each of the clans is precisely graded. Subclans within each clan are considered to be descended from a family of sisters and are ranked according to the relative age of their ancestresses (Garvin and Riesenberg 1952). Thus, relationships among clan members are marked according to seniority of matrilineal descent, which provides the basic pattern for the acquisition of titles by male members (counterpart titles are given to spouses), although many other factors can also influence the procurement of titles, for example, prestige competition among families based on presentations to chiefs at celebratory feasts and funerals (see chapter 7, in this volume). Because of the ranking of chiefdoms, clans, and subclans, the same title held by members of different chiefdoms and sections is not equivalent, and thus no two Pohnpeians have the same rank. Although birth into a high-ranking clan is the major qualification for titles, some upward mobility is possible, as the highest chiefs of each district use titles to encourage men and women to make great displays of tribute to them. New titles may also be created when new subdistricts are formed (cf. Petersen 1982). In a survey taken by Martha Ward of 1,200 Pohnpeians, 95 percent of those in the sample eligible held titles (Hughes 1982). Privileges of rank include a large share of redistribution of the tribute brought to the chiefs at feasts and funerals and increased prestige; responsibilities include sharing large amounts of produce with the chief and other community members.

The paramount chiefs control hundreds of chiefdom titles (*mwaren wehi*) and section titles (*mwaren kousapw*) (Mauricio 1993:59). The paramount chief is the highest title in a hierarchy of over thirty titles controlled by the ruling clan (Petersen 1982:17). The first twelve of these are *sohpeidi* titles. Sohpeidi means literally "to face downwards," and it refers to the facing relation between the chiefs and the people; that is, the chiefs face downward toward the people; the people face upward toward the chief. The title of paramount chief is ordinarily given to the senior male member of the ruling matrilineage of the ruling subclan or the ruling clan within the chiefdom (Mauricio 1993:60). The relationship between the paramount chief and the secondary chief is likened by Pohnpeians to a father–son kinship relation (Mauricio 1993:63). The secondary chief is of a different clan and controls a different but parallel line of titles. There are titles at the section level as well as the chiefdom level; currently section chief leadership positions number 250, and section chiefs control a set of lesser titles which they can bestow or confiscate with or without the consent of the paramount or secondary chiefs (Mauricio 1993:67). Each male title has a female counterpart title, and women have been described as having "complementary" spheres of activity and domains of power (Kihleng 1996:41); however, a woman loses her title and concomitant social position if her husband dies. An exception to this are females born of a chief and chieftess during their reign, and certain female titles bestowed by chiefs as recognition of high status. According to oral tradition, priestly titles antedated the political ones (Mauricio 1993:64).

Oceanic chiefdom organization

Although this study focuses on processes as they emerge in interaction, background on structures and classifications is helpful for understanding the relationship between structure and agency in Pohnpei and also how the hierarchical social organization of many Pacific societies has been viewed by earlier anthropologists. In the past, a strong tendency to classify chiefdom societies as intermediate (on an evolutionary scale between kinship organization and state organization) obscured the richness and complexity of social life in the Pacific. Oceania has been a focus of numerous anthropological investigations about systems of political organization.[2] Contradictions and problems in describing and analyzing Oceanic political systems have resulted partly from the view that chiefdoms are lower on the evolutionary ladder or "less complex" than modern states, partly on Western notions of political processes as formal and public, and partly from a reliance on data collection methods such as interviews and participant observation. This study shows that close interactional analysis based on video recordings of face-to-face or co-present interaction improves our understanding of the emergent, dynamic, and complex nature of political processes in Oceania.

The concept of chiefdom did not emerge as a theoretically important concept in anthropology until 1955 (Earle 1991). Before that, anthropologists recognized kinship and state as the two major stages in the evolution of society. Chiefdoms were defined as more complex sociopolitical organizations than tribal or kinship level organizations, with increases in productivity and in centrality of organization and less complexity than "civil society" (Service 1962:159). Fried (1967) classified chiefdoms as intermediate based on social control. As noted by A. Johnson and Earle (1987), both schemes emphasized classification over process. The Pohnpeian chiefdoms are clearly complex, highly stratified social organizations, which nevertheless accommodate a high degree of individual autonomy (see Petersen, 1982). This autonomy has not been previously examined or integrated into discussions of hierarchical systems.

Oceanic chiefdoms exhibit a characteristic redistribution of goods from the top of the rank hierarchy and a tendency toward decreasing participation of high-ranking individuals in the primary productive labor of the society (Sahlins 1958). However, variation is noted in that the highest-ranking person might have to be the hardest working to fulfill obligations to show generosity (Firth 1939; Fried 1967) and the necessarily collaborative construction of leadership in a ranked society, where few instruments for forcing compliance are available (Fried 1967). This dialogic nature of the "chiefly contract" (A. Johnson and Earle 1987:209) is important for an understanding of the role of language in constructing social asymmetries.

A dichotomy between "chiefs/chieftesses" and "commoners" has been reified in discussions of Oceanic political organization, despite the fact that our Western notion of "chief" did not always accurately represent the role we were trying to describe (e.g., the Oceanic chiefs have a combination of sacred and secular power, in some ways more like priests than chiefs) and no word for "commoner" exists in many so-called chiefdoms, where all claim descent from a chiefly, founding ancestor, or deity. As observed by other ethnographers in the Pacific, it is often hard to find anyone who classifies himself or herself as a commoner. On Pohnpei, I observed the term for commoner, *aramas mwahl*, used only in an insulting manner, although Mauricio (1993) reports that people with no titles and lesser titles are thought of as commoners. At the same time, he states "the generalization that the majority of Pohnpeians are potentially eligible to attain a high leadership position is a valid one" (69), because all Pohnpeians belong to one of thirteen clans, nine of which are considered chiefly clans.

The importance of mana (manaman on Pohnpei)

Historically on Pohnpei the highest chief and chieftess were nonparticipants in social interaction. Feast houses were built facing the direction of prevailing winds and fires were strategically built so that smoke would blow inside and obscure the visibility of the high chiefs on the feast house platform. Some sources report that the Nanmwarki sat behind a wall or a screen and smoke was directed between him and the public. The manaman, or sacred power of the chief, was considered extremely potent and dangerous.

Mana, a term with cognates throughout the Pacific (manaman on Pohnpei), describes the sacred power that flows from the deities through chiefs and chieftesses to the people. Specifically, mana flows matrilineally to descendants within chiefly clans. In the traditional Hawaiian monarchy, brother-sister marriages were sometimes contracted to build the potency of mana and to limit outsider participation in it. In Pohnpei in former times, high chief and secondary chief subclans intermarried exclusively (Reisenberg 1968) to conserve and increase sacred power; thus, because of matrilineal descent, all the title holders in the Nanmwarki line were either fathers or sons of those in the Nahnken line and vice versa. In Samoa, a sacred sister's mana conferred ancestral sanctity and power on the highest titles (Weiner 1992:82).

The concept of mana is often not fully understood by Westerners, whose idea of sacred does not also encompass the concept of danger. For example Keopuolani, the first and most sacred wife of Kamehameha I of Hawaii, whose parents were sister and half-brother to each other and whose grandmother was of the highest rank, had such powerful mana that if a man inadvertently came into contact with her or her possessions, he would be killed. The extension of mana to possessions and linkage of power and spatial distance are important for understanding the importance of bodily movement in space and possessive constructions for status marking on Pohnpei (see chapters 3 and 4, in this volume). Even though dangerous, mana is a force that is admired and sought after. Rituals symbolically contain and organize the "unbound potency" of mana (Shore 1989:153), which is both inherited through blood and acquired through position. Firth (1940) concluded that mana meant "success" to the Tikopia, as it is often ascribed after the fact, after its efficacy has emerged in interaction.

Mana is seen as a productive, efficacious force, not a force of repression, and it is linked to generative potency and to the sources of organic creation as well as destruction. Watson-Gegeo (personal communication) describes the concept of mana in Kwaterae (Solomon Islands) society as encompassing the idea of truth as well as the idea of power (see also Sahlins 1983). One Pohnpeian oral historian, Silten, cor-relates manaman with the physical energy force of lightning. "According to him, this force 'went into' or saturated Pohnpei and in part gives the island its *sarawi* ['sa-credness'] and manaman" (Mauricio 1993:92). Later this force was transferred to the chiefs; after the overthrow of the Saudeleur dynasty in Pohnpei, the "media embodying the deities were changed from inanimate and animate objects of the land and the sea to the human leaders" (Mauricio 1993:159).

Though the concept of mana is shared among many Pacific societies, and a cog-nate word can be reconstructed for a Proto-Oceanic language, its effects in status negotiations can vary. For example, Weiner notes that "in Hawaii everything of political significance is controlled through those who claim the highest mana; in Samoa this control can only be effected by claiming the highest titles; in the Trobriands only the claim of an ancestral conception belief allows such control" (Weiner 1992:83).

The authority of a chief and chieftess is supported by protective spirits, ances-tral ghosts, or clan deities, who possess the power to punish those who anger or dis-please them through *riahla,* a special punitive disease. Women are connected to chiefly power on Pohnpei not only through clan affiliation and marriage but also because, symbolically, the deities are in the position of mother (*ihn*) or mother's brother (*uhlap*) to members of the clan (Reisenberg 1968). That female deities and spirits inhabit the Pohnpeian world signifies that powerful positions are not open to males alone. In honorific language on Pohnpei, the link between the chiefly clan and the deities is materialized when third person plural forms are used in place of second person sin-gular to address or refer to chiefs, in order to include the spiritual world. The super-natural is further concretized in the humble, metaphorical lowering of other partici-pants, closer to the earth and in the special handling of possessions, which change semantic category when a shift to honorific register occurs.

The deities live in the sky world, and the human spirits in the undersea world. Traditional ideology indicated that when paramount chiefs die, their spirits go to heaven, whereas the spirits of the people and the lower chiefs go to the undersea (Mauricio 1993:432). A Pohnpeian historian describes the world of spirits as follows:

> Here are the places of the various spirits. The Underworld was the land for the spirits
> of the people who had died and been buried in graves or sunk in the sea or streams, or
> burned up in fire or killed, etc. Their spirits would go and live there for a while and
> then afterwards they would continue on from it. [Pueliko, the Second Heaven] was
> the place for the people who had poor voices. (Bernart, quoted in Mauricio 1993:119)

An Irishman who lived in Pohnpei during the 1820s and wrote extensively of his experiences there described his interpretations of 1820s Pohnpeian religious ideol-ogy and practice as follows:

> The whole theology of the island, the singular most imaginable for such a people,
> appears to be a worship of mind, intelligence, or life. They appear to have an idea
> of its action, independently of the body—to imagine it a separate and superior
> existence—a guiding genius over the conduct of the body. They have no [elaborate]
> temples, no idols, no altars, no offerings, no sacrifices; but worship a world of spirits,

Figure 1.1 Preparation for a feast in the nahs of the Paramount Cheif of Madolenihmw.

the disembodied souls, if I may so speak, or more properly, the exalted minds of their dead chiefs. (O'Connell 1972:152)

The first Christian missionaries arrived in Pohnpei in 1852, and current ideas reflect this influence as well as traditional thought. Most Pohnpeians would now identify themselves as Christian, either Catholic or Protestant.

Much of the traditional religious heritage of the political system is, however, still represented in part by the community meeting house or *nahs* (Mauricio 1993), discussed next, as well as in many other practices.

Space and rank: The nahs

Studies on social deixis (the communication of social status difference in language) and the communication of respect have shown the importance of integrating linguistic and ethnographic information with an understanding of the social organization of the space in which language is used (e.g., Firth 1970, 1972; Hanks 1990). It has long been recognized (e.g., Goffman 1967) that both verbal and nonverbal behavior are important in displaying deference to others' presence and in assessing social meaning. Spatial symbolism is extremely important in constructing status inequality on Pohnpei. The overall space in the *nahs* or feast house is ordered hierarchically, with certain portions of space reserved for the chiefs and other high-status persons. For example, one particular area is reserved for children born of a paramount chief and chieftess during their reign. However, the nahs is used for many everyday, unceremonial activities, such as drying laundry, playing bingo, and sewing. During such activities, the hierarchy of space is not observed. When sakau is not being served, for example, the sakau stones or stone may be turned on edge and leaned up against one side.

Each nahs is rectangular in shape, typically with a floor plan that is U-shaped, that is, one side is completely open to the outside (see diagram). The walls on three sides extend halfway to the roof. The U-shaped configuration results from the fact that the floor is raised on three sides above the middle, a bare earth floor. Low-status people usually enter the nahs at the ground level in the open front; they also may not step on the beam that forms the inner edge of a side platform. The furthest interior platform is reserved for the two highest ranking chiefs and chieftesses. The hierarchy of space can be mapped onto locales outside the feast house as well, as shown in chapter 5 (in this volume).

A U-shaped nahs with three center posts is called *mwengintik*, literally, "to whisper," whereas one with five center posts is called *koupahleng*, literally "to erect or build under heaven" (see figure 1.2). A number of Pohnpeian oral historians have equated the nahs with a church because it embodies sacred symbolic elements (Mauricio 1993:124).

The diagram (figure 1.2, in this volume, adapted from Mauricio 1993) shows the type of nahs called Koupahleng. Roof posts, entryways, and floor areas have names and statuses attached to them (the following description is based on that of Mauricio 1993). The first floor area on the upper platform (top of diagram) is the area of highest status and is called Woun Kerehlap, or "place of the honored one." The Enihlap or Great Deity is represented by the paramount chief when he is seated in this area. The second area (often represented by a height difference, i.e., lower) is referred to as Pahn Eririso, "in the attendance of the honored one." The third area is composed of an area called Wounken (literally "in honor of the Secondary Chief"), and Woulap ("the great honor of the paramount chief"). The remaining platform area (the white space on the diagram below Woulap and Wounken) is called Salada Mwahu, "orderly and calm attendance." The ground-level, dirt-floor area where *sakau* is often prepared and cooked food is redistributed is called Nankadeni Limes Ras Ie; the cooking area is Pahpeiso or Pehsen Pwel ("ash of the land"). The hearth is also shown on the diagram.

The roof support posts in the nahs have great symbolic and status value; they are divided into primary posts (*keidu*) and secondary posts (*uhr*). The post at the top of the diagram (labeled A) is called Saladien Enihlap. The name of the post literally translates as "facing downward of the Great Spirit (Dau Katau and Nahnsapwe)." The wall panel attached to the post is called *werekleng*, or "spouse of heaven." Only the paramount chief is allowed to sit against this post and face downward to the crowd. The post called Saladahn Leng (labeled B) is where the principal attendant, guard, or server (*erir*) of sakau to the paramount chief sits and works. The name means "facing the heavens." The post called Saladahn Enihlap (C in the diagram), meaning "facing forward toward the Great Deity," is where the person in charge of the redis-

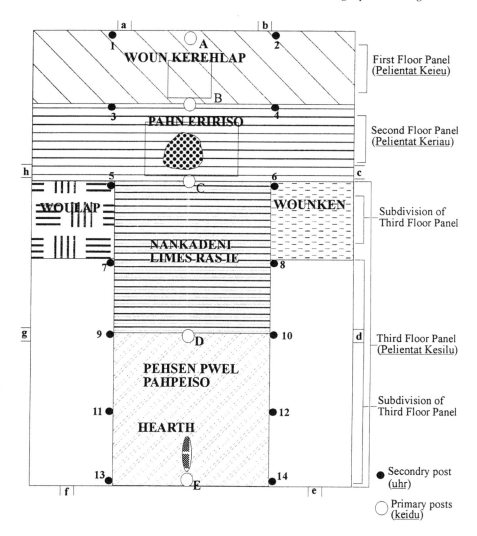

Figure 1.2 A Pohnpeian Nahs (adapted from Mauricio 1993).

tribution activities and the sakau ceremony works. The post called Oloapwoud (D), meaning "man-spouse," is where the person in charge of the hearth and the cooking works. The post at the entrance of the nahs is called Oahpwin (E). Secondary roof posts are also significant and are named although some of their literal meanings are no longer available (Mauricio 1993:417). They are as follows: Kienwoulap (on the diagram, number 1), Kienwounken (2), Saladak (3, "face upward or rising"), Uhdak (4, "stand erect or rising"), Pwoakinloak (5), Uhloak (6), Semendakenloak (7), Semenloak (8), Dakehnloak (9), Ririnsemenloak (10), Mehnloak (11), Ririnloak (12), Soaroaloak (13), and Uhroaloak (14).

Entryways of the nahs are labeled "a" through "h" on the diagram. Each has status relevant attributes. Entryway a is called Pelik Iso. It is used only by the secondary chief and his children. It is also referred to as "sacred entryway or door." Pelik Woau (b) is another "sacred entryway," this one used only by the Paramount Chief and his children. Likadahd (c) is the entryway for the women in the attendance of the paramount chief, that is, those invited to sit in the second floor panel (Pahn Eririso) on the upper platform of the meeting house. The entryway for men in the attendance of the paramount chief is Wahnmeimei (h). The general entryway for women is d, called Peilpein or Paliepein. The general entryway for men is Peilmwahn (g). The entryway for the nobility or those who have high ranking titles in the Paramount Chief's line is e, Oloiso. The entryway for those who have high ranking titles in the secondary chief's line is f, Serihso.

The beams, rafters, posts, and other lumber used for the construction of a *nahs* should add up to 333 representing Isohkelekel and his warriors. Chapters 3 and 5 also refer to the spatial symbolism of the *nahs*.

Kava (sakau) practices

In several of the transcript segments discussed, the participants are engaged in the preparation and consumption of sakau, a nonalcoholic, soporific beverage made from the pounded root of the pepper plant (*piper methysticum*) and water. In Pacific societies, the ritual sharing of kava (sakau on Pohnpei) is a natural setting for the use of honorific terms and for their acquisition by younger members of the society. Although kava drinking is widespread in stratified Polynesia (e.g., Tonga and Samoa), Pohnpei is the only country in Micronesia to have both the kava ceremony and a highly developed honorific lexicon. As Geraghty (1994) observes, although the name sakau indicates a non-Samoan source for kava drinking, the associated term *ahmwadang* ("food or kava served before the formal meal or kava ceremony") appears to be of Samoan origin (244). That the ritual use of *piper methysticum* was well developed by the ancestral inhabitants of Polynesia, is evidenced by archaeological data and by the Proto-Polynesian term *taano'a*, a bowl for mixing and serving the kava infusion (Kirch 1984:67).

The importance of kava drinking and its related ceremonial contexts is often mentioned in Pacific islands literature (Firth 1940; Oliver 1951; Bascom 1965; Marshall 1979; Kirch 1984). A number of ethnographers have, for example, recognized the relationship between kava drinking practices and local hierarchies (Holmes 1967; Bott 1972; Duranti 1981, 1994). Although missionaries completely eradicated the practice of kava drinking on the nearby island of Kosrae (the only other Micronesian island where the ceremony was observed), sakau drinking on Pohnpei survives in a variety of contexts, including the newest form, commercial sakau bars, loosely modeled after the American institution. Even in this newest, less traditional context, rank has enormous influence, and lower-ranking participants often wait until the highest-ranking participant takes his first drink (Petersen 1977:156).

To the Pohnpeians, sakau drinking is one of the most important daily social events. Because Pohnpeians live in scattered homesteads rather than villages, evening sakau is a time for all members of a neighborhood to meet and talk. The preparation of sakau is lengthy and ongoing: As pounded roots lose their potency, fresh roots are pounded and prepared as members of the community sit, smoke, and talk around the sakau stone. Concepts of person in Pacific societies are embedded in a matrix of social relations and involve such collaborative reconstruction of community (Kirkpatrick and White 1985; Watson-Gegeo and White 1990).

The preparation of sakau is similar to the methods described for making medicine; curers on Pohnpei identified to Reisenberg (1948) three acts in the preparations of their medicines—plucking leaves, pounding them, and wringing out the infusion (409). Typically, four men sit on logs on the earth floor of the nahs (feast house) around a large, flat stone and pound sakau roots until they are pulverized. Water is added and one designate performs the task of squeezing the mass through soaked hibiscus fibers. As the men pound, the pounding stones clang rhythmically on the large sakau stone in front of them. This sound alerts anyone on surrounding homesteads that sakau is in preparation. In formal settings, following a signal by the *menindei* (master of ceremonies) all the pounding goes through a final rhythmic, musical cycle and then stops in unison.

Although the status of the participants appears to be an important component keying the sakau event, certain customary sequences inherent in the practice of sakau lend themselves to establishing an ad hoc hierarchy from among whomever is present. For example, the first four cups of sakau are designated to specific high-ranking individuals. Although the exact designation of the four cups varies according to municipality and context, their importance is uniformly observed. Examples of the variety of specific designation include whether both high-ranking chiefs are in attendance, whether the chieftesses are in attendance, and guests to be especially honored. The first cup of sakau is always designated for the highest-ranking person present. When the chief is offered the cup, the erir's (server to the chief) right arm is placed over his left, and he looks back, averting his gaze from the chief. The four-cup sequence may be repeated many times during a feast (*kamadipw*) or funeral (*mehla*), again serving as an enactment of the relative status of those in attendance. Even in less formal settings the implications of the sequence of the first cups is attended to; if no high-ranking person is present and the differences in rank of those drinking are not substantial, Pohnpeians sometimes enact a competitive modesty, insisting that others accept the first cup (cf. Petersen 1977, 1982). Modesty is an important part of strategies for constructing and negotiating hierarchy from below and is discussed in later chapters.

That the first four cups constitute an important relational meaning is apparent in the rule, taken with great seriousness, that once the hibiscus bark (through which the drink is strained) is put down on the pounding stone, no one may leave until four cups have been served. This ritual suggests that even though the four cups are ranked in importance, their relationship carries an additional significance. The boundary between number four and five is often the boundary between the chiefs' (and their wives') cups and those of the lesser-ranking titleholders.

Though Protestants are exhorted from partaking of sakau by a rule against drinking intoxicants or smoking, the role of the erir, or server, allows high-ranking Protestants to participate in sakau without compromising either role. For example, the secondary chief of the district of Uh at the time of my fieldwork did not drink sakau because of his role as a Protestant minister, but he designated his erir (server) to drink for him. In this case, the erir offers the cup to the chief, the chief shakes his head, the erir then drinks. In this way the institutionalized use of a mediator has served to make the sakau practice flexible in terms of change and allowed it to retain its power to reproduce hierarchy.

The Pohnpeian language

Here I briefly describe some characteristics of Pohnpeian, especially those particularly relevant to specific aspects of status-marked language (for a complete description of Pohnpeian grammar, see Rehg 1981). Pohnpeian is similar to English in that the order of words in a sentence determines grammatical relationships. The basic word order is subject-verb-object, like English. No distinctions of gender are made with pronouns. Temporal relationships are indicated with what linguists call aspect. Aspect focuses on how the verb action is regarded or experienced with respect to time, for example, whether an action is completed or uncompleted. In Pohnpeian the suffix *-ehr* signifies an action that is already completed, whereas the word *pahn* preceding a verb indicates the action has not been completed yet. Verbs without aspectual marking signify an ongoing action; the reduplicated (repeated) form of the verb indicates a durative action (that has been going on for some time). The term *kin* preceding a verb signifies habitual action. As mentioned previously, verbs are important sites for status marking.

Whereas one language may use different specific verbs for indicating different ways in which a given action is performed (for example, "go" and "come" in English), other languages may keep the same verb root for both actions and add different morphemes or particles to convey different meanings, as in Pohnpeian, *kohdo* ("come") *kohla* ("go"), *-la* signifying directionality away from the speaker and addressee, and *-do* signifying directionality toward the speaker. In English we say "kill" or "die" to differentiate between acts caused by a person and other forms of causality. In Pohnpeian, a causative prefix (*ka-*) is used, so that *mehla* ("die") becomes *kamehla* ("kill"). Chapter 3 (in this volume) discusses verbs in more detail.

A distinction between transitive and intransitive verbs is made in translations of some status-marked verbs. In transitivity, an activity is carried over or transferred from an agent (e.g., subject) to a patient (e.g., object). The following are examples: the woman caught the fish; the man planted the banana tree. An example of an intransitive construction (without a direct object) is the following: the woman smiled. In Pohnpeian, speaking of low-status eating (*tungoal*), the intransitive (no direct object) is shown in the sentence—"so they can eat" *re en tungoale*—whereas a transitive sentence, for example "do you habitually eat [drink] sakau?" is *komw kin iang tungoal sakau?* The intransitive form of the verb is marked with the suffix *-e*. Many verb roots in Pohnpeian are used only either transitively or intransitively, but some can occur as both, with the addition of a suffix which adds transitive meaning. Rehg (1981) believes transitive forms derived from intransitive ones through suffix deletion (203).

Pohnpeian evidences a rich system of what linguists call classifiers, a set of specialized words that are obligatory parts of certain noun phrases. The semantic range of a classifier can be quite general (e.g., in Pohnpeian a classifier for small things considered precious) or quite specific (e.g., the Pohnpeian classifier for enumerating gusts of wind). Pohnpeian has numeral classifiers and noun classifiers (chapter 4 discusses the latter in some detail). Both systems divide nouns up into various categories. Classifier systems are common to many languages (including, for example, American Sign Language) and code additional information about nouns referred to in the noun phrase. Noun classification systems are rich sites for examining how languages categorize objects and relationships and for examining how experience is meaningfully and culturally structured. For example, there are more than thirty ways to count in Pohnpeian, depending on what is being counted. Categories are delineated primarily according to shape ("strand of," "pile of," "oblong piece of," "stalk of," "slice of," "small round object," "long object") but also according to such concepts as animacy, body parts, and food cooked in a stone oven. A speaker using the three phrases *uht riau* ("banana two") *uht rioapwoat* ("banana two.trees")[3] and *uht rioumw* ("banana two.bunches") is using different forms of classifiers suffixed to "two" to signify differences between two bananas, two banana trees, and two bunches of bananas (examples from Rehg 1981).

The Pohnpeian possessive classifiers also divide nouns into different categories; however, these are not organized according to shape but differentiate such meanings as natural state, harvested state, temporary versus permanent state, and kinship relations. As with numeral classifiers, speakers can decide to emphasize a certain aspect of meaning through choice of classifier. For example, it is possible to say *kene uht* meaning "his or her banana to eat" or *nah uht* meaning "his or her banana tree," and *ah uht* "his or her banana harvested." As discussed in chapter 4, possessive relationships expressed in Pohnpeian common speech are resorted and reclassified in honorific speech, and much of the specific information encoded in classifiers is "bleached" out. Microinteractions that index status are thus linked to cultural ideologies about control and the relationships of chiefs to the people. Pohnpeian honorific possessive construction entails a re-creation of social relations and systems of relations.

Another feature of Pohnpeian relevant to this study is the distinction between inclusive and exclusive pronouns. In the second person, dual (two people) or plural (more than two) inclusivity or exclusivity can be marked. That is, the speaker can exclude or include the addressee, to mean "we two, including you" (*kita*) or "we all, including you" (*kitail*) as opposed to "we two/all, excluding you" (*kiht*). As is shown in chapter 7, in oratory speakers can manipulate the inclusive/exclusive dimension to construct interesting status relationships and to link low-status and high-status members of the community together, as well as to distinguish between them.

Though there are many nouns for indicating high-status entities, only two nouns indicate low-status entities; food and speech. Nouns are often modified with deictic suffixes meaning "this" or "that," for example *liho* ("woman.that") or *lihe* ("woman.this").

The second person singular pronoun form can be marked for high status, and the third person plural pronoun is used as a status-raising form for chiefs (instead of the second person singular), but there are no subject or object pronouns denoting low status. The structure of certain aspects of the language is discussed in more detail in following chapters.

Two dialects of Pohnpeian are recognized by native speakers, the Kiti or southern dialect and the main dialect (cf. Rehg 1981), the principal difference being in the vowel sounds (see Rehg 1981:46). Borrowings from a succession of colonial rulers from 1852 to 1983 are evident in the lexicon: Spanish (e.g. *kana* from ganar, "to win"; *mihsa* from misa, "[Catholic] mass"; *pahdire* from padre, "priest"); German (e.g., *mahlen* from malen, "to paint, draw"; *sirangk* from Schrank, "locker, cupboard"), Japanese (e.g., *dengki* from denki, "electricity/flashlight"; *iakiu* from yakyu, "baseball"; *mai* from umai, "skillful"; *sarmada* from sarumata, "underwear/boxer shorts"; *sidohsa* from jidoosha, "automobile"), and American English (*ainpwoat* from ironpot/cooking pot, *Koht* from God, *pwuhk* from book, *sukuhl* from school, *tipaker* from tobacco, *kulok* from clock, etc.).

The German convention of indicating a long vowel by writing "h" after it was adopted for the Pohnpeian spelling system (Rehg 1981). Contrast between short and long vowel lengths is meaningful in Pohnpeian. In addition, extended vowel lengthening can be a sign of high status, as when a more pronounced lengthening of the third syllable (*leh*) in the greeting *kaselehlia* is used when greeting chiefs and chieftesses.

Methodology

Access to processes of building social inequality and the attitudes that inform these processes is made possible by analyzing audio and video recordings of particular interactions that are "enacted and lived through as accountable patterns of meaning, inference and action" (Drew and Heritage 1993:5). Together with traditional participant-observation and interview methods of anthropological research, this approach offers a way to address the problem associated with the frequent gap between self-reports of behavior and actual behavior, or between what people say and what they do (Drew and Heritage 1993:5). The use of videorecorded data and the now available tools for digitizing video to facilitate close analysis of talk in interaction, have created an opportunity to pose new questions and gain new insights into processes of human social organization.

My study combines ethnography with methodologies from a number of fields, including linguistic analysis, discourse analysis, conversation analysis,[4] the ethnography of speaking,[5] and linguists looking at relationships between metaphorical relationships and cognitive organization.[6]

The importance of studying spontaneous, ordinary face-to-face interaction as a key to understanding social organization was recognized in the work of Garfinkel (1967) and Goffman (1967, 1974). The interactionist approaches reflected in their work have been fruitful in focusing research in sociology and anthropology on how speakers and hearers disclose to each other and to overhearers (such as ethnographers) information about social categories. Interaction is recognized not as governed by fixed social rules but as a process affected by many contextual components that are constantly being analyzed and evaluated by participants. The emergence of "mundane," everyday conversation as a relevant activity for revealing both how participants construct context through talk and how recursively context shapes talk developed from this framework.

Work on face-to-face interaction inspired by the work of Goffman (1967, 1974) and Garfinkel (1967) gives considerable insight into how actors analyze and interpret social action. Conversation analysts have shown everyday speech to have a regularity and orderliness oriented to by speakers and hearers and important in co-constructing meaning.[7] Work on formal talk in institutions clearly indicates specific strategies actors use to construct asymmetries in interaction (cf. Drew and Heritage 1993). Work by linguistic anthropologists in the ethnography of communication tradition provides a basis for identifying speech events, including political speech events, participant roles, and the importance of context (cf. Hymes 1962; Gumperz and Hymes 1972; Bauman and Sherzer 1974). Data on how speech is organized provide critical details for the examination of social and political organization. Speech is recognized as social action rather than for its referential properties (Austin 1962; Searle 1969), but analysis is not limited to individual sentences in isolation.

The availability of a videotaped record allows for repeated and detailed examination of particular events in interactions and enables more precision in observations, in addition to giving readers an opportunity to look at the data themselves. Analysis is based on the recognition that the production of an utterance or turn at talk both embodies a definition of the situation and makes relevant some action or range of actions for the next speaker. If relevant action is not forthcoming from the next speaker, this too has meaning, as, for example, hesitation before accepting an invitation. This is social action at work, as speakers and hearers analyze and infer meaning and produce appropriate "next actions."

The explicit comparison (cf. Drew and Heritage 1993) in conversation analysis between institutional talk and "ordinary" conversation reveals points at which the context of institutions are constituted through the talk and may serve as a better tool for analysis of political process than categorizing whole societies as hierarchical or egalitarian in order to understand political organization. The value of an interactional analysis approach is in not reifying old dichotomies based on etic notions and oversimplifications of complex and dynamic social relations.[8]

Fieldwork

Fieldwork for this study was conducted for eleven months in 1992–93 and over the period of two summers in 1990 and 1991. I also spent two six-week periods in Pohnpei in 1995 collecting material on how spatial relationships are expressed in Pohnpeian and on narratives and gestures. During 1991 and the longer field stay in 1992–93, as well as in 1995, I made videotapes of activities in the daily life of Pohnpeians, with particular attention to those activities surrounding chiefs and chieftesses, forums for honorific language use. In almost every event or activity recorded, I filmed at least four or five hours to capture a range of activities and to accustom participants to the video camera. Video recording of human behavior is often subject to the criticism that filming somehow encourages people to behave in a way that is substantially different from their habitual ways of being. I believe, however, that if we take Bourdieu's (1977) notion of habitus seriously, we must acknowledge that a great deal of what participants in interaction are doing, and the interpretive strategies they are enacting, is at least partly beyond their level of awareness (see Silverstein 1981 for a discussion of limits of awareness of language use). In addition, I believe that any disadvantages of using video recording are far outweighed by the advantages of having a record that captures some of the rich complexity of human interaction in a medium that allows for continued observation and analysis by repeated viewing, by the ethnographer as well as by local consultants.

Transcriptions of portions of recorded material were done in the field with the help of Pohnpeian consultants, and continued in the United States. These sessions were extremely revealing about beliefs, practices, and actual behaviors, as well as language details.

Transcription conventions

Because I use video frames of Pohnpeian interactions in this book, it is not possible to provide some of the Pohnpeians with the anonymity that is conventional in these types of studies of language use (and, of course, many participants want to be recognized for their contributions to this study). In cases of spontaneous speech where video frames do not make identities known, I provide initials for names. The exception to this is in the case of the chiefs and chieftesses, who generously gave their permission, as did the other participants.

Of course, any transcript represents only an abstraction of the multilayered, complex nature of human communicative behavior. Transcripts privilege language over other communicative practice. In selecting certain segments of an activity to reproduce here, I am concentrating on a subset of the activities of speakers, and I no doubt simplify participants' performances. My choices are based on practical considerations (e.g., readability of transcripts) and established conventions within the field of linguistic anthropology and sociolinguistics as well as the goals of my research (cf. Ochs 1979), but they are nevertheless choices that influence this book. The issue of translation from Pohnpeian to English is also a process of interpretations and decisions (cf. Duranti 1997). Although for all translations I relied on Pohnpeian native speakers to either produce the translations or check my translations, translation itself is only a partial process. The issue of representation is an important one in anthropology and one not easily resolved. At the same time, transcripts permit a close analysis of language practices across a range of speakers and contexts and enable attention to the details of interaction that provides an opportunity to enrich our understanding of the processual nature of what we often take to be "givens" such as "social organization" and "culture," and hopefully will lead in the direction of an ever more rigorous investigation of human behavior.

In sections of transcripts from interactional data I provide three lines for each speaker's utterance: One line shows the Pohnpeian words, an interlinear gloss shows a literal translation of the Pohnpeian utterance, and a third line of text provides a "free" or idiomatic translation in English. I use the following abbreviations and transcription conventions:

[ ]	overlapped speech (two or more speakers at once)
(?words)	unclear stretch of talk
(?)	unintelligible stretch of talk
(?):	unclear who is speaking
W, M, S	capitalized initials indicate either names or titles of people
(())	author's comments
→	highlights portion for the reader
(. . .)	portions of transcribed data left out
COME!	capital letters indicate loud voice volume (e.g., shouting)
(1.0)	numbers between parenthesis silences in speech
-	cutoff
01	line numbers are used to direct the reader's attention to specific instances, and do not reflect an utterance relationship to the transcript as a whole
LocVerb	locative verb
TranVerb	transitive verb
Ps.Cl.	possessive classifier
afy&m	away from you (addressee) and me (speaker)
tm	toward me (speaker)
(S)	singular
(P)	plural
(D)	dual
(EXCL)	exclusive
(INCL)	inclusive
Interj.	interjection
[HUM]	humiliative honorific
[EXAL]	exaltive honorific
take.from	when periods appear between English words in the interlinear gloss this indicates that the English equivalent of the single Pohnpeian word is made up of a number of concepts rendered independently in English.

Notes

1. Fuller descriptions of Pohnpeian culture can be found in Fischer 1957, 1974; Mauricio 1993; Falgout 1984; Kihleng 1996; Reisenberg 1968; Petersen 1982; Shimizu 1982, 1987; and Hanlon 1988.

2. Goodenough 1957; Sahlins 1958, 1963; I. Goldman 1970; Friedman 1975; Earle 1977; Keesing 1978; Douglas 1979; Lindstrom 1981; Petersen 1982; Kirch 1984; Brenneis and Myers 1984; Gailey 1987; and others.

3. When periods appear between English translations of Pohnpeian words, this indicates that the English equivalent of the single Pohnpeian word is made up of a number of concepts rendered independently in English.

4. For example Schegloff 1968; Sacks, Schegloff and Jefferson 1974; Pomerantz 1978, 1984; C. Goodwin 1981; Atkinson and Heritage 1984; and others.

5. See Hymes 1962; Gumperz and Hymes 1972; Bauman and Sherzer 1974.

6. As in, for example, G. Lakoff 1987; G. Lakoff and Johnson 1980; Sweetser 1990.

7. See Sacks, Schegloff, and Jefferson 1974; Schegloff, Jefferson and Sacks 1977; C. Goodwin 1981; Pomerantz 1984.

8. For example, ideas of people as autonomous or intentional actors can be challenged (cf. Duranti 1988, 1997:226–36, 314–21; Hill and Irvine 1992; Rosaldo 1982).

Chapter 2

What Are Honorifics?

H onorifics" are systems of marking relative social status through grammatical choices. In languages with honorifics, expressions of differential status marking are actually part of the grammatical rules of the language. These contrasting expressions are isosemantic (Irvine 1992:252); that is, they are different ways of saying the same thing in terms of reference[1] or truth[2] values but offer speakers choices in terms of pragmatic[3] values. As Geertz (1960) states about Javanese:

> A number of words (and some affixes) are made to carry in addition to their normal linguistic meaning what might be called a "status meaning"; i.e., when used in actual conversation they convey not only their fixed detonative [sic] meaning ("house," "body," "eat," "walk," "you," "passive voice") but also a connotative meaning concerning the status of (and/or degree of familiarity between) the speaker and the listener. . . . Thus, for "house" we have three forms . . . each connoting a progressively higher relative status of the listener with respect to the speaker (248).

J. Errington (1988:11) recounts an elderly man describing Javanese language practices as including the following cognitive operations: "Whenever two people meet they should ask themselves: 'Who is this person? Who am I? What is this person to me?'" The man held up his hands as if they were parts of a scale. Living in Pohnpei, I found that part of each interaction involved analyzing my own status relative to others, and this was especially true in greeting situations. Not only linguistic behavior but other embodied behaviors such as bowing my head and taking care not to position myself in a higher vertical or horizontal relation than someone of high status were matters to be constantly attended to.

Grammaticalized status marking is evidenced in a wide range of genetically unrelated languages. Complex honorific systems (or registers) have, for example, been reported for African languages, Australian languages, Urdu-Hindi, Llasa Tibetan, Persian, Mongolian, Thai, Tamil, Burmese, Vietnamese, Zuni, Tewa (U.S.), Nahuatl (Mexico), Japanese, Korean, Javanese, Mongolian, and the Pacific languages Tongan and Samoan, as well as others (see Agha 1994 for a complete review of this literature).

Grammatically this status marking is realized in different ways. Status may be marked by independent words or by affixes (a general category that covers prefixes, infixes, and suffixes). Thus, in Korean, for example, there are different sets of endings for verbs, depending on the social relationship between the speaker and the addressee. In Pohnpeian, the verb stem is different depending on the status level to be conveyed. In Javanese, a sentence can be constructed to indicate at least six different speech "levels" and relationships between interactants. In Geertz's description of Java, an equivalent of the sentence "are you going to eat rice and cassava now?" can be rendered in the following ways (with lowest to highest) (1960:249):

are:	apa/napa/menapa
you:	kowé/sampéjan/pandjenengan
going:	arep/adjeng/baḍé
to eat:	mangan/neḍa/ḍahar
rice:	sega/sekul
and:	lan/kalijan
cassava:	kaspé
now:	saiki/saniki/samenika

Between the highest and lowest levels the above sentence would share only one word, *kaspé*, or "cassava." In Pohnpeian the sentence "will you go inside your house now?" can be stated in the following ways.

you:	ke/komwi/re
will:	pahn
go in:	patohlong/pidolong/ketlong
inside:	nan
your:	ihmwahmw/ahmw tungoal/sapwellimomwi/sapwellimahr
house:	ihmw/tehnpas
now?:	met?

Dunn (1996) reports six different status-indexing forms of the verb "to speak" in Japanese.

In some European languages, the contrast set is quite small, most commonly the second person pronoun. Using the second person plural rather than the second person singular denotes higher status for the person referred to or addressed, for example, French *tu/vous*. In German, the forms are *du* and *Sie* (note that the more honored form, Sie, is also capitalized, whereas *du* is not). In English only forms of address can index relative social status:

For the English speaker, the clearest linguistic markers of social relations are personal names, such as John and Mr. Brown. . . . John is used if there is high solidarity between the speaker and John Brown, and John Brown has less power than the speaker—in other words if John Brown is a *close subordinate*. A clear example is when John Brown is the speaker's son. On the other hand, Mr. Brown is used if there is low solidarity and John Brown has more power than the speaker—if he is a *distant superior*. . . . It seems unlikely that there would be any disagreement among English speakers as to the names appropriate to these two situations. (Hudson 1980:123–5)

Honorifics have captured the interest of anthropologists and linguists because they provide evidence about how people together construct a system of shared understandings about intergroup, intragroup, and individual ranked relationships. With social relationships explicitly marked in language, it is possible to have two data sets: (1) speakers' beliefs about how the system is organized and used, and (2) information about how speakers actually deploy these mechanisms, and negotiate social relations. As Irvine (1985) notes, "language levels are named and highly accessible to their speakers' conscious contemplation" (571) in a way that other grammatical practices are not. Speakers can report on their ideas about their particular language system; these ideas are valuable data about the link between cultural ideologies and the structure of language (Silverstein 1981). It is interesting, moreover, to note the specific limits of speaker awareness of these forms (Silverstein 1981). For example, in Philips's work in Tonga (Polynesia), government-sponsored tutorials in Tongan "respect vocabulary" emphasize only a limited set of honorific forms that are part of speakers' conscious repertoire. The real repertoire is only evident when actual language data are examined (see also Shibamoto 1987, for Japanese). In their analysis of different levels of respect in Nahuatl, Hill and Hill (1978) show that speakers' self-reports of how honorific speech is used in their conversations offer a very incomplete picture of how they actually show respect to one another. It becomes clear from actual speech behavior that the relationships conceptualized and expressed in language are not fixed and enduring but negotiated turn by turn between speakers in everyday conversations as well as in other contexts.

It is conventional among those working on honorifics to talk about them in terms of language "levels" to indicate the multiple nature of the social hierarchy that can be constructed with these forms. However, although such a term is useful, it also obscures some important aspects of honorific use, namely, the ways speakers can switch between levels within the same utterance (cf. J. Errington 1988:11) and to refer to the same person, and the important differences that can exist between levels (discussed in more detail in following chapters). J. Errington proposes speech styles rather than levels (1988:11; see also Wolfowitz 1991) to get away from any categorical rigidity. Style, however, does not capture the somewhat obligatory or hierarchical nature of many of these forms, although it suggests an important link with cultural esthetics and valued practices (see, for example, Beeman 1986:202; Keeler 1984:292). A term such as "layers" might be more able to capture the interrelatedness and complexity of these forms.

Sometimes honorifics are referred to as status indexing; at other times as indicative of respect or deference (irrespective of social status) or social features of the situation. Work on honorifics in different language systems shows that speakers use these resources not only to mark social relationships but to constitute other forms of meaning, for example, contextual variables such as level of formality. Honorifics can be used by speakers to demonstrate an understanding of appropriate comportment or demeanor (Ide 1989; Beeman 1986; Wolfowitz 1991; J. Errington 1988). Some authors (see Agha 1994) detach the role of honorifics in signaling deference and demeanor from status indexing on the grounds that it explains instances in which a superior uses an honorific to an inferior, something that happens in fact in the oratory of Pohnpeian chiefs. As Goffman (1956) notes, however, both deference and demeanor are indexes of status relations:

> Deference images tend to point to the wider society outside the interaction to the place the individual has achieved in the hierarchy of this society. Demeanor images tend to point to qualities which any social position gives its incumbents a chance to display during interaction, for these qualitites pertain more to the way in which the individual handles his position than to the rank and place of that position. (82–83)

Hill (1992) similarly characterizes "respect" in Nahuatl as "the proper observance of status relationships" (264). Close analysis of interactional behavior indicates that status is constructed by speakers to be a relationship that can be multiply indexical; that is, the pragmatic meanings that markers of status entail can be compound. When interactants use status-marked vocabulary in the service of constructing a particular type of context (e.g., formal or institutional) or a particular kind of speaker comportment (knowledge of appropriate social behavior and social structure), they are keying the socially indexical properties of these forms. Ervin-Tripp (ms) reports that "even before children are able to identify form contrasts as more polite, nicer, or bossier, they recognize them as indexing social features" and identify certain forms as appropriate for high-status addressees (Becker 1986).

I argue that when a Pohnpeian chief uses an exaltive form in oratory for the lower-status people, he is not just exhibiting deference or his own proper demeanor but is actually doing the act of raising their status. The fact that this does not alter the social superiority of the chief in the longer term is a result of the multiple ways the chief's higher status is continually constructed, for example, his position vertically and horizontally on the feast house platform as he delivers the status raising words of his speech, as well as his facing relation toward the people (from the side of the deities). Thus, though these forms may indeed be deferential, it is my position that they are first and foremost status indexing, but this use is expanded by speakers in multiply indexical ways.

Honorification and politeness

Honorific systems are considered to be a subset of behaviors identified under the rubric of politeness (P. Brown and Levinson 1978). For example, "[p]oliteness is demonstrated in Japanese through honorification" (Bonvillain 1997). Yet honorifics have posed some problems for politeness theories.

Cross-cultural research on politeness behaviors has assumed some similarities about the general nature of politeness phenomena and motivations for such behavior across languages and cultures. A number of authors (e.g., R. Lakoff 1973b; P. Brown and Levinson 1978; Leech 1983) have proposed universal principles. These include tact, agreement, sympathy, minimizing the cost to the other (Leech 1983), and not imposing as well as being friendly (R. Lakoff 1973b). P. Brown and Levinson (1978), in a landmark, cross-cultural study on politeness, argue that "negative" and "positive" politeness mediate between community members' sometimes conflicting desires for autonomy and approval (an example is a request for a favor, which impedes on another's freedom of action). Honorific speech is given as an example of negative politeness—an antidote to intrusion into another's personal space or freedom of action. Thus, for example, a person wishing to make a request of a high-status individual first expresses deference to that person's elevated social standing, which increases social distance, to offset infringement on autonomy resulting from the request (but see Duranti 1992; Irvine 1974).

As a number of authors have demonstrated, universal politeness theories have been overly dependent on the Western philosophical tradition and Western cultural ideas of the person as an autonomous agent existing apart from society. Matsumoto (1989), for example, argues that Brown and Levinson's linkage of negative face (concern with autonomy) to honorifics is problematic when analyzing Japanese culture, where dependence of inferiors already raises the status of superiors, and failure to show such dependence results in affront (cf. Wolfowitz 1991, for Suriname Javanese). Others have also suggested that use of honorifics in Japan is governed by a sense of obligation rather than strategic considerations. Ide (1989) remarks that honorifics in Japanese do not indicate speakers' intentions to enhance the other's esteem or avoid threatening the other but rather are an indication of an understanding of expectations of other group members (see also Rosaldo 1982). "For a Japanese speaker, to speak with the proper use of honorifics where it is required is to express that the speaker knows his or her expected place in terms of group membership (in group-out group), role structures (relative status, power relationship, specific role relationship such as selling and buying), and situational constraints (formal or non-formal settings)" (Ide 1989:241). Ide (1989) calls this "demonstrating socio-pragmatic concord" (242). Pohnpeians similarly feel that failure to use appropriate speech can result in loss of face for the speaker; however, this does not preclude the use of honorifics for strategic purposes (see also Beeman 1986:59 for Iran). As well, I argue, a speaker who is demonstrating that he or she "knows his or her expected place in terms of power relationship[s]" (Ide 1989:241) is continually constructing such a position and relation. Expressing proper demeanor also expresses rank, as when Goffman (1956) describes in his research on a mental ward: "[O]n Ward A, standards of demeanor were maintained that seem to be typical in American middle-class society" (79).

In Pohnpei and in other societies with honorific registers, honorific speech is used in all types of speech acts, including those described by Brown and Levinson's theory as positive politeness (addressing the desire to be approved of) (cf. J. Errington 1988 for Javanese) as well as those linked to negative politeness (autonomy). Honorifics are used in jokes, narratives, answers to questions from higher-status to lower-status persons, and so on. Duranti (1992) found that rather than recognizing the recipients' immunity to imposition, honorific speech in Samoa can coerce and oblige higher-status persons to behave in a certain way (e.g., with generosity or with a controlling demeanor) (93), thus directly impinging on their autonomy (see also Irvine 1974). The chief's nahs on Pohnpei is open to all in the community day and night, as problems develop or prestations are delivered. The chief's schedule is a round of funerals, feasts, and now meetings. Subordinates often have more privacy and autonomy than superordinates in daily life.

As Agha (1994) observes "Honorific usage appears to be independent of the notional rubric of politeness in a number of important respects" (288). Utterances can be deferential but impolite and vice versa (Hwang 1990), and in some languages the same honorific expression can be polite in certain contexts but impolite in others (e.g., Hijirada and Sohn 1986:367). At the same time, use of status-marked language, in those societies in which such language is part of the linguistic repertoire, is constructed as part of a range of appropriate behaviors in human interaction, which includes the notion of politeness. The linking of status-marked speech with politeness contributes to the reproduction of social stratification practices. The notion of rudeness can serve as a "potent social control" (Beeman 1986:85).

Honorific forms are among a set of resources for organizing aspects of human relationships, especially social difference and mediating inequalities. Honorific forms can be multiply indexical, marking not only status but also the relative *value* of high status, a value which can then be used to show appreciation and an especially valued relation through the use of the high-status form. When the use of honorific speech indexes proper demeanor or deference, this reflects local ideologies about the value of differing social strata. Honorific forms are not rigidly obligatory but are used as creative resources by speakers to encode aspects of social value that transcend structural role relations, acting as a symbolic means by which appreciation for individuals as well as ideologies of asymmetry are conveyed. Terms such as "honorifics," "deference," "respect vocabulary," and "politeness," which members of society are socialized to view as having very positive and laudatory connotations, tend to obscure our understanding of how these linguistic and social practices differentiate societies along status and rank lines, and how these social differences are valued, habituated, and naturalized. That these meanings are manipulated creatively in interactions between people shows the richness and complexity of the relationship between language and the constitution of society.

Cross-cultural classification schemes: Honorific types

Honorific systems have been subject to classification schemes not only by scholars but by native speakers. A frequently cited scheme by linguists for classifying honorifics is Comrie's (1976) tripartite categorization. This includes "referent" honorifics, signifying the relationship of the speaker to things or persons referred to, and "addressee" honorifics, which encode respect to the addressee without specifically referring to him or her, for example, by special intonation patterns (on Pohnpei, certain vowels are elongated to show respect). Languages such as Hindi, Malayalam, and Tibetan use only referent honorifics, whereas those such as Thai, Korean, Japanese, and Javanese use both referent and addressee honorifics (Irvine 1985). A third, more rare type in Comrie's classification—"bystander" honorifics are those used in the presence of specific persons to encode respect whether or not one is referring to or addressing such a person (Pohnpeian is often cited as an example as well as the vocabularies used traditionally between certain in-laws of indigenous Australian societies[4]). Actually, Pohnpeian evidences examples of all three types.

Although Pohnpeian is used as an example of bystander honorifics by Comrie (1976) and Levinson (1983), the term "bystander" is too passive in characterization to suit the data I collected in most cases. The term implies a person present but not taking part. Pohnpeian chiefs and chieftesses and others who are given deference without being addressed or directly referred to are *actively* partaking in events, and the significance of their participation is in fact constructed through the honorific words. So-called bystander honorifics constitute an environment in which the honored person is indexically included or pointed to in every interaction, whether or not he or she speaks. This is highly empowering of the honored person. Just how participation is defined obviously affects one's point of view on how active bystanders are. This again is an example of looking at language not necessarily for its referential meaning but in terms of what can be done with language. Bystander honorifics continually constitute differential status relations among participants, whether or not those participants are specifically referred to or addressed.

Identifying honorifics by referent, addressee, or bystander categories is useful for identifying the scope of honorifics cross-culturally, but as Duranti (1992) shows for Samoa, the use of respectful terms cannot be predicted merely on the basis of referent or addressee but is related to activity type and aspects of social relationships and social personae. Situational and contextual factors, as well as topic and stance (e.g., confrontational and epistemic), on Pohnpei can influence choice of honorific register, and as shown in an interaction discussed later, participant identity or role is not always a reliable guide.

Local classifications of honorific speech

Earlier researchers on Pohnpei, who relied on interviews with consultants and native speaker metapragmatic awareness, described honorific forms in terms of participant identity or role, as does Comrie, as well as according to levels. Garvin and Reisenberg (1952), for example, describe two levels of honorific speech, one high, but not including the two chiefs, the second for the chiefs alone. Rehg (1981) reports one scheme of three levels (two high and one common or unmarked) and one scheme of two levels, one high and one common or unmarked.

When I interviewed native speakers I received similar classification schemes (focusing on "high" and "common" or unmarked). Speakers conceptualize honorifics as divided into either two high levels similar to those mentioned by Garvin and Reisenberg and Rehg (high and very high) or into three different status levels: the two already mentioned (high and very high) and common or unmarked speech. However, looking at interactional data, I found the salient division to be not between the so-called two levels of higher status, or between high levels and common speech, but between a general class of high (for chiefs and sometimes others) and a general class of *low* (for myself and other nonchiefs). The low or *humiliative* form is mentioned by Garvin and Reisenberg (1952) and Rehg (1981) but not as part of a scheme of "levels." *Yet the humiliative form of honorific speech is unquestionably the most frequent form in interactional data*, where verbs and possessive classifiers of high status alternate with verbs and possessive classifiers of low status. For example, in fifty-one turns of talk in an interaction at the chief's home, twenty-six lexical items were expressed in "humiliative" speech whereas only six were expressed in what I term "exaltive" speech (what previous researchers call royal and/or respect). Six different speakers took turns at talk in the interaction, including the chief and chieftess. Obscuring the status-lowering form when talking about honorifics is a common phenomenon.

When self-lowering forms are described for other honorific vocabularies, it has been noted that they can operate independently of other-raising forms. Pohnpei's humiliatives can be either self- or other-lowering or both. The relationship between levels of honorific forms—for example between self- and other-lowering forms and other-raising forms—can be more clearly understood through a careful turn-by-turn analysis.

When interviewed, speakers told me that they used honorific speech only when in the presence of a chief. This shorthand description was repeated many times. Though they did not mention priests or ministers, I often witnessed honorific speech used toward members of the clergy. It is of course common for speakers to have only a limited awareness of their actual speech habits (cf. Hill and Hill 1978; Silverstein 1981). Pohnpeians are socialized into the use of honorific speech not through prescriptive rules or formal instruction but by their own observation and others' criticism of actual speech. Although honorific speech is part of nearly every radio broadcast, and the radio is the single most important information source on the island, speakers rarely report this as a context for honorific speech, nor do they report church services. Instead, they mention contexts in which chiefs are present, such as a visit to the chief's nahs (feast house) to receive permission for a burial or a funeral or feast where one would enter a nahs and greet the chiefs and chieftesses. These contexts are more conducive to the traditional learning methods, because church contexts are usually in the Western formal mode of passive listening as are radio broadcasts.

In contrast to local Pohnpeian taxonomies, elicited from informants and also reported in Rehg (1981) and Garvin and Reisenberg (1952), I talk about Pohnpeian honorifics on the basis of what they *do* in interaction, rather than on the role of the target of status marking, and how shared understandings about relative status are negotiated. In characterizing utterances by social act, I am following ideas developed in speech act theory (Austin 1962; Searle 1969) and interactionist approaches in sociology (Goffman 1964, 1967, 1974; Garfinkel 1967), as well as those who have studied conversation as social action,[5] including those who have studied discourse processes.[6] As Rosaldo (1982) points out, language is not only action but is used to exhibit and negotiate locally shared understandings. Language is a means for constructing ways of being and doing in the world.

I discuss honorific speech on Pohnpei as either humiliative or exaltive. Humiliative terms lower one's own or another's status, whereas exaltive terms raise another's status or in limited cases one's own (only done in conjunction with raising another's). This distinction is crucial because Pohnpeian humiliatives and exaltives are deployed in different ways and are organized structurally (e.g., morphologically and semantically) in different ways. They are not just different levels of the same phenomenon. These differences are significant in terms of how the Pohnpeians constitute an ideology about high and low status and about status relationships.

Pohnpeian honorific speech

Pohnpeian honorific speech is distinguished from common speech or speech unmarked for status. In other words, it is possible for an interaction in Pohnpei to be conducted entirely in common speech, without any honorific forms. In a context in which honorific speech is used, there is still a large portion of common speech terms. This is because not every Pohnpeian word has both a common and an honorific equivalent. When I first began collecting language data from interactions in which honorific speech was used, I found that only certain semantic domains appeared to be meaningful in terms of marking status. *Pohnpeian honorific vocabulary clusters around the domains of (1) verbs denoting location (including movement) in space, (2) possessive constructions, (3) verbs denoting mental states, especially knowledge, and references to speech itself, and (4) food and eating.* In this study I investigate these several domains through transcripts and video frames of recorded interaction. In Pohnpei, personal pronouns (the focus of honorification in European languages) are not significant sites of honorific marking. Rather, status marking is expressed in verb choice, choice of possessive classifier, and, much more rarely, noun choice. Cross-linguistically, verbs typically express actions, events, and states of affairs and in a high proportion of languages are the site of temporal marking. Possession is of course a relation between two noun phrases in which one "belongs to" the other. Possession can also be thought of as a type of locative, as in the case of "my village."

Personal pronouns only mark high status, not low status. *Komwi* is a second person singular pronoun used to mark high status. For paramount chiefs, the third person common speech pronoun ("they") is honorific according to Pohnpeians, rather than the second person singular or plural (though transcripts show more variety in use).

Although the focus of status marking is on verbs and possessive constructions (and these are covered in detail in the following chapters), two nouns are important sites for status marking: food and speech. Other nouns are honorific, but they only exist in *high*-status forms (e.g., *tehnpas*, or "high status feast house," or *tehnwahr*, "high status vehicle"). These nouns have no low-status equivalent. Table 2.1 gives examples of the important domains of honorific speech.

There is a basic pattern of Pohnpeian honorific verbs as follows: verbs with the stem *pato-* are humiliative, and verbs with the stem *ket-* are exaltive. To both of these verbs directional endings are suffixed in the usual way for Pohnpeian (e.g., *-do* "toward speaker"; *-la*, "away from speaker"; *-di*, "downward"; *-da*, "upward"; etc.). The basic pattern of possessive constructions involves using a common pronoun plus the classifier *tungoal* for humiliative marking and for exaltive marking using various

TABLE 2.1 Range of Domains of Honorific Marking

Common	Humiliative	Exaltive	Translation
kohdo	patohdo	ketdo	come (locative verb)
amwail	amwail tungoal	sapwellimomwail	your(P) (possessive)
ese	patohwan	mwangih	know (mental state verb)
nda	patohwan	poangoak	say (verb of speaking)
mwenge	tungoal	koanoat	food (noun)

exaltive classifier stems to which possessive pronouns are affixed (see chapter 5, in this volume). Throughout interactions, certain actions, relationships, and some mental states are indexed either as high- or low-status depending on the subject or agent. Speakers can raise or lower their own status or the status of others, for example, for themselves, *i patohla* "I go [low status]," and for others, *re patohla* "they go [low status]" or *Mohnsapw ketla* "the chief goes [high status]."

In the following example from an interaction involving the paramount chief, two verb forms are shown, the first one *humiliative*, the second *exaltive* (shown in boldface type). Because there are *many* persons of lower status and relatively *few* chiefs and chieftesses, the overwhelming incidence of honorific forms is the humiliative. The following example shows the action of movement to or from a location or at a location expressed in both humiliative and exaltive forms. For these polysemous verbs I use the interlinear gloss "Locative Verb," or "LocVerb," because the same verb form is used to describe any intransitive verb of motion (e.g., "go," "walk," "come," "climb") or stasis (e.g., "be," "stay"). A list of abbreviations and transcription notations can be found at the end of chapter 1.

(1) Sakau with the paramount chief

01 W: *S. ((title)) S, pwe   ma ice boxo   **pato-***
         S ((title)) S, because if ice box.there LocVerb[HUM]
         S. S, because if the ice box moves-

02   *ice ches' en **patohsang***
         ice ches' to LocVerb[HUM].from
         move the ice chest from

03   *mwo eri Mwohnsapw **ketla***
         there so the.chief   LocVerb[EXAL].there
         over there so the chief can go

04   *mwo ah komwi   ah ngehi.*
         there and you(S) [EXAL] and me
         there and you and me.

In the first and second lines, the movement of the ice box is indexed as humiliative through choice of verb with the pato- stem (the speaker cuts herself off to correct her use of "ice box" to "ice chest"). In the third line, the movement of the chief

(Mwohnsapw) is indexed as exaltive, through choice of the verb stem ket-. The paramount chieftess is addressed as komwi, "you(S)[EXAL]" (line 04).

Polysemy/metaphor in honorific speech

Across languages, honorific vocabularies evidence a restricted range of lexical resources compared to common speech (see, for example, Dixon 1971; Haviland 1978, 1979; Agha 1994). In Pohnpei, vocabulary items that lower speaker status evidence a high degree of referential ambiguity or polysemy. For example, the same verb form is used to describe any intransitive verb of motion ("go," "walk," "run," "come") in humiliative speech. In the case of humiliative transitive verbs, carrying is expressed with the same verb as "to speak" or "to know." Table 2.2 lists examples from both interactional data and consultants' reports.

The transitive *patohwan* appears to be a combination of *pato-* and *wa-* the verb "to carry." As can be seen from the list in table 2.2, the humiliative speech terms are more polysemous or ambiguous than the exaltive terms. For example, the same low-status verb stem is listed for all the items, whereas the honorific forms are much more diverse. In fact, there are *no* humiliative verb forms other than those beginning with the *pato-* stem, although the variety of exaltive verb forms is relatively larger, especially if one takes as data not only transcripts of interaction but written sources and oral reports of exaltive words (e.g., for chiefs' activities). Drew and Heritage (1993) note that institutional interaction tends to involve a selective reduction in the full range of conversational practices available for use. In this case, there is a greater reduction in the range of vocabulary items to index those terms that refer to *low*-status than to high-status individuals and groups. Haviland (1979) notes a restricted range of lexical resources for Guugu Yimidhirr respect vocabulary: "The Guugu Yimidhirr respectful style makes do with a very small number of distinct roots; it therefore pushes a formal mechanism like the case system to its expressive limits—to construct specific messages from restricted lexical raw material" (210). This is similar to what Dixon (1971) reports about the in-law language traditionally spoken by the Dyirbal people (Australia), where the brother-in-law vocabulary is limited and "syntactic and derivational devices are used heavily to express specific and detailed ideas" (Haviland 1979:218). Dixon (1971) characterizes the Dyirbal in-law language as having a one-

TABLE 2.2 Polysemy of Low-Status Compared to High-Status Verbs

Common	Humiliative	Exaltive	Translation
koh-	patoh-	ket-	locative verb
alu	patoh-	mahliel, ket-	walk
mwohndi	patohdi	mwoalehdi, ketdi	sit
dou-	patoh-	paleke, ket-	climb
wah-	patohwan-	limeh-, ketikih-	carry
ese	patohwan	mwahngih	know
nda	patohwan	mahsanih, poangoakih	say

Those verbs listed with a dash [-] indicate directional suffixes are added.

to-many correspondence to the unmarked or "everyday" language. The mother-in-law language utilizes "nuclear verbs"; a nuclear verb in English would be "look" (vs. "stare," which has a more particular meaning).

Agha (1993) notes that honorific vocabulary is denotationally (i.e., referentially and predicationally) less specific relative to nonhonorific vocabulary and that this lack of denotational specificity then leads to a greater contextual specificity. In Lhasa Tibetan, for example, "Various distinctions of denotational content in non-honorific verbs are neutralized in honorific register. Thus . . . we find a three-way denotational contrast in non-honorific speech ('come' vs. 'go' vs. 'arrive') neutralized to a single honorific form, *phee*" (Agha ms:7). The decrease in denotational specificity is accompanied by an increase in contextual specificity, for example, the indexing of social categories with honorific forms, and the restrictiveness of denotational specificity is interpreted by speakers as an indexical mark of social identity or role relation (Agha ms:12). In chapter 6 (in this volume), I discuss some strategies speakers use for reintroducing denotational specificity with the verbs "say" and "know" in humiliative speech. Ochs (1988) describes how in Samoa, lower-status persons are expected to assume the perspectives of higher-ranking persons and to bear the burden of resolving ambiguities (see also Duranti 1993), suggesting a possible relation between status and communicative specificity. As mentioned previously, the *humiliative* forms of Pohnpeian respect vocabulary are less denotationally specific than the *exaltive* forms.

It is possible that the ambiguity of the lower-status or humiliative terms is related to a lack of affect, or at least impoverishing of "manner" of activity (e.g., type of motion) in favor of the indexing of an attitude of deference. Shades of the meaning of acts referred to are bleached in favor of the act of status marking. Geertz (1960) has described Javanese speech levels as having a "flatness of affect" or "emotional equanimity" (240; cf. J. Errington 1988:12). Context becomes important in understanding meaning in honorific speech where one lexical item is often used for several concepts which are differentiated in common speech.

The limited humiliative inventory of nouns in Pohnpei is a stark contrast to the rich metaphorical language of the exaltive inventory listed in table 2.3. The chief's tears are a waterfall, his anger the wind, his breath a typhoon, his memories clouds in the sky (there are *always* clouds in the Pohnpeian sky due to the 200 inches of annual rainfall). The linkage of the chief's activities and emotions with the natural universe and some of its most prominent displays is explicit. Consultants describe two suffixes that can distinguish between items used by the two highest chiefs. For example, the morpheme -*iso* is used as an affix for terms referring to the Nahnken (second-ranking chief), and the morpheme -*leng* (a bound form of the noun -*lahng* or heaven) to refer to the Nanmwarki (paramount chief). Thus, when speaking about the Nanmwarki, the word for "cane" is *irareileng*, when speaking about the Nahnken, it is *irareiso* (Rehg 1981). In the humiliative, on the other hand, the term for activities is cognate with the word for flat, level ground (*patapat*).

As has been found in other Oceanic respect vocabularies (cf. Samoa and Tonga), the Pohnpeian honorific lexicon includes nouns that refer to chiefly body parts as well as specialized items for use. There are many such terms on Pohnpei; none have humiliative counterparts. Table 2.4 lists a few examples.

TABLE 2.3 Metaphorical High-Status Terms for Which There Is No Low-Status Equivalent

Common	Exaltive	Humiliative	Translation
lingeringer	engieng (lit. windy)	—	angry
pilen mese	tenihrlap (lit. big waterfall)	—	tears
pouk	malimalih (lit. typhoon)	—	blow
tamataman	ediedinloang (lit. cloudy sky)	—	remember
wadek	doaropwe	—	read

Though these words are rarely used in daily conversation, their existence serves to further sacralize the body of the chief.

J. Errington (1988) observes for Javanese that body parts are rarely expressed in honorifics and are "among the least widely recognized" forms (164). Javanese consultants report that these rather intimate terms, which would not likely be conversation topics, were most likely only known by royal servants who were caretakers of royal children and responsible for their health and cleanliness:

> Why should there be honorific terms glossable as "break wind," "phlegm," or "buttocks"? It seemed as peculiar to the Javanese I felt comfortable asking as it did to me that there should be honorific terms for genitalia, intercourse, defecation, and other topics one might expect to be avoided in speech about and perhaps with those of high status. . . . Today many *priyayi* find the semantic content of these honorifics presupposing of an intimacy at odds with the stylistic deference they convey as parts of the honorific vocabulary. But in traditional *priyayi* circles these were complementary rather than competing aspects of a social relationship: intimacy (physical or otherwise) did not necessarily mitigate status differences or the need for their linguistic diacritics. (165)

Errington reports that fewer terms for body parts have *krama* equivalents (krama words are those that educated [i.e., priyayi] speakers use when they speak polite addressee-exalting speech), and speakers more frequently choose between levels that have krama equivalents than between those that do not, suggesting the contrastive relationship of status.

TABLE 2.4 Examples of Status-Marked Nouns that Refer to Body Parts

Exaltive	Common	Translation	Humiliative
kahlap, erekiso	paliwar	body	—
wasaile, sihleng	mese	face	—
likinsekiri, likinoar, likinleng	likinpaiki	back of head	—
kotokot, tahta	seisei	haircut	—
keinuhnu, sisipwai	timwe	nose	—
tepinkasang	tepinwere	neck	—
aluweluwe	neh	leg, foot	—

From consultants and from Rehg 1981

Questions of power and solidarity

Based on the nature of the pronoun contrast (T/V) in some European languages, and on the co-occurrence of special registers with highly circumscribed relationships in other languages, it has become conventional to discuss honorifics in terms of their "social distancing" function, and in terms of a contrast set of intimate versus distant relations, or power versus solidarity. Whether a speaker "gives" *tu* or *vous* (i.e., addresses his or her interlocutor as *tu* or *vous*) and receives *tu* or *vous* (is addressed by his or her interlocutor as *tu* or *vous*), for example, constructs status relationships between the participants. The honorific use of plural personal pronouns (e.g., *vous*) for singular subjects "has a world-wide distribution in unrelated languages" (P. Brown and Levinson 1978:179). In an influential study, Brown and Gilman (1960) proposed that the contrasts between T/V could be understood in terms of two ideas: power and solidarity. Power, defined as the ability to control the behavior of the other (Brown and Gilman 1960:255), is indexed through the nonreciprocal use of pronouns, whereas solidarity, a symmetrical relation, is signaled through the use of reciprocal pronouns. The power and solidarity contrast is illustrated by Hudson (1980) for English and French:

> The norms for choosing between *tu* and *vous* in the singular are precisely the same as those for choosing between first name only and title plus family name in English, tu being used prototypically to a close subordinate and vous to a distant superior, with other situations resolved in relation to these . . . the form which expresses high solidarity also expresses greater power on the part of the speaker and vice versa. (123–5)

Brown and Ford (1961) suggest that this power versus solidarity contrast is a linguistic universal. Though Brown and Gilman's study focuses on the cultural significance of an historical move noted in speakers' behaviors away from indexing power relationships in language (i.e., wider use of reciprocal pronouns), the study represents the best known framework for promoting a relationship between intimacy and symmetrical status versus distance and asymmetrical status, a rubric that has been cited and used widely. Goffman (1956) also developed the idea that a measure of social distance is used to express deference and is explicitly made in some languages where deferential markers are the same as distance markers.

The power–solidarity contrast for honorific speech depends on seeing hierarchy and solidarity as opposing organizational schemes (sometimes visualized as horizontal versus vertical). It soon becomes clear in examining social interaction that these two concepts are hardly mutually exclusive or opposing/contradictory. In an interaction discussed in this chapter, I show that the participants, including the chief, use expressions of solidarity while organizing an event, but once the event is under way, speakers shift to honorific register or expressions of power differentials. *Thus, in the same interaction, among the same participants the polarities of solidarity (intimacy) and power (social distance) are reversed.* First participants establish solidarity, then they construct hierarchy. This suggests that building hierarchy depends on relations of solidarity or intimacy, and that the two notions of power and solidarity are knit together in a more complex way than a two-dimensional contrast set. In Pohnpei and perhaps other areas in the Pacific, a ranked hierarchy can be intimate in ways Westerners do not usually recognize, similar to a family model, where there is a high degree of responsibility and caregiving from high- to low-status individuals and a great deal of affection and unabashed dependency from lower-status persons to higher-status ones. Sahlins (1983) proposes a notion of "hierarchical solidarity" to account for what he calls the "common submission to the ruling power" in what he terms "heroic societies" (85).[7] In Suriname Javanese, relationships of respect signal intimacy and "social connectedness" (Wolfowitz 1991:50, 236). Urban (1991) notes the idea of different types of solidarity, one based on similarity the other on difference, for some South American groups (see also Tannen 1994 for American work environments).

Use of the plural as an index of power or status is an interesting strategy, and a number of authors have mentioned it. Brown and Levinson (1978) propose that honorifics in general are motivated by a strategy of "impersonalization" (1978/87:23), and that person–number switches in pronoun reference are a predictable result. The hearer is thought to have the option of understanding the utterance as directed to someone else, an associate, not specifically to him or her as an individual. Garvin and Reisenberg (1952) suggest that use of a plural pronoun in Pohnpei for the chief symbolically removes the chief being addressed from the normal speaker–hearer relationship. Bean (1978) suggests for India that it transforms a dyadic interaction into a triadic one. Hanks (1990) terms third person the "least inclusive" among a referential hierarchy of personal pronouns (186). Duranti (1992) notes for Samoa that speakers there show a tendency to obscure the individual in favor of the public and positional role a person is embodying (87).

In Pohnpei, pluralization of what we would describe as second person in the T/V contrast takes the form of the third person (they) rather than the second person (you). *Ihr* (object or independent pronoun) or *re* (subject pronoun) on Pohnpei (lit. "they"/"them") refers not only to the individual chief present but to others whose power that individual represents, that is, the very source (genealogically speaking) of his authority, which is plural. According to Pohnpeian speakers, the plural pronoun signifies that when one speaks to a chief, one speaks to his *eni* or clan spirits/ deities as well. Rather than an act of social distancing, this seems to be the reverse, bringing into the interactional space more participants, and in fact bringing into proximity the spirit world as language mediates between the invisible world and the visible.

Rather than *im*personalization, such use of third person plural can be interpreted as literally increasing the size and power of the referent. Haviland (1979) suggests similarly that "a plural form that literally makes more of the hearer is more deferential than a singular form" (221). The Pohnpeian paramount chief and others addressed as *vous* in T/V systems thus can be seen as representing a collaborative source, as Levinson (1988) puts it: "acting in *author* role but as representative of other like-minded *principals*" (203). Plurality *personally* ties the chief to institutionalized traditional authority; it is a linguistic resource for constructing legitimacy. Third person plural is how a deity, or nonvisible entity with no speech capability can enter an interaction. No answer or response is presupposed or expected from the invisible world by use of "they." Pluralization can create what Bakhtin (1981) calls "the authoritative word (religious, political, moral; the word of a father, of adults and of teachers, etc.)" (342):

> Its authority was already *acknowledged* in the past. It is a prior discourse. It is therefore not a question of choosing it from among other possible discourses that are its equal. It is given (it sounds) in lofty spheres, not those of familiar contact. Its language is a special (as it were hieratic[8]) language. It can be profaned. It is akin to taboo, i.e., a name that must not be taken in vain. (Bakhtin 1981:342)

The correct greeting for the paramount chieftesses and chiefs in Pohnpei is a plural form of their titles, Likendko and Mohnsapwko, respectively (-*ko*, signifying plurality). However, the prescriptive use of pronouns for high-status individuals in Pohnpei is more accurate for monologic contexts (i.e., oratory) than in spontaneous conversations, where speakers often use the singular of these forms in reference. Speakers also vary in their pronoun choice for the chief.

As is shown in chapter 7 (in this volume), plural subject pronouns, which include the chief and low-status participants, are frequently used in oratory with exaltive verbs and with exaltive possessive classifiers. Such usage intimately connects low status with chiefly status. In casual speech, a phrase such as "you and the chief can talk" is rendered with a high-status verb for "talk."

Though plural pronouns are prescribed for the chief, interactional data show a larger set of pronouns in use and variation according to speaker and context. Plural pronouns in interaction are anaphoric; that is, they follow an earlier speech reference in the form of a proper noun (individual title/address form). Examples are shown next from interactional data of an interaction videotaped at the home of the chief. The chieftess is teasing the chief about being hungry but reluctant to eat while being filmed or watched (a common antipathy on Pohnpei). One of the men preparing sakau also comments on the chief's reluctance. Line 03 shows the expected third person plural pronoun reference to the chief (re "they"). The pronoun used to refer to the chief is the second reference to the chief in a series, where the first reference is Mwohnsapw (line 01, lit. "before/in front of the land", the respectful address title and reference term used for the chief by many speakers in the Madolenihmw chiefdom). Re is the subject pronoun for third person plural.[9]

(2)

01 Chieftess: *Mwohnsapw pil kahng koanoat pwe*
                chief   also refuses eat[EXAL] because
                the chief also refuses to eat

02   *e de sansalada*
                 it lest clear.become
                 lest it show [in the video]

((laughter of other participants))

03 N: →   *ansouwet **re** ketin kupwurki koanoat*
                time.this they [EXAL] want[EXAL] eat[EXAL]
                now you want to eat

04   *mwohn   kasdohn*
            in.front.of movie.there.by.you
            in front of the movie

The next example shows the same series, with an additional common speech pronoun (*ke*, "you") used to refer to the chief last (line 05), showing that there is variation in the pronoun reference to the chief. References to the chief are in boldface
type.

(3)

01 Woman: *Mwohnsapw ketla   mwo*
            chief   LocVerb[EXAL].there there
            the chief goes there

02   *ah komwi   ah ngehi*
            and you(S)[EXAL] and me
            and you and me

(. . .)

03 Woman: *na **re** ketwei   mwo*
→   so they LocVerb[EXAL].there.toward.you there
            so you go there

04   *ah Likend me*
            and chieftess here.by.me
            and the chieftess here

(. . .)

05 Woman: ***ke** sou ketwei   kis*
→   you not LocVerb[EXAL].toward.you a.little
            can't you move out just a little

06   *ah Likend   me   ah-*
            and paramount chieftess here.by.me and
            and the paramount chieftess here and

In the following examples, the third person singular pronoun (*e*, "he") is also used
for the chief rather than the third person plural, but in these cases the chief is not
present.

(4)

01 Woman: *ia   Mwohnsapw?*
    (off camera) where paramount.chief
                  Where is the paramount chief

02 Boy: ***e** ketket   powe*
→   he staying[EXAL] above
              he's up there

A consultant described this use as permissible because the boy is not talking directly to the chief. The following example is similar:

(5)

01 N: *Mwohnsapw- Mwohnsapw poahngokih en wiawi keneinei*
         chief-   chief   says[EXAL] to doing   careful
         the chief- the chief says to do it carefully

02   *pwe   e pahn ketin   sakau*
     →   because he will [EXAL] sakau
         because he will [join] the sakau

These examples show that though Pohnpeian speakers report that the appropriate pronoun use is re, actual usage reflects a wider range of choices. Exaltive verbs are used throughout this interaction, yet the pronoun form for the chief varies. In example 3, a similar directive is given once with the nominal subject Mwohnsapw, once with the plural pronoun subject re ("they"), and once with the singular subject e ("he"). In example 3, the pronoun komwi ("you," sing., exaltive) is used to refer to the chieftess.

In the instances in which re is used (examples 2 and 3), it is sequentially after a more specific reference term (Mwohnsapw) and refers back to that. In many cases, pronoun reference to the highest chief, highest chieftess, secondary chief, secondary chieftess, or other very high-status participant would be clear from the choice of high-status verb. However, when multiple high-status persons are participants of an interaction, pronoun reference may require more specificity. These examples are cases of the important relationship of honorific speech and context. Clearly, Mwohnsapw and re are not semantically equivalent because Mwohnsapw is one individual and re is many, though they are referentially equivalent in these examples.

It is in oratory that the forms ihr and re (third person object pronoun and third person subject pronoun) appear to work as suggested by native speakers. The following example shows ihr used for God in a prayer during a speech by Soumakaka, the chief's representative in the kousapw (community) in which I lived:

(6) Soumakaka's speech

01 Soumakaka: *I pil kapingkiongihr ansouwet*
                I also praise.them   time.this
                I also praise you now

02   *pwe   sen ((se en)) kapinga ih*   (. . . .)
                 because we.to   praise   him
                 in order for us to praise him

03 (. . .)   *patohpene   rahnwet pwe*
                 LocVerb[HUM].toward.each.other today   because
                 come together today in order for us to

04   *sen wiahda aht   tungoal kapingohngihr.*
           we.to make   our(EXCL) [HUM]   praise.to.them
           make our humble praise/thanks to you

05   *re ketin[10] ieiang*
           they [EXAL] live[EXAL]
           you are among us

In his prayer, the speaker uses re and ihr as consultants described for references to chiefs. Genre, whether dialogic or monologic, affects use of plural pronouns as high-status honorific references.

The use of plural pronouns for high-status individuals has been linked by previous ethnographers and theorists not only to social distance but also to strategies of avoidance. A link between avoidance and honorific speech has been described for Pohnpei in particular (Garvin and Reisenberg 1952; Fischer 1969) and for Samoa. Milner (1961), for example, suggests for Samoa that honorific speech is the verbal equivalent of the taboo on physical contact with chiefs, thus creating an impediment to social contact between higher and lower interactants. Throughout Oceania, chiefly power (mana) is constructed as a dangerous force transmitted through touch (see chapter 1, in this volume).

In the respect vocabulary of Guugu Yimidhirr in Australia, a special register co-occurs with what are characterized as "avoidance" behaviors: "[B]oth men [one married to a woman the other classed as his granddaughter] not only use the respectful vocabulary; they sit far apart, orient their bodies so as not to face one another, and avoid direct eye contact" (Haviland 1979:170). Rather than looking at these behaviors in the conventional way as avoiding, however, I argue they are constitutive of a certain type of reiterated or overemphasized relation. I believe honorific language, far from *avoiding* sacred or taboo areas or realms of power, constitutes and reproduces them as contexts of *elaborated* and embellished behavior (sometimes including highly metaphorical and artistic expressions, such as commonly found in specialized registers). Through language, these consecrated domains are constituted as power-full; they are celebrated, differentiated, historicized, and institutionalized. Specialized vocabularies mark certain relationships as distinctive by prescribing discriminating terminological reference. This has come to be conceptualized as "avoidance," although in fact these relationships are constructed through nonavoidance, that is, in particular interactions.

Shore (1989) describes how it is important to ritually *transform* and properly *channel* the potency of divine mana for human purposes, not avoid it. Honorific speech constructs an environment in which social contact *is* appropriate. In fact, social distance can be decreased with honorifics, as shown in the following chapters—how lower-status participants give directives to the chief and chieftess using honorific speech (see excerpt 3), and how the use of plural second person subject pronouns ("we") that include low-status members of a gathering used with exaltive verbs can unite low status with chiefly status. The avoidance theory may be a product of local theories and ideologies rather than an accurate analysis of language in use. Some Pohnpeian consultants report that the term *wahu* in *lokaian wahu* ("speech of honor" or "high language") signifies a valley between the chiefs and the people. Speakers may try to avoid being in the presence of the chief (because of the elaborate prescriptions on behavior and vulnerability to mistakes and shame), but once there and once honorific register is invoked, they must acknowledge his presence and his status as well as their own through honorific speech; indeed, each participant is expected to formally greet the chief and chieftess. This reference and address cannot be avoided.

Status marking in everyday interactions: Testing theories

The nature of Pohnpeian use of honorific forms is highly fluid and context oriented and not as regularized as native speakers imply, or as theories would predict. The analysis of conversational interaction reveals that in the presence of the second-ranking chief, during the process of eliciting cooperation before a sakau event, honorific forms are not used; however, once the cooperation of community members has been achieved, and the event is about to begin, a change in register is accomplished. This suggests that asymmetries of status may be context specific in ways not revealed by generalized descriptions of Pohnpeian social organization or cross-cultural theories of politeness.

Although the secondary chief is present during the entire period of recruitment of pounders for sakau, participants do not use status-marked speech, as would be predicted by the chief's presence in the system described by Comrie (1976) and Levinson (1983) as "bystander honorifics" (appropriate in certain settings where bystanders, or over-hearers are of a certain status), and as reported by Pohnpeian speakers' metapragmatic judgments. Pohnpeian speakers prescribe honorific speech for any interaction with chiefs. However, table 2.5 shows which verbs were actually used in the first part of the interaction compared to what I expected, based on what my consultants told me and other researchers had reported. As chiefs do not use honorific speech (except in oratory), it is the woman's and man's speech that are notably lacking in honorific forms (*kohdo* is the common form of the verb "move toward speaker" or "come").

Excerpt 7 has no honorific speech. The first utterance by the chief would not be expected to contain any honorific forms, as chiefs do not use them (except in a limited way during oratory). However, that the woman's utterance does not contain any self-lowering forms is striking, given the rules for honorific use stated by consultants. In addition, the man sitting within a few feet of the chief does not use status-marked vocabulary. The honorific forms that would be expected in this context would be an honorific equivalent for the verb kohdo.

TABLE 2.5 Differences between Actual and Predicted Uses of Honorific Speech

	Actual	Predicted
Chief:	en *kohdo* iang sukusuk	en kohdo iang sukusuk
Woman:	en *kohdo* en iang kilele	en *patohdo* en iang kilele
Man:	*kohdo* mah kita iang suk sakau	*patohdo* mah kita iang suk sakau

(7) The chief and two men sit near the sakau stone. The chief is on the raised platform, while the two men sit on benches one level down, on the dirt floor. A woman is standing off camera watching.

01 Chief: *ia (.4) kisin pwutak me   mwohmwod mwo*
           where little boy   the.one sitting   there
           where (.4) is the little boy who was sitting there?

                      [

02 (?);   [(?)

((one of the men turns to look outside, toward the nahs entrance, as if attending to a speaker out there))

03 Chief: *en kohdo   iang sukusuk.*
           to LocVerb.here join pounding
           tell him[11] to come and join the pounding ((of sakau)).

04 W: *en **kohdo**   en iang kilele.*
→   to LocVerb.here to join picture.this.by.me
           tell him to come and join this movie.

05 Chief: *en kohdo   iang* [(?)
           to LocVerb.here join (?)
           tell him to come and join (?)

                    [   ]

06 M: ((shouting))
→   ***KOHDO**   MAH KITA IANG*
           LocVerb.here first   we(D) join
           Come here first let's join

07 W: ((laughter))

08 M: *SUK SAKAU*
           pound sakau
           the sakau pounding

When directional endings are added to *koh-* it means the English sense of "come" or "go," "come up," "go down," etc. The verb form that would have been predicted from honorific speech rules for the woman and the man in the presence of the chief would be *patohdo*. This form would be self/other-lowering, in this particular case other-lowering. Its absence is even more surprising given that the referent/addressee is a boy. It is clear that the social status or identity of the participants is not enough to key honorific usage. In fact, all speakers are using almost the same words as shown in table 2.6.

The appropriateness of the forms used is not challenged, even though conventions exist cross-culturally for the immediate alleviation of breakdowns, in the form of "next turn repair initiators" and a "repair as soon as possible" tenet (Schegloff, Jefferson and Sacks 1977). Participants in the interaction under study do not show in their analysis

TABLE 2.6 Comparison of Usage of Speech

Chief:	en	**kohdo**		**iang sukusuk**
Woman:	en	**kohdo**	en	**iang** kilele
Man:		**kohdo**	mah kita	**iang suk sakau**

of prior speech segments as the talk progresses that anything unusual is occurring in the lack of honorific forms. Neither the woman speaker nor the men, nor the young boys in the segment, use status-marked speech at this point in the interaction. Those seated near the chief as well as those on the periphery use common speech.

The use of honorifics in this case appears to be sensitive to a cluster of context features, not just to the presence of the chief. The first use of an honorific form coincides with a directive given by the *menindei* (master of ceremonies) to one of the participants, a man called W. The menindei directs W to move up very close to where the chief is seated. In fact, W is going to take the role of server to the chief—the *erir*. Erirs were traditionally responsible for performing a protective chant on the cup before giving it to the chief. The menindei tells W: "W go up there and position yourself. Take off your shirt." In this utterance the menindei uses three honorific forms: *patohdala* ("go up there") is used twice and the transitive humiliative form *patohwansang* ("take from") is used once. These are both status-lowering forms. In this instance they act as "other-lowering"; that is, the menindei lowers W's status in relation to the chief. Excerpt 8 presents the transcript segment.

(8) One of the men passes out pounding stones to the other three seated at the sakau stone.

01 Menindei: *W (name) **patohdala**   mah mwo*
              W (name) LocVerb[HUM].upward first there
              W go up there and position yourself.

                        [

02 Elizabeth: ((to person near camera))
                        I won't be able to see (?)

03 Menindei: ***patohwansang**   ahmw sehten*
              TranVerb[HUM].from your(S) shirt.that.by.you
              take off your shirt

04   *koh   **patohdala**   wiada udahn*
              you(S) LocVerb[HUM].upward.there do   truly
              you go up there and really

05   *mwohden erir   eh?*
              sit.of   server eh
              sit like a server eh?

06 N: *ehng, e pwung*
              yes   it correct
              yeah, that's it.

W's actions have previously been referred to with the word *kohdo*, but now his actions are referred to in honorific register, status-lowering form, *patohdala*.

This first use of honorific speech coincides with several other contextual features. First, all the required participants for a formal sakau have finally been assembled. In chapter 1, I discussed the relationship of kava drinking practices to local hierarchies and structures of prestige.[12] As noted in chapter 1, the customary sequences inherent in the practice of sakau on Pohnpei lend themselves to establishing an ad hoc hierarchy from among whomever is present (cf. Petersen 1977). The first cup is always offered to the highest-ranking participant present, and subsequent cups are ranked accordingly. It seems significant, then, that honorific speech forms indexing relative status of participants occur as a sakau event is about to begin. Second, the first honorific form occurs just after the chief has repositioned himself higher on the nahs (feast house) platform and has adopted a less casual seating pose. The organization of space on the nahs platform is symbolically and significantly changed. The overall space in the feast house is ordered hierarchically (see chapter 1), with certain portions of space reserved for the chiefs and other high-status persons. However, the nahs is also used for many everyday, unceremonial activities, such as drying laundry, sleeping, and playing. During such activities, the hierarchy of space is not observed. Therefore, it is significant that the chief both moves to his ceremonial seating space and adopts a more formal seating position (the interaction of hierarchy of space and hierarchy in language in this particular interaction is discussed in more detail in chapter 3, in this volume). Third, the pounding stones have been passed out to all the pounders. These stones are specially quarried and specially handled. Once the pounders have them in hand, they typically begin pounding. Fourth, W is moving into a symbolically and ritually high space on the nahs platform next to the chief. The other-lowering of W seems to mark to him and to others that although he is moving into a ritually high space, he himself is of low status. W's low status is clear from the transcript in two other ways: (1) he is not called by a title, and people with titles are called by their title, not their name; and (2) he does not know the proper way to sit, and must be instructed by the chief. The following example shows the menindei referring to the chief's speech by an exaltive verb (line 01) and also shows the chief's directives to W about how to sit (lines 04–06).

(9)

```
01 Menindei:  ohlen          nek  masanihonguhk
→             man.that.by.you could tell[EXAL].to.you(S)
              that man (the chief) could tell you

02            dahme pwungen ahmw  pahn mwohd
              what  right.of  your(S) will  sit
              the correct way for you to sit

      (2.0) ((woman laughing softly in background))

03 Menindei:  keidawei                    ekis
              move.upward.there.toward.you a.little
              move up a little
```

04 Chief: *keidado   keidado*
                move.upward.here move.upward.here
                move up here move up here

05   *keida   keila   ekis   me*
                move.upward move.there a.little here.by.me
                move up move there a little here

06   *men.   ke   pahn nda   mwo*
                there.by.you you(s) will say/do there
                that's it. you will do it like that

07 W: *mwo?*
                there.away.from.you.and.me?
                there?

08 Chief: *me, ((W moves his legs)) men*
                this.one.by.me   that.one.by.you
                like this, that's it.

09 Menindei: *NA   SUKUSUK!* ((loudly to the pounders))
                so.then pounding
                so start pounding

The ritual formula *na sukusuk* (line 09) is the command to start pounding. Not only do co-occurring features create a context deemed appropriate for honorifics by the menindei, but by employing honorifics the menindei contextualizes the interaction as one in which relative status is a salient feature. The participants are now dependent on an institutionalized organizational scheme and are no longer independent.

The interaction leading up to the beginning of the sakau pounding was not contextualized as status salient. In the first part of the interaction (without status-marked verbs) the chief, the menindei, and other participants solicited cooperation from other men to join as partners in the sakau making. Collaborative strategies were used to invite participation and did not index status differentials. The transcript reveals a striking use of the words for partner (*ianget*) and the verb "join" (*iang*) as well as affiliative terms such as *nahn* ("buddy"). These terms are highlighted in boldface type.

(10)

01 Menindei: *kohdo   **nahn** pwe   sohte **ianget**.*
               LocVerb.here **buddy** because no   **partner**.
               come on buddy, because we've got no partner.

        (1.0)

02   *mehlel!*
               truly!

(11)

01 Chief: *en kohdo   **iang** sukusuk.*
               to LocVerb.here **join** pounding
               tell him to come and pound.

02 W: *en kohdo   en **iang** kilele.*
             to LocVerb.here to **join** picture.this.by.me
             tell him to come and join this movie.

03 Chief: *en kohdo   [**iang** (?)*
             to LocVerb.here **join** (?)
             to come and join (?)

                          [   ]

04 M: *KOHDO   MAH KITA **IANG***
                          LocVerb.here first   we(D) **join**
                          come here first let's join

05 W: ((laughter))

06 M: *SUK SAKAU*
             pound sakau
             the sakau pounding

07 Chief: *ia- **iangete** sukedi.*
             joi-join only pound.downward
             join only in the pounding.

08 W: ((laughs; other laughter in the background))

09 Chief: (?)   ((laughter in background))

10 M: ((looks down at the sakau pounding stone, shouts))
         MWADANG NAHN!
         HURRY   **BUDDY!**

Excerpt 11 shows the use of affiliative terms (solidarity/intimacy), terms that will precede the use of so-called distancing forms (or power/distance) among the same participants in a matter of minutes. This shows that the indexing of solidarity and power relationships can be sequentially related. A status or power relationship is constituted *after* the requests to come and join have been heeded. Solidarity is achieved before power/hierarchy is invoked. The order of the relationship between these two is, I believe, significant for understanding exactly how power hierarchies are constructed in moment-by-moment interaction.

Although a switch to honorific register occurs, it is not uniform. Possessive classifiers are not marked in honorific register, as might be expected. For example, when the menindei directs W to take off his shirt (with the humiliative verb *patohwansang*), he does not use the humiliative possessive classifier *tungoal*; instead, he uses the common form *ahmw* in line 01 (possessive classifiers are discussed in more detail in chapter 4, in this volume). It is customary to pound sakau without shirts.

(12)

01 Menindei: *patohwansang   **ahmw** sehten*
             TranVerb[HUM].from your(S) shirt.that.by.you
             take off your shirt

02   *koh   patohdala   wiada*
                you(S) LocVerb[HUM].upward.there do
                you go up there and

03   *udahn mwohden erir   eh*
                truly   sit.of   server eh
                really sit like a server eh

This indicates that registers can vary within a single utterance and among references to a single person. Because directives are issued both before and after honorific speech register is invoked, the particular speech act involved cannot be said to determine honorific usage, as theories might presuppose. Rather, it is clearly context that is being attended to.

Not all participants use honorific forms. One participant, N (shown in excerpt 13), does not use honorific forms even though they are used by the menindei. N says "*kihsang sehten*" ("take off your shirt") in line 09, whereas the menindei said moments earlier, line 01, "*patohwansang ahmw sehten*" ("take [HUM]-off your shirt").

(13)

01 Menindei: *patohwansang   ahmw sehten*
                TranVerb[HUM].from your(S) shirt.that.by.you
                take off your shirt

02   *koh   patohdala   wiada*
                you(S) LocVerb[HUM].upward.there do
                go up there and

03   *udahn mwohden erir   eh*
                truly   sit.of   server eh
                really sit like a server eh

04 N: *eung, e pwung*
                yes   it correct
                yes, that's it.

05 Woman: *heh heh heh ha A* ((name))

((W sits on nahs in front of the chief, starts to take off his shirt))

06 Chief: *men,   men   kadilong apali*
                that.one.by.you that.one.by.you tuck.in   one
                that way, that way tuck in one side of

07   *nemwen pwe   soangen eriren*
                leg.your because type.of   server.that.by.you
                your leg because that type of sitting as a server

08   *i kilang e sapwung nahn*
                I see   it wrong   buddy/friend
                I see it is incorrect buddy

09 N: **kihsang** *sehten*
                take from shirt.that.by.you
                take off your shirt

10 Menindei: *ohlen   nek* **mahsenihong***uhk dahme*
                man.that.by.you could tell[EXAL].to.you(S) what
                that man ((the chief)) will tell you

11   *pwungen ahmw pahn mwohd*
                correct.of your(S) will   sit
                the correct way for you to sit

Note that in the utterance directly following N's use of common speech (line 09), the menindei uses another honorific, *mahsenihong* (line 10). In this way, he recontextualizes the event at honorific level, after N's use of common speech, and introduces another distinct status level, exaltive (previously he used humiliative). In using the word "mahsenihong," he invokes the first other-raising honorific form. The importance of the menindei as an intermediary is evident. The chief cannot initiate high language, as he himself does not employ it. In this interaction, it is the role of the menindei, a lower-status person, to define relative social identities and contexts of use.

During most sakau events in which I participated at the secondary chief's home, the sakau pounders typically casually arrived one or two at a time in the late after-noon and began preparation and pounding of pepper roots, even if the customarily required number of four men was not constituted. In the more casual setting I ob-served for the entire week before I set up the camera to make the video, the menindei role was not constituted, nor was the role of erir (server to the chief) performed by one of the participants. However, because of the making of the video, the chief wished to have the sakau ritual proceed along more "customary" lines. In the transcript, there-fore, the menindei directs various men and boys who are hanging about to "come and pound," as the filming of "customary" sakau cannot begin until four men are situated as pounders and one is situated as erir, or server to the chief. Because of this unusual mixture of casual (in terms of the event setting, that is, evening at the chief's nahs) and formal (in terms of presentation) constitution of the event, this is an excel-lent setting for analyzing which contextual features co-occur with a shift in register.

This is an example of the ethnographic video recording of an event having con-sequences for the organization of an event. Although some might argue that the data collected under such conditions would be unsuitable, to the contrary, the presence of the camera in many cases made many aspects of Pohnpeian social practice more explicit. Participants often vocalized to me and to their co-participants ideas about how the event should proceed; these notions were then negotiated among the par-ticipants. The various solutions proposed presented a range of appropriateness far richer than individual consultants' accounts. I found that the beginnings of events were a rich site for understanding relationships between language and context in Pohnpei, as well as the situated nature of cultural performance. These event begin-nings also provided an opportunity for interesting and informative discussions with consultants watching the tape at a later date.

Out of eighty-one turns at talk before all the men are finally assembled and directed with the ritual phrase "na sukusuk" to begin pounding, thirty-seven turns, or 45 percent, are directives. The most directives are issued by the menindei (sixteen in total), who is responsible for the orderly succession of events. The secondary chief himself is the second most frequent issuer of directives (eight in total), his directives are often repeated by the menindei and others, as shown in excerpt 7. Of the menindei's directives, though only two are sequentially repeats of the chief's directives, all are issued in his role as master of ceremonies. That is, it is the menindei's job to gather the required number of men and the erir to serve the chief, and his directives are an attempt to achieve this goal. Failure to comply with the directives is not evidenced by any verbal disagreement, with the exception of one case, but by avoidance behavior (persons withdrawing themselves from sight of the menindei or the chief) or delay. In excerpt 14 the menindei is trying to stop someone from disappearing into the bush:

(14)

01 Menindei: ((shouting)) *UH UH UH nahn kohdo!*
                          UH UH UH buddy LocVerb.here.toward.me
                          UH UH UH buddy come here!

In the one case in which there is verbal disagreement to a directive, two other participants respond to such disagreement with surprise, and both give accounts (shown in excerpt 15, lines 04–07). Note that it is the chief who first issues the directive, perhaps making the young man's disagreement so surprising to the two older adults who respond, a woman and the menindei.

(15)

01 Chief: *en kohdo ih kihsang ah sehten.*
                  to come   he take.from his shirt.that.by.you
                  ((tell him)) to come and take his shirt off.

02 Woman: *kohdo   kihsang ahmw sehten.*
                  LocVerb.here take.from your(S) shirt.that.by.you
                  come take your shirt off.

03 Young Man: *ah sit!*
                  oh shit! ((borrowed English))

04 Woman: *ekei!*
                  ((Surprise exclamation))
                  what!

05 Menindei: *ekei!*   *seht pahn kapwuhrsang*
                  ((Surprise exclam.)) shirt will   cause.undress.from
                  what! the shirt will be taken off

          ((the young man begins to take his shirt off))

06 Woman: *kumwa pahn kihsang ahmwa seht kan*
             you(D)   will   take.from your(D) shirt those.by.you
             you two will take off your shirts

07   *pwe   lihe   pahn wiada kasdo.*
             because woman.this.by.me will   make   movie
             because this woman will be making a movie.

In this particular corpus of data, appeals to affiliative goals (we need a partner) are employed (see excerpt 10, "come on buddy, because we've got no partner"). The activity is constructed as a partnership, and yet, when honorific register is invoked, the partnership is reconstituted as a hierarchy of status which will determine who may stand, who may sit and where, who may leave and when, and the order of consuming sakau. Spatial positions indicate that no two participants have equal status. Pohnpeians appear to utilize structures present in their everyday life, both those of traditional hierarchy and those of a more egalitarian notion of reciprocity, to solve problems and are flexible enough to incorporate new facets of the environment, such as the video camera, in their strategies.

Acquiescence to a particular social organization (showing proper demeanor) is an act of solidarity (with rules) as well as an act of reconstitution of such rules. The Pohnpeian interactional data show the importance of solidarity in building a ranked structure. The first step is persuasion through solidarity, leading to acquiescence to participate, and a second step of the construction of hierarchy within that fellowship or order. Delinking honorifics from social distancing strategies allows for a more complex and complete understanding of the role of honorifics in building a social order. Viewing honorifics solely as "creating social distance" does not indicate that honorifics are productive mechanisms for structuring dependent intimacy and relationships of responsibility. Social theories about goal-directed actors and polarities of intimacy and hierarchy do not adequately predict speaker behavior.

Summary

The Pohnpeian interactional data demonstrate that although speakers believe the use of honorifics to be obligatory and regularized, asymmetries of status are context specific in ways not previously revealed by generalized descriptions of Pohnpeian social organization. The nature of the activity as well as the social identities of the participants are relevant to the employment of honorific forms.

Cross-cultural classification schemes and theories of status-marked linguistic behavior have tended to reify local ideologies of honorifics as forms that distance social actors from each other. I am suggesting that honorific speech can construct an interdependent intimacy rather than social distance. It is an etiquette of power relations that allows agents to transform and channel power and negotiate a status hierarchy. Honorifics index *shared* values, or solidarity, which interactional data show is an important first step in constructing systems of social inequality and resolving contradictions within such systems.

Both the English term "honorifics" and the Pohnpeian gloss of meing or lokaian wahu into "high language" negatively affect our understanding of these forms as indexes of status depreciation as well as honor. Pohnpeian honorific speech does not just give honor to higher-status persons. It is a pragmatic force which can constrain the actions of higher-status persons (Duranti 1992), coerce their generosity (Irvine 1974, 1992) and protection, reduce the prestige of lower-status speakers, and of course constitute and reproduce a system of inequality—a system co-constructed from the bottom, by the very speakers whose status is inferiorized. That a process that subordinates a large majority of speakers is called high is significant. In contrast, Guugu Yimidhirr speakers in Australia gloss the English word "deep" to describe the words of their respectful speech toward in-laws (Haviland 1979:217). Deep is the opposite of high and suggests something buried or hidden from view; this is significant given the taboo or forbidden ethos described by Guugu Yimidhirr speakers as appropriate for these interactions.

In fact, local ideologies of honorific use have been influential in shaping scholarly discussions of honorific speech because of researchers' reliance on interviews and participant observation rather than recorded speech data. Studying interactional data can reveal how stratification is organized and reorganized through language in interaction and how linguistic forms contribute to the naturalization of hierarchical relationships and the collaborative construction of meaning.

In the next several chapters I discuss in detail the domains of movement/location in space, possession, women's role in the constitution of hierarchy, and verbs denoting mental states and speaking.

Notes

1. The term "reference" is used in linguistics for the entity (object, state of affairs, etc.) in the external world to which a linguistic expression refers, for example, the referent of the word feast house is the physical object "feast house."

2. Linguists use the idea of truth values to suggest that meaning can be defined in terms of the conditions in the "real world" under which a person can use a sentence to make a true statement. This approach to meaning is different from other approaches such as speech act theory, which defines meaning in terms of the use of sentences in communication.

3. Pragmatics refers to the study of language usage and choices speakers make.

4. See Dixon 1971; Haviland 1978, 1979.

5. For example, Sacks 1974; Sacks, Schegloff and Jefferson 1974; Schegloff, Jefferson, and Sacks 1977; Schegloff and Sacks 1973; Jefferson 1972, 1979, 1987; Pomerantz 1978, 1984; C. Goodwin 1981; M. Goodwin 1990; Duranti and Goodwin 1992; Drew and Heritage 1993.

6. Hymes 1962, 1974; Gumperz and Hymes 1972; Cicourel 1980; Gumperz 1982; Ochs 1988; and others.

7. Rumsey (1996) discusses a similar notion, the uses of the first person pronoun in reference to an entire clan.

8. Hieratic: highly stylized or formal.

9. Ihr is an independent pronoun (that can stand alone as a one-word sentence) alternate for ira ("they two" or irail, "they plural"). In status-marked speech, ihr is also used as an object pronoun, suffixed to a verb form.

10. Chapter 3 describes ketin. Used serially with verbs it is a way to status-mark verbs that do not have a status-marked equivalent, as well as to increase the status-marking force of some high-status verbs.

11. In this construction, the verb *nda* ("say") is understood but not stated, as in *nda en kohdo*.

12. See also Firth 1940; Oliver 1951; Bascom 1965; Bott 1972; Petersen 1977, 1982; Marshall 1979; Duranti 1981, 1994; Kirch 1984; and others.

Chapter 3

Paths and Regions in Honorific Speech

Hierarchy of Place and Access to Status

Perhaps the most frequent site of Pohnpeian honorifics is in expressing common-place verbs of motion and stasis (i.e., a person's relative position or path to a goal position in space). Grammar constitutes at least two status levels or planes of movement and location, one high and one low. These verbally constructed levels complement a nonverbal, visual structuring of space, in which the concepts of high and low (vertical) are imposed or mapped onto a horizontal plane (the floor or ground). This chapter, along with chapter 5, examines the relationship between the verbal and nonverbal spatial organizational schemes—how relationships between discourse organization and spatial organization create a collaboratively achieved, cognitively shared world. In addition, I discuss an important construction in which any common verb can be made honorific through the use of an additional verb. This construction appears to be highly context sensitive and in the humiliative form to have inter-actional significance beyond lowering the status of participants' activities (e.g., conflict avoidance or mitigation). I also examine inclusive and exclusive strategies in honorific speech through choice of verbs and the implications for constraining access to power. Although verbs denoting speech and knowledge states have an identical morphology to transitive humiliative movement verbs, these domains are discussed in chapter 6. For the present, I concentrate on the *paths* and *regions* constituted for people in honorific speech by honorific verbs and the use of the special status-raising verbs used with common speech verbs.

As mentioned in previous chapters, two status levels are primarily expressed by honorific movement verbs: exaltive and humiliative. This polarity contrasts with *multiple* gradations of status constituted by the nonverbal ordering of space. It suggests that verbal symbols may be most powerful when ordered in terms of polar opposites (cf. markedness in languages), whereas visual symbolism is capable of a far greater complexity.

Because there are no *humiliative* pronouns (and very few nouns[1]), verb forms are important sites for the expression of low status. Low status is a relative state, a property of actions, whereas high status is something that not only is a property of actions but also adheres to nouns (including places) and pronouns, because there *are* exaltive nouns and pronouns (see chapter 2, in this volume). Activities therefore, not agents themselves, are coded for status in humiliative speech, whereas in exaltive speech both agents and actions are coded. Differences between these two speech levels (humiliative and exaltive) are emphasized in other parts of this chapter. The two speech levels differ in salient ways to constitute cultural ideologies of status. High status and low status are not just constituted as polarities but as states with differing degrees of agency and/or causality.

In this chapter, I first lay the groundwork for an understanding of the operation of honorific verbs. I then discuss how status can be constituted in inclusive and ex- clusive ways through choice of verbs and agents, and how different constructions of agency can empower or constrain access (expressed through verbs) to positions of dominance. Finally, I discuss the symbolic use of space to delineate hierarchy and how this symbolism and honorific speech terms interact.

Honorific verbs: An overview

Verbs of motion are expressed in honorific register by using one of two stems, ket- (exaltive) or pato- (humiliative), to which directional and/or transitive suffixes are added. The directional suffixes are important because they add specificity and make the polysemous stems (which replace multiple movement verbs) less ambiguous by providing deictic (i.e., pointing) references. Status marking includes not only com- monplace movement verbs but also verbs denoting stasis: The stems pato and ket used without directional suffixes indicate this. The English term "stasis" does not quite capture the Pohnpeian notion of the *achievement* of position as the result of activity, that is, the notion of place and status requiring continual attention and activity rather than an absence of movement. Though many languages distinguish between locative and directional along the lines of an opposition between static and dynamic, I am not concerned with these as oppositional concepts. Pato and ket can be thought of as expressing location as well as goal locations. Lyons (1968) as well notes a "parallelism" between static and dynamic states:

> The opposition of "locative" and "directional" [in/at versus to or from—ed.] may be regarded as a particular manifestation of a more general distinction between *static* and *dynamic* . . . as location is to motion, so being in a certain state or condition is to change into (or from) that state or condition: in other words there is a notional parallelism between such static expressions as "(be) in London," "(happen) on Tuesday," "(be) a teacher" and their dynamic counterparts "(go/come) to London," "(last) until Tuesday," "(become) a teacher." (Lyons 1968:300)

Location and status are linked through honorific language as well as in seating arrangements in honorific and other contexts. The Nanmwarki (paramount chief) is sometimes called Wasa Lapalap (lit. "**place** high-ranking"). Lapalap is the reduplicated form of *lap*, "large in stature; important or physically large." In certain contexts on Pohnpei, *location has a social status* which attaches to the person occupying the location (but not vice versa), thus the importance of such points in space. This is also noted by Duranti (1992, 1994) and Ochs (1988) for Samoa, where seating position can override other indicators of status. Access to identity- and status-producing goal locations is marked and ranked through honorific verbs of motion; occupation and border crossing into symbolically high areas are marked by both verbal and visual status guides.

Placement and direction

The examples from interactional data in table 3.1 illustrate the honorific locative verb stems pato- (humiliative) and ket- (exaltive) with directional and/or transitive suffixes and without. The construction of stem + suffix allows for a range of meanings to be expressed with a minimum of vocabulary. As mentioned in chapter 1 (in this volume), Pohnpeian marks temporal relations with aspect marking; that is, what speakers and hearers attend to temporally is whether an action is completed or not.

The importance of the directional suffixes can be seen in excerpt 1 in which the stem pato- takes four different endings: -long ("inward"),-sang ("from"), -di ("down-

TABLE 3.1 Honorific Locative Verb Stems with Suffixes

Humiliative		*Exaltive*
pato	locative verb	ket
pat-pat	locating (durative aspect)	ket-ket
patoh-do	locative verb—toward speaker	ket-do
patoh-la	locative verb—there	ket-la
pat-patoh-la	locating away from addressee and spkr	ket-ket-la
patoh-di	locative verb—downward	ket-di
patoh-da	locative verb—upward	ket-da
patoh-long	locative verb—inward	ket-long
patoh-sang	locative verb—from	ket-sang
patoh-wei	locative verb—toward addressee	ket-wei
patoh-wei-sang	locative verb—toward addressee–from	ket-wei-sang
patoh-di-wei	locative verb—downward–toward addressee	ket-di-wei
patoh-di-la	locative verb—downward–there	ket-di-la
patoh-long-ala	locative verb—inside–there	ket-long-ala
pat-patoh-ki	locating with	ket-ket-ki
patoh-wan	transitive verb	ket-ki
patoh-wan-ehng	transitive verb—toward	ket-ieng
patoh-wan-do	transitive verb—here toward speaker	ket-kih-do
patoh-wan-da	transitive verb—upward	ket-kih-da
patoh-wan-la	transitive verb—there	ket-kih-la
patoh-wan-sang	transitive verb—from	ket-kih-sang

ward") and -wei ("there by you"). Each verb phrase also contains an additional deictic (i.e., pointing) reference, such as "here by me" (*me*) or "there toward you"(*men*).

(1)

01 Chief: *ah pwe   ma ke   mihmi me*
          but because if   you(S) staying here
          but if you stay here

02 N: *ah pwe   ma e   **patohlong**   me*
          but because if   she LocVerb[HUM].inward here
          but if she goes inside here

03 L: ((to another participant))

          *ah kowe.   **patohsang**   men*
          andyou(S) LocVerb[HUM].from there.by.you
          and you. move from there

04 LA: *soh I pahn **patohdiwei**   men*
          no I will   LocVerb[HUM].down.toward.you there.by.you
          no I will go down there

Note that the chief in line 01 uses *mihmi* ("staying") in common speech; all verbs by other speakers are in humiliative form. Excerpt 2 presents another example of the use of directional suffixes:

(2)

01 N: **patohdi**
      LocVerb[HUM].down
      sit down

02 L: **patohsang**   *men*   *mwowei*
      LocVerb[HUM].from   there.by.you in.front.of.me
      move from in front of me

(. . . .)

03 S: *ke   kak **patohdo***
      you(S) can LocVerb[HUM].toward me
      you can move here

04   *pohn   kehle*
      on   wall/fence.this.by.me
      on the wall here ((there is a low cement wall on which he sits))

Some of the verbs of motion or relative location in space which are commonly expressed in honorific speech by pato and ket are go/come, move, put, sit, stay, carry/take/give. Verbs not marked by honorific register in interactional data where honorific register is found include join, change, do/make, use, organize, work, rest, fight, show, meet, can, find, lose, be slow, wait, hurry, need, want, understand, get wet, untie, twist, turn, cut, break, buy, jump, lean, feel sorry for, get angry, stop, invite, ride, refuse, begin, stare, cover, plant, try hard, send, run, make fire, face (a certain direction), and the existential marker *mie*. Pato and ket can also take other suffixes, such as that marking perfective or completed aspect (*-ehr*).

Transitive movement: Movement with objects

A difference is expressed in humiliative speech between transitive and intransitive forms, the former expressed by pato- plus suffixes and the latter by *patohwan* with or without directional suffixes. Patohwan appears to be a compound of pato plus wa, the verb "to carry." Transitive verbs are verbs that can take a direct object (i.e., goal or patient). Excerpt 3 shows uses of the transitive patohwan:

(3)

01 L: *Nansou,* **patohwando**   *mah*
         Nansou,   TranVerb[HUM].here.toward.me first/please
         Nansou, bring please

02   *pihlen*   *pwe*
         water.there.by.you because
         the water there because

(4)

01 LA: *kumwail patohda*   **patohwan**
         you(P)   LocVerb[HUM].upward   TranVerb[HUM]
         you all come up and take

02   *ahmwa tungoalaka*
         your(D) food[HUM].these.by.me
         your food

(5)

01 ND: *ke*   *nek*   **patohwan**   *two-by-fourko*
         you(S) could   TranVerb[HUM]   two-by-four.those
         you could take those two-by-fours

The transitive exaltive form is *ketki, ket* plus the instrumental suffix *-ki*.

(6)

01 Soumakaka: ((a prayer to God))

                sapwellimahr kalahngan   **ketkihdo**
                their(P)[EXAL] kindness/mercy give[EXAL].here
                your mercy that you give to us

Although I concentrate primarily on movement verbs in this chapter, an honorific verb construction exists for making potentially any activity status relevant. Ket and pato occur with the conjunctive adverb -n in front of other verbs that do not have an honorific form, or as Rehg (1981:367) reports where the honorific form is unknown to the speaker. This way of making any act (verb) status relevant is an important feature of the Pohnpeian honorific verb repertoire, and examples from interactional data show some important differences in the way Pohnpeians use this construction to constitute high status and low status. These verb forms operate strategically to raise or lower individuals' actions. The humiliative verb form *patohwen*, for example, can be used with the list of verbs provided earlier, which do not have humiliative equivalents ("change," "do/make," "get angry," etc). The use of the humiliative patohwen in a sort of serial construction with other verbs appears to correlate with verbs expressing high agency as well as with potential conflict (e.g., the verb "argue") or situations in which power is contested or status/power is a focal point of the utterance. This use discussed further later.

Other activities: The honorific verbs patohwen and ketin

Theoretically speaking, any verb can become an honorific verb by using the construction of pato or ket plus the conjunctive adverb -n/-en before a common verb, as discussed previously (i.e., patohwen [humiliative] or ketin [exaltive]. Some examples are patohwen + "argue," patohwen + "don't laugh," patohwen + "criticize/explain," patohwen + "take another's place," ketin + "teach," ketin + "recall past history." Using patohwen or ketin means that activities that typically are not marked in honorific speech can be so marked if a speaker chooses (patohwen used in this way is different from patohwan, the transitive humiliative verb, distinguished by the vowel /e/ rather than /a/ in the final syllable). Instances of patohwen and ketin are interesting because they are less obligatory (because choosing an uncommon verb is one way to avoid honorific speech). Ketin and patohwen are most frequent in oratory, with patohwen occurring in youth oratory and ketin in adult oratory. The two terms, ketin and patohwen, are not completely functionally equivalent, however. Although patohwen occurs before common verbs, ketin often occurs before verbs already in honorific exaltive register. The majority of verbs (other than locative verbs and transitive verbs involving location, knowledge, and speaking) are not marked for low status during casual interactions; hence the occurrences of status marking with patohwen calls attention to low status as a particularly relevant concern in a particular utterance.

Garvin and Riesenberg (1952) refer to the use of patohwen and ketin before common verbs as an honorific determinant. Rehg (1981) suggests that ketin and patohwen can be used as a strategy for speakers who do not know the proper honorific verb. However, the fact that this phenomenon occurs in oratory suggests that the use of patohwen may not just be an indication of lack of speaker competence but audience competence as well, because in the cases recorded, the speeches were prepared in writing beforehand and the proper words could have been ascertained from elders. Interactional data also show a correlation between the use of patohwen in oratory and transitive verbs (verbs denoting highest agency). Patohwen also co-occurs with verbs in utterances that are potentially offensive or antagonistic in casual speech. Thus interactional data show that these verbs can be strategically employed and have pragmatic consequences beyond indexing status, and further that ketin and patohwen operate in quite different ways and are not necessarily equivalent terms as far as usage goes.

In speeches, the chief and others frequently use ketin with other honorific verbs, such as in the construction *ketin kupwurki* (see excerpt 7). Here ketin appears to increase the exaltive force of kupwurki, already an exaltive term for the thoughts, feelings, and desires of the highest chief. In the following example of the speech of the leader of the small community in which I lived, ketin is used once with a common verb and twice with an exaltive verb. Ketin is used before the common verb *padahkieng* ("teach") and also before the exaltive verb kupwurki ("desire, think, feel") and the exaltive verb *pilerehrekieng* ("promise"). The speaker is an accomplished orator and honorific language speaker, a leader of the community, and a minister of the Protestant Church.

(7)

01 → *kauno*   **ketin**   *padahkiengkitailier dahme*
       leader.that [EXAL] teach.to.us(P).already what
       God has already taught us what is

02   *mwahu eri iet   me kauno   pil*
       good so here.by.me that leader.that also
       good so this is what God

03 → **ketin**   *kupwurki*
       [EXAL]   desire[EXAL].about
       wants

(. . . . .)

04 → *ihr* **ketin**   *pilerehrekidieng*   *kiht*
       they [EXAL] promise[EXAL].about.down.to us(EXCL)
       you (God) promise us

05   *rahnwet en pwurehng nenehng*
       today   to return   distribute.to
       today to return what is distributed among us

One consultant regularly translated ketin in a perfective or completed sense, even before common verbs. This "already accomplished" aspect is usually signaled in Pohnpeian by the suffix *-ehr/-ahr*, as in *serio kohlahr palio* (lit. "child-there go-already side-there," "the child already went to the other side").

In the following instances, ketin appears both with the common verbs (*wiada*, "do"; *kadaudoute*, "recall past history"), and with the exaltive verbs (*mwahngih*, "know"; *sapwellimaniki*, "have"). Co-occurrence of *ketin* with possession and knowledge states (and eating/drinking in excerpt 8) repeats the pattern of special marking for these domains noted in honorific speech in general and sets these exaltive activities apart from other activities expressed in exaltive form.

(8)

01 *wahuele   mwein kitail koaros* **ketin**   *mwahngih*
    honor maybe perhaps we(P) all   [EXAL] know[EXAL]
    honor: maybe perhaps we all know about

02 *wahu samatail   ko   me **ketin   wiada***
   honor father.our(P) those that [EXAL] does/makes
   the honor that our ancestors made

(. . .)

03 *ih mwo   kitail **ketin   sapwellimaniki***
   it there.afy&m we(P) [EXAL] have[EXAL]
   that's what we all have

04 *rahnwet wahu*
   day.this honor
   today honor

(. . .)

05 *kitail pil **ketin   kadakadaurdote***
   we(P) also [EXAL] recall.past.history.only
   we also still recall past history

In excerpt 9, ketin is used as the only verb (i.e., not in a serial fashion) to refer to the fact that the chief is going to eat (i.e., drink) sakau:

(9)

01 N: *Mwohnsapw— Mwohnsapw poahngokih en wiawi keneinei*
     chief—   chief   says[EXAL] to doing careful
     the chief says to do it carefully

02   *pwe   e pahn **ketin   sakau***
     because he will [EXAL] sakau
     because he's going to drink the sakau

The humiliative patohwen in contrast never appears serially with a verb already in humiliative register. In the following example of casual speech, patohwen is used with *sansal* ("clear, be clear") (following Rehg 1981, adjectives are classed as intransitive verbs in some contexts). Sansal is not typically expressed with patohwen but S (the second speaker) uses patohwen before the verb *sansal* to humble his own action (which is a boast).

(10)

01 Chieftess: *S,((title)), komw   keida   ekis*
           S ((title)) you(S)[EXAL] move.upward a.little
           S, move up a little because

02   *pwe   komw   sohte **sansal***
            because you(S)[EXAL] not   clear
            you are not clearly showing ((in the video))

03→ S: *ahka   ngehi   me   keiehu* **patohwen   sansal**
           of.course I   the.one first [HUM]   clear
           of course I'm the one who will show up the best

There are numerous instances of sansal in interactional data of honorific register without the use of patohwen. The chieftess (who uses humiliative speech throughout the interaction in the presence of the chief), for example, in an utterance preceding S's chooses not to use patohwen before the verb sansal (see line 02). S, however, explicitly self-lowers by adding patohwen before sansal. His utterance is a boast ("I am the most clear/I will show up the best"); boasting is disapproved of on Pohnpei. The use of the humiliative *patohwen* moderates the force of the boast and modifies the claim of superiority. Though S claims he shows up the best, he acknowledges the presence of higher-status people by choosing the humiliative *patohwen*. He thus renders his act at the same time boastful and humble.

In excerpts 11 and 12, patohwen is used before the verb "count," and before the verb "laugh." In excerpt 12, the speaker lowers another, in excerpt 11 the speaker self-lowers. As in the previous example, one speaker does not use the humiliative for a verb (e.g., with *wadek*), but the next speaker does use the humiliative marking. (In the first line of excerpt 11, speaker LA uses patohla with wadek—this expresses the action "go," as in "go (and) count.")

(11)

01 LA: *na patohla   wadek en L ((name)) beisen*
          so LocVerb[HUM].there count of L ((name)) basin
          so then go count L's drawer

02   *en rausis depe   io*
          of trousers how.many there.away.from.you.&.me
          how many trousers are there

03 N:→   *ah meh isuh   me   i* **patohwen   wadekada**
          but ones seven that I [HUM]   count.up
          but I counted seven

04 LA: *owwww ((laughs))*

Excerpt 11 is a competitive comparing of numbers of trousers. N contests LA's claims about the number of trousers her husband L has; however, N self-lowers his own act of counting on which he bases his argument. Several turns later, N also uses patohwen in front of the verb "laugh" when he says "don't (you) laugh":

(12)

01 N: *ke   dehr* **patohwen   kourouhr**
         you(S) don't [HUM]   laugh
         don't laugh

It is not clear specifically to whom N directs this utterance (other than it is obviously not the chief or chieftess because a humiliative verb is chosen). In the video, a number of people are laughing, including N himself, at a comment N has made to L, who is putting the sakau in the hibiscus bark. Use of patohwen restores the proper hierarchical order broken by the frame break (cf. Goffman 1974) of laughter. Laughter is not appropriate during the preparation of the first four cups of sakau, and in general those preparing sakau for the chief are expected to have a composed, serious demeanor.

In excerpt 13, speaker LA criticizes the behavior of two men who are arguing about expertise in local medicine and curing practices. She uses patohwen with the reduplicated form of *akamai* ("argue"):

(13)

01→ LA: *kumwa pahn **patohwen akakamai** nan kasdohn*
you(D) will [HUM] arguing in movie.that.by.you
if you two are going to argue in the movie

02 *ah kumwa patohweisang*
but you(D) LocVerb[HUM].toward you.from
then you two move from

03 *men pwe ngehi P ((name)) masak kumwa*
that.by.you because me P ((name)) fear you(D)
there because P and I are becoming afraid of you

04 *da*
suddenly/becoming

(Lines 03–04 are delivered in a sarcastic manner.) The arguing, like laughing while preparing sakau for the chief, challenges and threatens to subvert situated hierarchy. All three excerpts involve potential conflict or disagreement: who has more trousers, who is foolish, and whose behavior is appropriate. Thus using an honorific verb before a common speech verb can have interactional significance—drawing a participant's attention to status as a relevant concern and moderating potential conflict by invoking low status and putting limits on agency. In Pohnpeian honorific speech, dominance can be contested and status and power manifest during conflict.

The previous examples show patohwen used before common verbs in potentially antagonistic utterances (some involving intransitive verbs). There also appears to be a correlation between the use of patohwen and transitive verbs, in contexts other than conflict-laden ones. Transitive verbs are those indicating the most agency on the part of the subject or actor in the sentence and indicate a change made in the state of some entity. In excerpt 14, the same verb ("squeeze") is used twice, once in the intransitive form and once in the transitive form. The humiliative patohwen is used only before the transitive form (reflecting highest agency) of the verb "squeezing." (*Pediped* is the intransitive form, *padik* the transitive.)

(14)

01 N: *re palang oh patohwaneng*
they dry.in.the.sun and TranVerb[HUM].toward
they dry it in the sun and put it into

02   *nan   pihl ahpw nan   kisin ehd*
       inside water but   inside small bag
       the water but it is in the small bag

03   *re   patohwaneng   nan   kisin ehd kei   duerte*
       they TranVerb[HUM].to inside small bag some same
       they put it in some small bags which are like a

04 →   *ami   ahpw pediped. pediped pediped.*
       screen but   squeezing. squeezing squeezing
       screen but it is squeezed, squeezed, squeezed.

05 →   *ihr **patohwen** padik padikediehng   nan pihl*
       they [HUM]   squeeze squeeze.down.toward in   water
       they sqeeze it and squeeze it down in the water

06   *oh eri powdero   te*
       and so powder.there only
       and so it's only the powder

07   *re   tungtungoale ah re widewidekilawehu eri*
       they(P) eating[HUM]   but they pouring.there.one   so
       they are drinking but they are pouring out

08   *ahr   tungoal sakau pwe   re sohte soahng me*
       Ps.Cl.3P [HUM] sakau because they not   type   that
       their sakau because they are not the type that

In lines 04 and 05, the same verb ("squeeze") is used, first in the intransitive form (pediped) and then second in the transitive form (padik). Note that a humiliative patohwen precedes only the second use (transitive). Use of patohwen in the second instance also disambiguates the subject because the subject, the pronoun ihr, "they," can refer in exaltive speech to the chief (see chapter 2). Use of the humiliative verb *patohwen*, however, makes clear that ihr could not be the exaltive pronoun ihr but the common one. The second squeezing verb refers to a goal-directed activity (squeezing into the water) where an agent is changing the state of an entity, as opposed to the first, just squeezing. Goal-directed activity expressed by a transitive verb coincides with humiliative marking.

A similar use of patohwen to lower the status of transitive verbs is noted in the speeches of members of Catholic youth groups at an island-wide celebration in February 1993. Several examples are shown. The verbs are all used in a transitive way: "explain," "ask," and "replace." They are not typically expressed in humiliative register in interactional data. Patohwen explicitly describes an additional speech act, that of self-lowering, in addition to the act performed by the verb (e.g., "explain," "ask"). The act of lowering sequentially precedes another specified act, for instance, in the example patohwen *weliandi*, "I lower myself + I replace" (see excerpt 16). The verb *kawehwe* (excerpt 14) glossed in English as "explain" is a reduplicated form of the verb *kawe*, "to criticize." A correlation between criticism and the verb *patohwen* was shown in earlier examples in casual speech.

(15)   Girl from Wene

01 *eri   I   pahn **patohwen kawehwe** lepin   mahsen*
    so   I   will   [HUM]   explain   small   speech[EXAL].that.by.you
    so I will explain the word ((the Bible))

(16)   Boy from Tamoroi

01 *I   pahn **patohwen pehki** rehn   pwihn pwulopwul*
    I   will   [HUM]   ask   location.of group   youth
    I will ask the youth group

(17)   Boy from Paiess

01 *i   pahn **patohwen weliandi** kiht   pwihn   pwulopwul*
    I   will   [HUM]   replace   us(EXCL) group   youth
    I will represent us the youth group

In my corpus of *oratory*, the use of patohwen in a serial construction correlates with transitive verbs in nearly all cases. An exception is a case of patohwen + the intransitive *pehm* ("perceive," "think," "feel") and a case of patohwen + *doula* ("climb up") in youth speeches, the latter, however, used as a way of saying "continue (my speech)," a transitive action. In the case of *pehm*, as seen in chapter 6, verbs denoting interior mental states are typically marked in honorific register.

In the preceding section I discussed some of the ways common speech is marked for status using the honorific verbs patowen and ketin. Speakers thus have a range of resources to make status relevant in certain interactions. In the following section I discuss how interactional data show that exaltive status marking of verbs and humiliative status marking of verbs differ in terms of obligatoriness or variability.

Differences in status marking of verbs in humiliative and exaltive

As noted in the previous section, not all activities (verbs) are status-marked in honorific contexts. The following examples show segments from interactional data in which some verbs are in honorific speech and others are not. What becomes clear in examining these cases is that the verbs that are unmarked for status refer to activities of *low-status* persons, and the activities of the chief or God within an utterance are *all* status-marked.

In excerpts 18 and 19, verbs *not* marked in humiliative are in boldface. Humiliative verbs are marked in the interlinear gloss.

(18)

01 Lepen: *Nansou, patohwando*
              Nansou,   TranVerb[HUM].here.toward.me
              Nansou, bring

02   *pihlen   pwe   en **lekidekdi***
         water.that.by.you because to drop.down
         the water in order to drop ((the sakau))

03   *loale pwe   en mwur **ngalangalda***
         inside because to a.little drying.up.become
         in it so that it can dry up a little

((note the speaker makes a mistake in the last line—he most likely means to say *mwakelekelehda*, "become clean," rather than "dry up a little"—and laughs about his mistake in a subsequent utterance))

Excerpt 18 shows "bring" in honorific register and "drop down" and "dry up" in common speech. The following segment shows "go" and "stay" in honorific speech and "refuse," "begin," "sit," "cause to depart," "refuse," and "go" in common speech.

(19)

01 LA: *kisin pwutako **kahng** patohseli*
       small boy.there refuse   LocVerb[HUM].around
       the little boy refuses to go around visiting

02   *ah ihme se   kin*
         and it.this we(EXCL) habitually
         that's why we always

03   *patpatohki   reh   pwe   e*
         LocVerb[HUM].with location.of.him because he
         stay with him because he

04   ***kahng** patohseli.   dene   e sohte pahn*
         refuses LocVerb[HUM].around it.is. said he not   will
         refuses to go around he says he will not

05   ***iang** wasahn (?mehla)*
         join   place.of (?funeral)
         go to the place where (?the funeral is)

06   *e patpatohdote   mwo ih L ((name))*
         he LocVerb[HUM].here.only there he L ((name))
         he only stays there he and L

07   *me   ira   kin   **tapiada** ah   ira*
         the ones they(D) habitually start   however they(D)
         are the ones who started it and they

08   *kin (1.0) **mwohmwod** i kin   **kamwasal** ira*
         habitually sitting   I habitually cause.depart them(D)
         are always sitting around. I always make them go out

09   *ah ira   kin   **kahng** me **kohseli**.*
         but they(D) habitually refuse   that go.about
         but they always refuse to go about.

In the last line of excerpt 19, the verb *kohseli* is used, the common speech form of *patohseli*, which was used two times previously in this utterance by the same speaker. This shows that in the same utterance the same verb may occur in both honorific and common speech. The common form co-occurs with a change in subject or topic from "he" or "the small boy" to "they" (he and L), and also with a drop in the volume and projection of the speaker's voice. The speaker thus humbles the boy but not L and the boy. In the first example discussed in this section, the action of carrying something into the location of the speaker is marked for status, but the activity of putting roots into water *at* the location is not status marked. Similarly, in the second example, the boy's movement from and location is marked as low status, whereas the habitual actions of the two of them *at* the location are not marked as low. Status marking changes with a shift in subject focus as well as a shift in location. *Mwohmwod* is also not in honorific speech (the humiliative of mwohmwod is *patohdi*) and also has a dual subject (*ira*, "they"). Some common strategies of plural subject constructions with honorific verbs will be discussed below.

The following example shows common and *exaltive* speech verbs in the same utterance. Common speech verbs are again marked in boldface type, whereas exaltive verbs are identified in the interlinear gloss.

(20)

01 N: *Mwohnsapw- Mwohnsapw poahngokih en* **wiawi** *keneinei*
      chief-   chief   says[EXAL] to doing careful
      the chief- the chief says to do it carefully

02   *pwe   e pahn ketin   sakau*
      because he will   [EXAL] sakau
      because he will drink the sakau

This example is different from the humiliative speech examples (excerpts 18 and 19). The common speech verb in line 01 (*wiawi*) does not refer to the chief's actions but to the peoples'. The subject of wiawi is understood to be "us" rather than the chief (i.e., "the chief said for us to do it carefully"). All verbs referring to the chief's actions are in exaltive speech. Similarly, in the following example where the subject is God (*kauno*, lit. leader), all verbs referring to God's actions are expressed in exaltive form:

(21)

01 *wasa me kauno   kupkupwure   nektehn*
     place that leader (God) thinking[EXAL] almost
     the place that God had in mind that he had almost

02 *ketin   ketieng   irail pwe   **koasoan** loale*
     [EXAL] give[EXAL].to them because inhabit   inside
     given them to live in

03 ***koasoan*** *loale oh* **sapwenikihda**
     inhabit   inside and own.land
     to live in and to have the land

04 *ah   ih pilerehre   wet   me   e*
   however that promise[EXAL] this.by.me the one he
   however that promise the one he

05 *poahngokieng Moses en* **katamanken** *irail*
   say[EXAL].to   Moses   to   remind.to   them
   gave to Moses to remind them

The common verbs *koasoan* ("inhabit") and *sapwenikida* ("to own land") refer to the actions of the people, and the common verb *ketemen* ("remind") refers to actions of the biblical figure Moses. In the case of exaltive subjects, more of their activities are marked for high status than are activities of humiliative subjects marked for low status. Thus, the status of high people is unvaryingly constituted in activities, whereas the status of low people is only constituted in specific activities, most frequently those related to relative position or goal position in space.

    Another way that low-status marking varies is according to speaker. Two different speakers may differ in their choice of humiliative versus common verbs; that is, they may choose different status levels for the same activity by the same agent, as noted in excerpt 22 for the act of buying (trousers):

(22)

01→ N: **I ale kihda**   *rausis eisek paiehu*
            I take give.up ((exchange)) trousers ten   four
            I bought fourteen pairs of trousers

          (. . . .)

02   Boy: *cents isihsek limau mwo*   ((he smiles))
            cents seventy five   those
            the ones for seventy five cents

03   N: *ekei!*   *aphw rausis!*
            ((exclamation)) but   trousers
            what! but for trousers!

04→ LA: *ke   patohwansang   ia?*
            you(S) TranVerb[HUM].from where?
            where did you buy them?

N refers to buying (exchanging) as *ale kihda*, whereas LA refers to the buying as *patohwansang*. This excerpt is an example of a speaker not choosing to self-lower while another participant lowers the status of the same actions. Thus, through language a participant's activities can be constituted to have two different status levels. This is not possible in spatial arrangements, indicating the importance of language as well as the contestable nature of status in language.

    The previous sections described interactional uses of honorific verbs and discussed some differences in usage between humiliative and exaltive marking. In the next section I discuss a phenomenon noted in interactional data whereby honorific verb forms can be constituted inclusively or exclusively to index differential access to high-status locations or positions. In oratory, the chief sometimes raises low-status persons by using an exaltive verb for theirs and his collective action, notably the action of paying honor or respect.

Verbs and access: Inclusive and exclusive strategies in honorific speech

Exclusivity and inclusivity are concepts expressed by various grammatical means in Pacific languages, most notably by pronouns such as "we two, but not you," in other words excluding the addressee. In Pohnpeian honorific speech, exclusivity and inclusivity can be expressed through both pronoun choice and choice of exaltive or humiliative verb in some instances, and thus differential access to certain domains is indexed (pointed to). Access is of course a key component in issues of dominant and subordinate status differentials, especially when space is indexical of status.

Access to exaltive position can be limited and delimited in honorific speech in several ways. Two different verbs, one low and one high, may be used for the same plural subject (excerpts 27 and 28), lower-status subjects may share the high status of chiefs with an inclusively high verb (excerpts 23, 24, 25, and 26), and, conversely, joining a high-status person's location can be exclusively marked for lower status (excerpt 29). Excerpt 23 shows an example of honorific speech used *inclusively*. The subject *kumwail*, "you (P)," which refers to the whole gathering (high and low status), is followed by the exaltive verb ket. Both words are shown in boldface type (in this section both subject pronouns and status marked verbs are shown in boldface type).

(23) Drinking sakau at the chief's home

01 N: *suwedla   kumwail peneinei ah* **kumwail**
         bad.become you(P)   family   but you(P)
         it's bad that you all are one family and you all

02   *pahn pwonte* **ket**   *nan kasdo*
         will   entire.only LocVerb[EXAL] inside movie
         will be in the movie

The use of ket raises the status of the whole family, which includes the chief and high-status ancestors/deities, as well as lower-status persons who have been referred to by low-status verbs in previous talk. The speaker refers to the fact that those pounding sakau traditionally are not supposed to be members of the same clan as the chief.

Similarly, a dual subject in excerpt 24 includes the chief and another man. A high-status verb of speech is used for their collaborative action. The utterance begins with a humiliative verb, pato ("stay/be"), addressed to the lower-status man as a singular subject, but then a high-status verb, *poapoangoak* ("talking"), is used when he joins the chief as a dual subject (*kumwa*, "you two").

(24)

01 S: *I! ((title)) **pato**   *pahn*   *kupwur*
       I! ((title)) LocVerb[HUM] under.of desire/heart[EXAL]
       I! sit under the authority of the chief here

02   *me*   *pwe **kumwan** (kumwa en) **poapoangoak***
       here.by.me because   you(D)   to   talking[EXAL]
       so you two can talk

These examples show that in cases of multiple subjects of the same verb, the
highest-status verb is chosen for all parties. This is significant in that much of the
literature on honorifics stresses distance-creating and avoidance strategies claimed
to be social goals in honorific use (see chapter 2, in this volume). Pacific concepts of
political/divine power as both a sacred and dangerous force, to be avoided *and yet
employed* as the vital source of life, are not contradictory. Honorific speech in interaction shows how lower-status individuals gain symbolic power through proximity
and sharing of verbal symbols of status.

In excerpt 25, the chief uses the subject *kitail koaros* ("we all" or "let's all"), but
he chooses a status-raising verb for all.

(25)

01 Chief: *wahu. ele   mwein **kitail** koaros **ketin   mwahngih***
          honor. maybe perhaps we(P) all   [EXAL] know[EXAL]
          honor: maybe perhaps we all know about it

Although "we" (*kitail*) includes himself, self-raising is considered arrogant in
Pohnpeian society, even for chiefs. By using a plural pronoun, however, the chief
can raise himself by raising others with him. In excerpt 26, a high-ranking woman
combines all statuses, including children, with a single exaltive verb. Neither chief
was present in the interaction in excerpt 26, but the Soumas was present, the representative of the chief in the local community.

(26)

01 Woman: *kumwail mwahngih   kihs?*
          you(P)   know[EXAL] octopus?
          you know the story of the octopus?

(. . .)

02   *kitail ketkipene   wahu*
        we(P) take[EXAL].toward.each.other honor
        we honor each other

Both adult orators cited previously are speaking about the institutionalized practice
of honor. The status of the group is raised to pay tribute to traditions and the hierarchical status system. Paying tribute attaches increased honor to those paying homage.

In young people's oratory, however, *exclusive* strategies are used. The young speechmakers (see excerpts 27 and 28) do not combine plural subjects into the highest-status verb applicable. Instead they use two different verbs joined with the conjunction "or" (*de*) to signify two different status levels. The conjunction "or" signifies no collaboration or permeability of boundaries from high to low status (see excerpt 27 for an example):

(27) Boy from Tamoroi

01 *oh koarosie me ketket   de pato*
   and all.here   that LocVerb[EXAL] or LocVerb[HUM]
   and all of you that are here or are here

02 *wasa kiset*
   place this.by.me
   in this place

(. . . . .)

03 *kitail en tepda kupwukupwure de medemedewe*
   we(P) to begin thinking[EXAL] or thinking
   let's all start thinking or thinking

The first subject is *koarosie* ("all here") in line 01, but two verbs are used (ketket, exaltive and pato, humiliative), thus subdividing the plural subject into different status groups: high and low. When the subject is *kitail* ("we") in line 03, two different status levels of the verb "thinking" are used: *kupwukupwure* (exaltive) and *mede-medewe* (common speech). Excerpt 28 also shows this strategy with the subject *koarosie* ("all here") and the verbs "ket" and "pato."

(28) Girl from Wene

01 *oh koarosie me iang ket   de pato*
   and all.here   that join LocVerb[EXAL] or LocVerb[HUM]
   and all of you who join being or being

02 *wasa kiset*
   place this.by.me
   here

This example is very similar to the previous one, giving an idea of the rhetorical strategies used in young peoples' speechmaking. The exaltive verb always occurs first, then the humiliative, suggesting the significance of syntactic and linear order in connection with status. The youthful speakers do not raise the status of the whole group by choosing a verb to represent the whole as the paramount chief and titled adults do. Young people use exclusive strategies and do not constitute themselves as able to bridge dominant/subordinate relations.

    The following example of an utterance by the chieftess (not involving a plural subject pronoun) shows another exclusive strategy—how honorific speech can be used to disjoin status from location or limit access. The chieftess invites a lower-status person to share her vertically high location (in a chair) but not her status. The chieftess expresses the lower-status person's activity of sitting on the chair using a humiliative verb (pato).

(29)

```
01  Chieftess:  ke      pahn iang pato          pohn
                you(S) will   join  LocVerb[HUM] on
                you will join me and sit on

02                     dewei                    sehro
                position/location/rank.my  chair.that
                my chair over there
```

Here status is separated from the position itself through language and becomes something that adheres to the activity of the humble person (i.e., that the humble person carries along with him or her). Status is divorced from location by lowering the status of the person crossing a border and entering a high space (this is similar to examples in chapter 5, in this volume). Thus because of honorific speech, lower-status persons can occupy ritually high positions and explicitly not receive the commensurate status. In this instance, honorific speech works to redefine and to limit access: Movement does not mean change in status. The chieftess, unlike the chief, uses honorific speech and therefore can lower others in a way that the chief cannot.

The previous examples showed how status can be constituted in inclusive and exclusive ways through choice of verbs. The following section examines how verbs can signal different constructions of agency which can empower or constrain access to positions of power.

Agency

In honorific speech, the powerful immanent agency[2] of the chief is signified when verb-level choice changes the chief's semantic role. In the following utterance, in the phrase "then (you) try and ask the chief," the chief is not the actor or agent (i.e., initiator of the action). However, as the following example shows, use of an exaltive verb reclassifies the chief's role as that of agent of the action "ask." The high-status verb of speaking/asking is used, as if the agent were the chief; the chief's role is redefined as one necessitating status agreement with the verb, normally the role of subject or agent. Asking the chief a question is expressed as a chiefly activity even though the agent in the sentence is a low-status person.

(30)

```
01  N:  ke      kahng? na   song keinemwe rehn
         you(S) refuse?  then try    ask[EXAL] location.of
         you don't believe me? then try and ask

02         Mwohnsapwo
           chief.there
           the chief
```

Other studies on honorifics have noted an association between honorifics and passive construction and reduced agency or agentlessness (cf. Brown and Levinson 1978) and intransitive rather than transitive constructions. As shown previously, the use of patohwen as a status-lowering verb occurs frequently in transitive (i.e., highest agency) sentence constructions, thus modifying or lowering the force of the agency. Fischer (1969) observed a relationship between honorific forms and causatives and passives in Pohnpeian: "[I]nterestingly there are honorific forms of some verbs which appear analogous to forms of other verbs which are causative or a sort of passive, e.g., the verb itek 'to ask' which has both a pseudo-causative honorific form ke-idek 'to ask' and a pseudo-passive honorific form pe-itek 'to ask' (also used as a nominalized form meaning 'a question')" (Fischer 1969:420).

Positing a relationship between the causative prefix *ke-* or *ka-* and the exaltive verb stem *ket-* is an intriguing one, with implications about high-status persons being perceived as direct instigators of actions. The pseudo-passive prefix *pe-* may be similarly related to the humiliative *pato*. Pato- is similar to words for ground (the lowest-status location), including *patapat*, "level ground," and *patehn neh*, "foot." In many cultures, diminutives are used to protect individuals from harmful spirits. Lowering oneself or others in Pohnpeian therefore could be seen both as humble behavior and protective behavior, particularly in the presence of the chief, who is surrounded by powerful spirits and who has high amounts of manaman or sacred power.

Before proceeding to an analysis of how verbal signs and spatial signs combine to create status hierarchy in Pohnpei, I briefly mention subjects of honorific verbs as noted in interaction to show the frequency of other-lowering.

Subjects of honorific verbs

Table 3.2 shows the different distribution of person and number in subjects of honorific verbs for a sixty-minute segment of a sakau interaction.

Speakers do not self-raise, although they self-lower (first person, singular and plural subjects of humiliative verbs = thirty-one, subjects of exaltive verbs = zero). Other-lowering is twice as frequent as self-lowering (second and third person subjects of humiliative verbs = sixty-four, first person subjects of humiliative verbs = thirty-one). It is important to note that this other-lowering is never done by the chief but primarily by *same-status members of their own low-status group*. In exaltive speech, the third person plural pronoun is often used for second person; thus total second person singular (you) should be twelve, showing this to be the largest category.

Constituting spatial hierarchy through honorific verbs

Hierarchy of social space

In this section I show that spatial proximity can express finer gradations of status on Pohnpei than the use of honorific verbs permits. One's proximity to the chief and others in formal seating arrangements signifies a complex *individualized* hierarchy

TABLE 3.2 Distribution of Person and Number in Subjects of Honorific
Verbs for a Sixty-Minute Segment of a Sakau Interaction

Subjects		Humiliative Verbs	Exaltive Verbs
I	i	23	0
you (S)	ke, komw	28	3
he, she, it	e	22	8
we (D,P)	se, kita, kitail	8	0
you (D,P)	kumwa, kumwail	7	1
they	ira, irail, re	7	1
total 1st person	i, se, kita, kitail	31	0
total 2nd person	ke, komw, kumwa, kumwail	35	4
total 3rd person	e, ira, irail, re	29	9

of status, states achieved through both birthright and achievement. Verbs can only
reference two different degrees of status (high or low) or, in rare cases, three (as in
separate food terms for the paramount chief, paramount chieftess, and the secondary
chief). Humiliative verbs for example reference people as *members of a group* of
low-status individuals, not differentiated. The actions of boys and girls as well as
titled men and women are status marked as low by the same humiliative verb in the
presence of the chief. The spatial design of the feast house, however, can signal each
individual's relative social status.

That the allocation of space is often a more salient guide to relations of relative
status than is speech in Pacific societies has been noted by Duranti (1981, 1994) for
Samoa. On Pohnpei in particular, not only space is important but relative height (see
Toren 1990 for a discussion of the significance of space in constructing hierarchical
relations in Figi). Where seating arrangements in the *fono* or Samoan political meeting can influence rights of participation in talk, similarly, the side platforms of the
Pohnpeian nahs (i.e., low status) are called *mwengintik* (lit. "whisper little"), which
indicates that here too is a relationship between status and not only amount but volume of talk.

The nahs

The Pohnpeian nahs or feast house is typically rectangular in shape, with a floor
plan that is U-shaped. One side is completely open to the outside. The U-shaped
configuration results from the fact that the floor is raised on three sides above the
middle, a bare earth floor (see chapter 1, figure 1.2, in this volume). The walls on
three sides extend only halfway to the roof. Sometimes the chief's family or owner's
family lives in the nahs. When I first lived with the second-ranking chief's family
in 1991, the chief used the back rooms and the rest of us slept on the main platform
at night.

A traditional nahs is built of mangrove wood, pandanus leaves, and *pwehl* (sen-
nit). According to oral history, the configuration of the nahs was influenced by the

culture hero Isokelekel, who overthrew the ruling class of Saudeleurs inhabiting the stone fortress of Nan Madol, the abandoned ruins of which are located in Madolenihmw. While the Saudeleurs were in power only chiefs were sheltered in a smaller type of nahs, and all offerings of tribute took place outside the structure, where lower-status people stayed during feasts and funerals. Isokelekel introduced the current structure with a central sheltered place for the people and their activities (Hambruch 1936; Hanlon 1988), still, however, lower than the chiefs or in raised areas classed as low. A description of a Pohnpeian nahs follows:

> The Nach or Council Lodge was a lofty, wide, long and spacious building with a raised platform, at the end of which there was often a room for the sleeping place of the Chief and his family, railed off by shutters of cane sometimes called Pel or Ueip; the partition is called Mech-en-tet. On this raised platform, about six feet in height (Lempantam or Leppantam), ascended by a rude ladder (Kantake), sat the chiefs and distinguished men. Along both sides within the Lodge ran a wooden terrace or platform, with reed-grass or cane flooring, where the women and children and those of lower estate sat. In the open space below were several huge flat slightly concave basalt stones, upon which the Chakau, Choko, or Kava root was pounded (Christian 1899:141).

Today, nahs structures are made of a combination of Western and traditional materials. Most nahs platforms are uniform in height; that is, the side platforms are the same height as the rear one. However, the traditional status symbolism is still relevant. The rear of the platform is reserved for the paramount chief (Nanmwarki), the paramount chieftess (Likend), the secondary chief (Nahnken), and the secondary chieftess (Nahnken Iai) and those of highest title during ceremonial occasions. No one may pass behind the chiefs and chieftesses in the nahs, as that is the highest space reserved for the ancestor spirits. Today high-status women sit on part of the main platform. When a new nahs is constructed it may not be used until a feast has been held during which the paramount chief or secondary chief dedicates/blesses the structure.

Each part of the nahs has a name and a status attached to it (see figure 1.2 for details). Locations as well as doors, the site of entrances into and exits out of hierarchized space, are named and reserved for certain high-status individuals. For example, only a man with the title Keraun en Ledau can lean on a certain post; only a man with the title Nahlaimw can use the opposite post. Only specifically titled women can sit near the two chieftesses. The platform floor as well as the earth floor are portioned into sections, each with a name and status. Certain boundaries may not be crossed; for example, a low-status person cannot hang his or her legs over the platform (the boundary between where chiefs sit and where sakau pounders sit) or step on the beam which forms the inner edge of a side platform. Sakau, however, is a boundary-crossing force; when carrying a cup of sakau, one can go anywhere.

Despite the prescriptions about spatial hierarchy, however, a nahs serves many functions, including canoe storage, laundry drying, and living quarters. Thus the hierarchical spatial symbolism only holds in certain contexts. When sakau is not being served, the sakau stones or stone may be turned on edge and leaned up against one side. With such multiple-use patterns, the transition from common use with no prohibitions or hierarchy to ritual use with prescriptions is made using honorific speech as well as gestures and body position.

The interaction discussed in the following section shows just how in a matter of a few minutes the symbol-neutral living space, where earlier in the day the family slept, laundry was hung, and children played, is transformed into an historical, symbolic hierarchy where prescriptions govern *speech, movement, and location* in space. These three domains are the very ones that are sites of honorific speech. The encoding of space with hierarchical symbolism is achieved with the use of honorific verbs.

Talk in interaction: Assigning ranked social space

The following segments illustrate a relationship between verbal status marking in honorific speech and visual status marking in spatial symbolism. Action and participation status are connected, and body movement and speech are coordinated. Previously I discussed how honorific verb forms focus on movement to and from as well as location in space, whereas many activities within the space are not marked for

Figure 3.1 The Nahs of the Paramount Chief of Madolenihmw

low status but only for high status. Two different speakers may choose different strategies in low-status speech, but high-status indexing is less variable. Verb forms limit access and degrees of agency. The following discussions connect the limiting of access to status in speech with the limiting of access to status in spatial symbolism.

An interaction with the second-ranking chief

In the following segment (discussed also in chapter 5, in this volume), a shift to honorific speech register occurs as a reconfiguration of space is constructed using the cultural symbolism of the nahs. Whereas at the beginning of the interaction Nahnken, the second-ranking chief, sits at the edge of the nahs platform in a casual pose, with one leg vertical and one arm resting on his knee (see figure 3.2, frame 1), coincident with the beginning of honorific speech register he has moved several feet back and adopted a more formal seating pose with both legs crossed (see figure 3.5, frame 4). Honorific speech is used by the man who is acting as the menindei (master of ceremonies) to direct a low-status person into the chief's area. Through a series of video frames I describe the coordination of speech and seating positions.

When the chief is in a casual pose, and before the hierarchical symbolism of the nahs is constructed, no honorific words are used, even though prescriptively humiliative speech by the man and boy sitting on stools on the dirt floor would be appropriate.

Chief

Figure 3.2 Video Frame 1

(31)

Chief: *ah ia   ih*   ((first video frame action occurs here))
             but where he
             so where is he

Woman: *ie   ih*
             here by me he
             here he is

Chief: *en kohdo e kihsang ah sehten*
             to come he take from his shirt that by you
             tell him to come and take off his shirt

Woman: **kohdo** *kihsang ahmw sehten*
             come   take from your(S) shirt that by you
             come and take off your shirt

The woman's second utterance uses the common speech form of the verb "to come" (kohdo), just as the chief does.

In the next frame I have selected, a few minutes later, the chief stands up and leaves to go to his private room (where he sleeps) in the back of the nahs to get a pack of cigarettes. He can be seen leaving in the second video frame. The other participants are still getting organized. Both the chief and the menindei use common speech in assigning places.

Chief

Figure 3.3 Video Frame 2

(32)

Chief: *aramas pahn mih wasao*
       person   will   stay place there
       someone should stay over there

((chief gets up and walks off—second video frame action occurs here))

Menindei: *na Mwar kumwa keido   me*
          so Mwar you(D)   move.here here by me
          so Mwar you two move over here

In the next video frame (figure 3.4, frame 3) the chief returns, and stands briefly on the platform before sitting in a new position and pose. The others have organized themselves into appropriate positions for the pounding of sakau, and the pounding stones are being passed out by the only one of the pounders who remains standing. Just as the chief returns from the back room, the menindei utters the first honorific words (in boldface type)—verbs of movement:

(33)

((the chief is walking back))

Menindei: *W ((name))* ***patohdala***   *mah dehu*
          W ((name))   Loc.Verb[HUM].upward.there first   location
          W go up there first and position yourself

Chief

Figure 3.4 Video Frame 3

((third video frame action occurs here))

> **patohwansang**   *ahmw sehten*
> Tran.Verb.[HUM].from your(S) shirt.that.by.you
> take off your shirt

> **patohdala**   *wiada udahn*
> Loc.Verb[HUM].upward.there do   truly
> go up there and sit the way

> *mwohden erir   eh*
> sit.of   server eh
> a server sits eh

The menindei uses three humiliative verb forms for the actions he wants W to do: go up there, take off your shirt, and go up there. These verbs contrast with verbs used earlier before the chief left (e.g., *kihsang ahmw sehten* is now *patohwansang ahmw sehten*). It is obvious that these are still preparatory measures (getting into position, getting properly dressed or undressed), and that the honorifics do not occur because preparations are finished. Honorifics occur when the chief arrives to take up his appropriate sitting *position* and when W is directed to move *up* to his appropriate sitting position on the feast house platform. Prior to this, the only moving about by low-status participants was on the dirt floor. Though W will occupy a high position, it is symbolically lower than the chief, being closer to the entrance of the feast house. W's lower position is also indicated in the use of humiliative verbs by the menindei to direct his actions. The space in the feast house is inscribed with hierarchical meanings through honorific speech.

In the fourth video frame (figure 3.5, frame 4), the chief sits, not in the position he occupied before leaving to get his cigarettes but several feet farther back on the platform. W has also begun to position himself on the platform in the fourth and fifth video frames. The chief talks to him as he does so:

(34)

Chief: *men,   men   kadilong apali nemwen*
     that by you that by you tuck in   one   leg your
     that, that, tuck in one leg

> *pwe   soahngen eriren*
> because type.of   server.that.by.you
> because that type of [sitting as]

> *i kilang* ((fourth video frame action here)) *e sapwung*
> I see   it wrong
> server I see is incorrect

Erirs (those who sit in front of the chiefs and chieftesses and serve them sakau) have a unique way of sitting, with legs not crossed but bent sideways. Apparently the chief has seen W or others doing it the wrong way, and he aims to teach W the correct way, with both knees facing the same direction, feet toward the lower-status area. Figure 3.5, frame 4 shows clearly the chief's position farther back with his legs crossed

Figure 3.5 Video Frame 4

in front of him. This pose contrasts with both his former pose in the first frame and W's pose. The status differential between the chief and his server is thus mapped onto body pose as well as speech and relative location.

The fifth frame (figure 3.6, frame 5) shows W taking his shirt off as he has been instructed by the menindei. It is culturally appropriate for those serving the chiefs to have their shirts off. The other pounders are waiting, with their pounding stones in hand. They sit lower than the chief, both in their position closer to the entrance of the nahs and in their position lower on the dirt floor. As W takes his shirt off the menindei tells him that the chief is going to explain to him the proper way to sit. The menindei uses the exaltive verb *masanih* plus the suffix *-ong* to refer to the chief's activity of talking.

(35)

Menindei: *ohlen   nek   **mahsanihong**uhk dahme*
man.that could say[EXAL].to.you(S) what
that man ((the chief)) could tell you

pwungen ahmw pahn mwohd
correct.of your(S) will   sit
the correct way for you to sit

The construction *nek mahsanihong* moderates the force of what otherwise might be seen as a directive by the menindei to the chief. Rather than "that man will tell you . . ." the construction is "that man could tell you. . . ." The chief is a person with

W

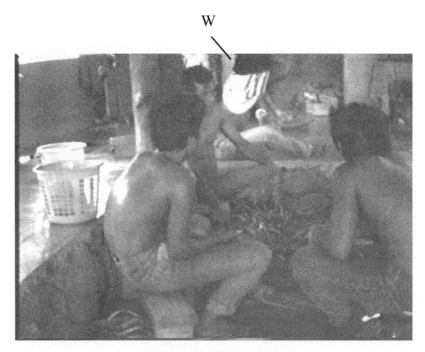

Figure 3.6 Video Frame 5

many options from which to choose, whose actions cannot be predicted or directed, unlike W who must sit a certain way.

W has moved up closer to the chief and is positioning his legs in the way appropriate for the erir (server). His role will be to take cups of sakau from the menindei and give them, in a stylized hand and arm movement with eyes averted, to the chief. The chief instructs W to move up even more (i.e., higher). Appropriate humble behavior dictates taking a low position and then being urged by someone else to take a higher one. In this case W is raised up to a higher position by the chief. The chief in assigning position uses common speech. The chief thus does not other-lower. Rather, chiefs in this and other contexts seem to engage in acts of *raising* the status of others (see chapter 7). Lowering is done by similar-status peers.

(36)

Chief: *keidado*   *keidado*
　　　　move.upward.here.toward.me move.upward.here
　　　　move up here, move up here

The reference point for position is not only the floor of the nahs platform but the location of the chief. The sixth video frame (figure 3.7, frame 6) shows the position of the four pounders, the erir, and the chief as well as the menindei. The menindei has given the command to begin pounding, and all talk has ceased.

N   W   Chief   Menendei

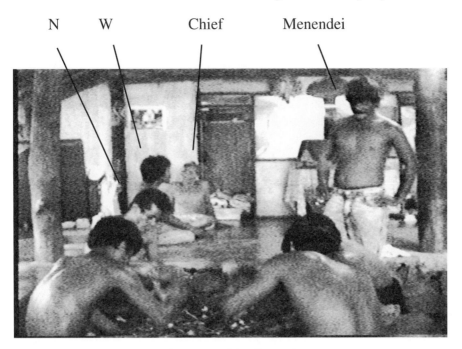

Figure 3.7 Video Frame 6

The sixth frame contrasts sharply with the first frame in terms of the number of participants (including two more pounders, a server for the chief, and the master of ceremonies) and the seating position of the chief and W. The meaning of space has changed. Spatial organization is closely related to the organization of discourse; at the same time, language can be a powerful force for altering the meaning of space for the participants. Positional identities are constituted from among a group of men through honorific language which assigns low- and high-status positions and dictates actions within those positions. Polarities in speech are used to assign a hierarchy of space.

A similar sequence of positioning involving women and men is discussed in chapter 5, with the paramount chief.

Summary

Honorific verbs status-mark journeys from source areas to goal areas, as well as the areas themselves. The relationships between verbal and nonverbal spatial domains and organizational schemes is a complex dialogic one. Visual maps can reproduce finer gradations in status than honorific speech is able to do. For example, all low-status social actors are grouped into one class by honorific verbs, when in fact their seating position indicates that they inhabit positions in a complex hierarchy, where no two positions are equal. However, in speech two different status levels can be constituted (and contested) for the same person, depending on activity and other factors, and these gradations or qualities cannot be expressed visually. Language can also constitute different degrees of agency for social actors of different statuses; low-status persons can occupy ritually high positions in the visual sphere without the concomitant status if they are lowered in status by verbal means. Low-status individuals' activities can also be joined with high-status individuals' activities through plural subject verbs. This is significant because much of the previous scholarship on honorifics stresses distance-creating and avoidance strategies as motivating honor-ific use. Honorific speech in interaction shows how lower-status individuals gain access to status through proximity and sharing of verbal symbols of status. How-ever, strategies are also employed to express exclusivity or nonsharing of dominant, socially valued positions.

The two speech levels, humiliative and exaltive, differ in the ways they consti-tute cultural ideologies of status. High status and low status are not just constituted as polarities but as states with differing degrees of agency and/or causality. Low sta-tus is a property of actions, whereas high status can also be expressed in nominal exaltive forms. Differences are also evident in the use of the verbal patohwen or ketin forms in exaltive versus humiliative speech.

Notes

1. Sometimes the term *pato* is used as a noun.
2. The agent in a sentence is the instigator of an action or initiator of an event.

Chapter 4

Honorific Possession

Grammatical Relations of
Control and Permanence

In the previous chapter I described status marking of paths and locations in space through verbs of movement. In this chapter I discuss honorific possessive constructions, which signify status marked relations of ownership as well as relations of proximity. I incorporate linguistic and interactional data with ethnographic data about Pohnpeian society and cultural beliefs, particularly notions about the meaning and construction of ranked social relationships. Pohnpeian possessive constructions not only constitute cultural categories of rank and power relations but dynamically resort or reclassify these categories through honorific speech. In this chapter I show how Pohnpeian possessive classifiers provide data for understanding the importance of certain domains of power transfer and power sharing, and the importance of rank to cognitive organization schemes in Pohnpei.

Microinteractions which index status are linked both to larger cultural ideologies about power and metaphorically to the experiential domain. The overt arrangement of entities into classes exhibited by the Pohnpeian possessive classifiers provides productive data for understanding the importance of selected concepts and relationships within a language system and within a culture. Work in linguistic anthropology on categorization schemes (e.g., Berlin and Kay 1969) and by semanticists (Bolinger 1965; G. Lakoff 1973) provides insights into cognitive organization patterns and shows that metaphorical extensions are one of the essential processes at work in language (Givon 1986). Mental categorization schemes such as noun classification systems can be productive sites for examining how experience is meaningfully and culturally structured through metaphorical and metonymic associations.

Pohnpeian speakers organize relationships of possession into different categories using an elaborate system of noun classifiers. This overt distribution of entities
into classes (expressed in Pohnpeian possessive classifiers) affords a view of how
Pohnpeians constitute their world and which properties of and relations between
entities are constituted as meaningful. In classifying, some distinctive features are
noted for similarities and differences while others are ignored. When speakers shift
into honorific or status-indexing speech, possessive classifiers are different from those
used in common speech, and the categories formed by the different possessive classifiers are reshaped, including part–whole relationships for the body. Differences
between common speech and honorific speech possessives and between the two levels
of honorific speech, for example, indicate how Pohnpeians constitute status levels
not only as asymmetrical but with different properties of control, temporality, and
dominance. Possessive classifiers contribute to constituting a culturally specific,
dependent relationship between the chiefs and the people. As Duranti and Ochs (1990)
observe, "genitive [possessive] constructions have not been studied for the richness
of their semantic and pragmatic implications" (18). In this chapter, metaphorical
connections between the honorific possessive classifiers and the experiential base of
the human environment, particularly the harvesting of food from the land, are related to other cultural practices which connect food and land with rank. The possessive classifiers also provide data for understanding cultural ideologies of the interdependent relationship between low and high status.

Classifiers are an important feature of many languages (e.g., Chinese, Vietnamese, and Hopi), and mark words as belonging to the same semantic class based on
such attributes as shape, size, color, animacy, status, and so on. Classifier systems
categorize nouns into different and/or additional classes than those given by the nouns
(Denny 1976) and encode additional data within the noun phrase. Besides possessive classifiers, Pohnpeian has a system of numeral classifiers, organized for the most
part by physical attributes of the noun, primarily shape, but not status (see chapter
1). I limit my discussion to possessive classifiers.

Some details about Pohnpeian possessives are given next, including implications
of semantic properties shared between classifiers and the entities classified. A brief
discussion[1] of common speech possession is necessary because the changes that occur
when speakers move from one register to another are significant in terms of structure and meaning. I am making distinctions (1) between common speech and honorific speech and (2) within honorific speech, to differences between low-status indexing
(humiliative) and high-status indexing (exaltive). I discuss how Pohnpeians construct
a relationship between low status and high status through metaphorical connections
suggested in the honorific constructions.

The morphological and semantic changes in the way possession is signified when
a shift from common speech to honorific register occurs are made significant by
local ideologies about manaman (power) which resides in high-status persons and is
transferred to their possessions (see chapter 1). Errington has noted for Javanese that
possessions that come in close contact with high-status individuals, such as pillows
and blankets, are marked in honorific language (J. Errington 1988:164–5). The relation is also made significant by the cultural association between location and status.
Grammarians have noted that possessives often express relationships of spatial prox-

imity or attachment (e.g., "my village") rather than possession, for example, as noted by Lyons:

> The term "possessive," as it is traditionally employed by linguists, is somewhat misleading: it suggests that the basic function of the so-called possessive constructions that are found in many languages is the expression of possession or ownership. Generally speaking, however, a phrase like "'X's Y" means no more than "the Y that is associated with X"; the referent of "(the) Y" with the referent of "(the) X" is frequently one of spatial proximity or attachment. It can be argued that so-called possessive expressions are to be regarded as a subclass of locatives (as they very obviously are, in terms of their grammatical structure, in certain languages). (Lyons 1977:473)

A linkage between possessive constructions and location points again to the spatial domain as a salient site for constructing social asymmetry. Thus important relationships between hierarchy and possession can already be established: (1) through the cultural belief in the transference of high-status sacred/dangerous power to possessions, and (2) through the importance of spatial relations to status symbolism. This chapter examines phenomenological relationships between bodily activities and possession, by looking at metaphorical links between the honorific possessive classifiers and local ideologies about sharing food and land, as well as transmission of sacred power.

Polarities of control and noncontrol

Many Polynesian languages (cf. Samoan, Hawaiian, Tongan, and others) grammatically distinguish between possessive categories of control and noncontrol, marking relationships initiated with a possessor's control and without, and specifying more precisely some relationships of the former, such as possession as drink or source of food, personal kin, and certain artifacts for personal use (see Wilson 1982:123).

> The heart of the Polynesian possessive systems is a contrast between A and O pairs. The semantic function of this contrast has been poorly understood in the past. We have found that in Proto-Polynesian, A-forms marked relationships initiated with a possessor's control and the O-forms marked relationships initiated without a possessor's control. O-forms had secondary functions, however, as markers of *specified* relationships initiated with a possessor's control. *Among these specified relationships were possession as drink or source of drink, possession as source of food, possession as personal kin, and possession of certain artifacts for personal use.* (Wilson 1982:123 [emphasis added])

Possessive constructions constitute multiple relationships in Pohnpeian. These relations include dominance versus nondominance (degrees of control), temporality (temporary vs. permanent), locative associations, and status, as well as of course ownership.

Pohnpeian expresses the idea of control versus noncontrol in possessive marking. An important meaning encoded in the humiliative or low-status speech classifier is noncontrol and nonpermanence. Harrison (1988) reconstructs the following

Oceanic possessive classifiers and their meanings which show a relationship to the Pohnpeian ones:

na   dominant possession
ka   subordinate or uncontrolled possession; edible possession, intimate
          property
ma   drinkable possession (Fiji and the New Hebrides)

Although a part–whole relationship (e.g., body parts) can be expressed by directly suffixing possessive morphemes to nouns in Pohnpeian (i.e., without using a classifier), in the majority of cases of possession possessive classifiers (discussed in more detail later) are used. Possession can also be formed by adding -*n* to the third person singular possessed form (e.g., *mese-n liho*, "the face **of** the woman"), similar to the English usage. In a survey of three taped interactions among men and women, formal and informal, possession with classifiers occurs in 89 percent of cases, the remaining 11 percent is made up of part–whole possessive constructions. Whereas some Micronesian languages might have between fifteen and twenty possessive classifiers (Harrison 1988), Pohnpeian has twenty-nine, counting the honorific possessive classifiers. Table 4.1 lists the spectrum of Pohnpeian *common* (non–status-indexed) speech possessive classifiers and provides examples of each.

Table 4.2, which I constructed based on data from Rehg (1981) and interactional data, illustrates a close morphological and semantic relationship between the classifier and the objects classified. For example, the verb to drink is *nim* and the possessive classifier for things to drink is *nime-* as in *nimei uhpw* ("my drinking coconut") (see literal meanings in the right-hand column). This is not unusual in the phenomenon of noun classification across languages; as Craig and others have observed, "the forms used as classifiers come from words used as names of concrete, discrete, moveable objects" (Craig 1986:6) or, as in the case of the Pohnpeian nime-, from verbs. The implications of this semantic relationship between classifier and classified in the cases of the honorific classifiers *sapwellime* and *tungoal* are a focus of this chapter.

The common (non–status-marked) possessive classifiers appear to fall into three main groups: (1) relatives or kin (e.g., maternal uncle or child of one's sister), (2) items for personal use, and (3) edibles and drinkables. The organization of these categories is of course culturally specific; for example, siblings, nieces, clan members, and maternal uncles could be subsumed under the class of relatives to Americans, but they are constituted as distinctive categories in the Pohnpeian world. Additional information is coded with the nouns in table 4.2 when they are expressed in "possessive" relationships. A person's catch of fish and her share at a feast are classified differently from other food. The sense relations common to many noun classifier systems (Lyons 1977:332) appear not to be salient here for encoding distinctions. Whereas the Pohnpeian *numeral* classifiers fit the paradigm of the most common principle of sortal classification—shape (Lyons 1977:464)—the possessive classifiers appear to express a different principle, one I believe is connected to rank, power transfer, or conduits of mana. For example, *maternal* relatives have specific classifiers (*ullap*, "maternal uncle" and *wahwah*, "man's sister's child"), but paternal rela-

TABLE 4.1 Common Speech Possessive Classifiers

Classifier (3rd pers. sg.)	Category	Example of 3rd Person + Noun	Translation
ah	general	ah pwoud	his/her spouse
nah	general, dominant	nah seri	her/his child
kene	edible things	kene uht	his/her banana
nime	drinkable things	nime uhpw	his/her drinking coconut
sapwe	land	sapwe deke	his/her island
imwe	buildings	imwe nahs	her/his feast house
were	vehicles	were sidohsa	her/his car
kie	sleeping pads	kie lohs	her/his mat
ipe	sleeping covers	ipe tehi	his/her sheet
ulunge	pillows	ulunge uluhl	her/his pillow
rie	siblings	rie serepein	her/his sister
kiseh	relatives	kiseh ohl	his/her male relative
ullepe	maternal uncles	ullepe ohl	her/his maternal uncle
wahwah	nieces, nephews	wahwah serepein	his/her niece
sawi	clan members	sawi pwutak	her/his boy clan member
pelie	peers, opponents	pelie ohl	his/her male peer
seike	catch	seike ah	his/her catch of mullet
pwekidah	share of feast food	pwekidah pwihk	her/his share of pig
mware	name, title, garland	mware mwaramwar	her/his garland
ede	names	ede aditik	his/her nickname
tie	earrings	tie kisin kohl	her/his earring
dewe	location	dewe sehr	his/her chair

Adapted from Rehg 1981.

tives do not. Rank is inherited matrilineally on Pohnpei; a man's rank traditionally passed to his sister's son; for example, in the case of the paramount chief his sister's son (not his own) is in line to become the next Nanmwarki. Matrilineal genealogy entitles an individual not only to rank but to lands. Traditionally, a title and the land it represented passed from ullap to wahwah. Maternal relatives, land, and titles all represent relationships to power and status. Edibles and drinkables are also related to rank, because on Pohnpei, food share is determined hierarchically according to rank, both within the family and at community events. One's catch, for example, should be shared hierarchically, the best presented to the chief and others of higher status. One's share at a feast is also linked to one's status. Personal items can also be conduits of power, especially those that spend a large amount of time close to the body, such as pillows, sheets, sleeping mats, and earrings (cf. J. Errington 1988: 164–5). It appears that the Pohnpeian classifiers organize linkages to rank and power in common speech genealogically through relatives, physically through contact with the body, and through food and drink.

TABLE 4.2 Possible Sources of Classifiers

Classifier	Translation	Possible Lexical Source (lit. = literally)
	Food/drink	
kene	food	possibly from causative prefix ke/ka + ne, "to be divided"
nime	drink	nim, lit. "drink"
seike	catch	sei, lit. "paddle"
pwekidah	share	pwekpwek, lit. "to formally distribute food at feast"
	People/relatives	
sawi	clan member	sawas, lit. "help"; sou, lit. "clan"
pelie	peers, opponents	pelie, lit. "member of a matched pair"
rie	siblings	rie, lit. "two"
kiseh	relative	kiseh, lit. "relative"
ullepe	maternal uncle	ullap, lit. "maternal uncle"
wahwah	niece, nephew	wahwah, lit. "man's sister's child"; wah, lit. "offspring"
	Items for personal use	
mware	title/garland	mwar, lit. "title"
ede	name	ahd, lit. "name"
tie	earrings	tie, lit. "to wear earrings"; ti, lit. "spirit"
imwe	buildings	ihmw, lit. "home, dwelling"
kie	sleeping pads	—
ipe	sleeping covers	ipir, lit. "to blow at, as the wind"
ullunge	pillows	ulung, lit. "to use a pillow"
sapwe	land	sahpw, lit. "land"
were	canoe/vehicles	wahr, lit. "canoe"
	Location/position	
dewe	location	dehu, lit. "rank, station, area or location"
	Honorific, humiliative	
tungoal	all possessions	lit. "food, eating"
	Honorific, exaltive	
sapwellime	general	sahpw, lit. "land" + lime, lit. "hand[EXAL]"
nillime	land	ni lit. "at," lime, lit. "hand[EXAL]"
tehnpese	dwellings	tehnpahs, lit. "empty nest"
tehnwere	vehicles	tehn, lit. "empty"; wahr, lit. "canoe"
moatoare	sleeping gear	lit. "mat, sleeping place[EXAL]"
koanoat	food, drink	lit. "food, eat[EXAL] for paramount chief"
pwenieu	food, drink	lit. "food, eat[EXAL] for paramount chieftess"
sahk	food, drink	lit. "food, eat[EXAL] for secondary chief"

These categories are transformed, however, in honorific register, and the organization of high-status possession is different from the organization of low-status possession. In the presence of the chiefs and chieftesses, different classifications of possessive relationships are constituted. Common power relations and relations between people and between people and things are reclassified, and a specific relation (in addition to status) is encoded (by the honorific classifiers) between the chief and the people, linking the chief to land and the people to food or the offspring of the land.

The contrast between relationships initiated with a possessor's control and without, as well as the notion of permanence and special distinctions for food/drink and certain kin, is important in the following discussion of Pohnpeian possessive classifiers and status marked possessive construction. The changes that occur in status-indexing speech in terms of the polarities of control versus noncontrol are significant, as these relationships are altered in a shift to honorific register.

Classifiers and meaning

The *ah* and *nah* classifiers (ah signifying general, nondominant possessive relationships; nah general, dominant possessive relationships) are the two most commonly used possessive classifiers in Pohnpeian common speech. In a survey across three taped events, ah classified possessives made up 58 percent of the total possessive marking, whereas nah was used 22 percent of the time. The remaining percentage (20 percent) consisted of other noun classifiers. The nah classifier (inflected or marked for person) is generally used with people or things over which the possessor has a *dominant* relationship, plus small items considered precious, for example, *nah pwutak* ("her boy"), *noumw dengki* ("your flashlight"), *nei pwihk* ("my pig"), *noumw masis* ("your matches"), *noumw sent* ("your money"). This classifier is not used in honorific possessive constructions, either humiliative or exaltive.

The ah classifier is a "general" one. Numerous classifier languages have such a general or residual category (cf. Craig 1986). Many of the nouns that take the ah classifier in common speech are imported terms, which perhaps supports the impression that it is a classifier for terms that do not fit other classification schemes. Examples are zorie (*sohrie* [Japanese]), *seht* (shirt [English]), *sehr* (chair [English]), and *sirangk* (cupboard [German *Schrank*]). However, the common terms for father, mother, and spouse are also included in this category. *Ah* also indexes relationships as temporary. The *ah* classifier is used in Pohnpeian humiliative constructions.

In common speech, the ah/nah (dominant/nondominant) contrast can be used to indicate different perspectives on the temporal relationship between the noun and the possessor. The classifier ah is used when the relationship between the possessor and the thing possessed is temporary, for example, when someone is pounding sakau using a particular sakau stone (locative). This is in contrast to nah, which signifies a relationship of permanence (i.e., ownership).

| ah moahl | his sakau pounding stone that he is working with (temporary, nondominant) |
| nah moahl | his sakau pounding stone that he owns (permanent, dominant) |

The ah/nah contrast can also differentiate between edible, unharvested, and just harvested food:

nah kehp	her yam, unharvested
ah kehp	her yam, harvested
kene kehp	her yam, to eat

(from Rehg 1981)

A connection between ah and temporary states links the organization of humiliative possession (which uses only the ah classifier plus the humiliative classifier) to both temporary and nondominant states. Possessive classifiers index *specific* categorizations within the domain of possessive relationships, including dominance, permanence, control, and rights to consumption.

Though humiliative speech is restricted to a single possessive construction (*ah tungoal*), exaltive speech in contrast evidences a wider range of semantic choices because of a larger set of possessive classifiers (eight). Table 4.2 lists the eight exaltive classifiers.

Differences between common and status-marked possession

The following examples introduce the specifics of differences in Pohnpeian possessive construction between **common** (un-status-marked) speech and the status-marked **humiliative** honorific and **exaltive** honorific speech. All three examples from interactional data show the relationship of a person to his or her son. Excerpt 1 shows the exaltive form of this relationship (the possessor is a very high status man). Excerpt 2 shows the humiliative form of possession (the possessor is of lesser rank than another person present, in this case the paramount chief). Excerpt 3 is from a common speech discussion between several women in which no honorifics are used (boldface indicates possessive).[2]

(1) Exaltive honorific speech

01→ *dene   L ((name)) oh **sapwellimen**   N ((title)) pwutak*
     it is said L ((name))   and Ps.Cl.[EXAL].of N ((title))   boy
     they say that L and N's boy are

02   *kin   patpato   rehra ((re ira))*
     habitually LocVerb[HUM].there location.of.them(D)
     always staying with the two of them

(2) Humiliative honorific speech

01→ *en S ((title)) **ah**   **tungoal**   pwutako*
     of S ((title)) Ps.Cl.3S Ps.Cl.[HUM] boy.there
     S's boy is

02   *me   ale ira*
     the one take them(D)
     the one who took the two of them

(3) Common speech

01   *liho   pahn kin   kadarado*
     woman.there will   habitually send.here
     that woman always sends

02→ **nah**   *kisin pwutako en kohdo en peki*
     Ps.Cl.3S small boy.there to come to ask
     her small boy over here to come and ask

Following is a summary of these differences:

1. **sapwellimen** N pwutak   (exaltive, high status)   N's boy
2. **ah tungoal** pwutak   (humiliative, low status)   his/her boy
3. **nah** pwutak   (common speech,   her/his boy
    unmarked for status)

There are significant differences between humiliative (low status) and exaltive (high status) possessive constructions. These two status domains are constituted as not only asymmetrical but with different properties of control and temporality, and they are linked to different experiential domains. These differences are discussed in more detail next.

Humiliative possessive construction (*a-/e- tungoal*)

Humiliative possessive construction (i.e., references to the possessions of low-status persons) is different from both common speech and exaltive honorific possessive constructions: Only one classification of possession is observed and two classifiers are used simultaneously. The correct person form of the general classifier ah- (or its phonological variant *e-*) is followed by the humiliative classifier tungoal. Those nouns that usually take a specific classifier, such as a food classifier, are reclassified (e.g., *kene mwahng*, "her taro," becomes *ah tungoal mwahng*) (see following table):

Common Speech	Humiliative Speech	
kene mwahng	ah tungoal mwahng	her taro
nah pwihk	ah tungoal pwihk	her pig
were sidohsa	ah tungoal sidohsa	her car

You can see by the previous examples that the categorizations observed in common speech between a vehicle and food are not observed in humiliative honorific speech (they **are** observed in exaltive honorific speech, as I discuss in more detail shortly). *Common* classifiers distinguish between food that is about to be eaten and food that is in the tree, whereas the humiliative classifier does not, as shown next.

Common Speech			Humiliative Speech
nah kehp	her yam, unharvested	)	
		>	ah tungoal kehp
kene kehp	her yam, to eat	)	

Even nouns that would normally not take a possessive classifier (i.e., body parts; usually possessive morphemes are directly suffixed to body parts) are reclassified in humiliative, low-status constructions as nondominant, general (not fitting any category), and temporary. They are expressed in humiliative speech with the general classifier *a-* (or its phonological variant *e-*) inflected for person, plus tungoal.

Common Speech	Humiliative Speech	
moahngei[3]	ei tungoal moahng	my head
ngihlei	ei tungoal ngihl	my voice

(4) Body part expressed as humiliative

01 Woman: *ma i patohwante   i pahn wiada*
                if   I   TranVerb[HUM].only I will   do.up
                if I had only known I would have done up

02→   ***ei   tungoal***   *moange*
                Ps.Cl.1S Ps.Cl.[HUM] hair
                my hair

In humiliative talk, therefore, part–whole classifications (possessive suffixed to noun) are reconfigured. However, in exaltive speech part–whole constructions are retained. Exaltive nouns such as for chiefs' and chieftesses' body parts can index status (there are only two humiliative nouns and none for body parts).

One of the consequences of the differences between humiliative and exaltive possessive classifiers is that humiliative classifiers for low-status possession are less semantically rich than classifiers used in common speech and exaltive speech (for high-status possession). In humiliative speech, speakers lose the potential for expressing gradations of meaning. Humiliative speech is restricted to a single possessive construction, ah tungoal, the general classifier inflected for person and the humiliative classifier. Exaltive speech in contrast evidences a wider range of semantic choices because of a larger set of possessive classifiers than humiliative speech (i.e., eight, but smaller than the range of common speech classifiers, twenty-two). As demonstrated shortly, the use of the classifier tungoal links all low-status possessions semantically with food and eating.

Although the humiliative construction is impoverished in terms of categories it can delineate (such as a difference between control and noncontrol), it is enriched in its status-indexing potential: It can index more than one level of status in the same construction because of the a- tungoal formation. Two words are used in series; it is therefore possible with this double, concurrent classifier construction to express two different levels of status simultaneously, targeting two interactional participants (this is possible in the second person singular only, however). For example, an addressee and a bystander can be indexed as having two different statuses, as can a referent and an addressee. One status level can be expressed with the first classifier and another with the second classifier. In example (a), the suffix of the general classifier (*owmw/ahmw*, "your [s.]") contains an honorific form, the suffix *-i*. This pronoun signifies exaltive status, whereas the humiliative classifier tungoal signals low status.

(a) omw**i**   tungoal   moahng   your (s.) head
      high[EXAL] *low*[HUM]
(b) ahmw   tungoal   moahng   your (s.) head
      common low [HUM]

Thus the addressee in example (a) is simultaneously exalted (omwi) and humbled (tungoal) in the phrase *omwi tungoal moahng* "your ^{exalted} _{humbled} head." In example (b), the first classifier is in common form (unmarked for status) and the second in humiliative form. Excerpt 5 shows an example of this phenomenon from interactional data. One low-status man (S) is addressing another (N) in the presence of the chief. The speaker (S) is of lower status than the man to whom he is offering a cigarette. But the man to whom he is offering a cigarette (N) is also of lower status than the chief, who is present.

(5) High + low status in the same construction

```
01  S:  N ((title)). omwi         tungoal     sikah
        N ((title))   your(S)[EXAL] Ps.Cl.[HUM] cigarette
        N your cigarette ((offering him a cigarette))
```

High status is being constructed for the addressee (N), yet another higher-status person's presence (the chief's) is acknowledged by the added use of tungoal (low status) for the addressee. The status of the person is separated from the status of his/her possession/body part in example (a), and from his cigarette in excerpt 5. Thus two noun classifiers can place nouns into two additional (and contrasting) informational classes. In the case of excerpt 5, two classifiers simultaneously communicate relative rank between speaker and addressee, as well as between addressee and bystander and between speaker and bystander.

In the same interaction with the highest chief (see excerpt 6) the classifier tungoal is used for a low-status speaker's house in the first excerpt and for a referent's in-law (*mwah*, "opposite sex sibling of one's spouse" or "the spouse of one's opposite sex sibling") in the second.

(6) Conversation during sakau

```
01  Chief:  ia      N ((title)) eh?
            where N ((title))   eh?
            where's N eh?

02  L:      i sohte i sohte patohwan        mwein e
            I don't I don't TranVerb[HUM] maybe  she
            I don't, I don't know maybe she

03  →       patopato          ni  aht              tungoal
            LocVerb[HUM] there at  Ps.Cl.1P(EXCL) Ps.Cl.[HUM]
            is at our

04          ihmwo
            house there
            house

(. . .)

05  Chief:  P ((name)) ia?
            P ((name))   where?
            P from where?
```

06 L: →   *en S ((title)) **ah**   **tungoal**   mwah*
           of S ((title)) Ps.Cl.3S Ps.Cl.[HUM] in-law
           S's in-law

07 M: *P ((name)) e kohsang   Uhke*
           P ((name))   he comes.from Uhke
           P, the one who comes from Uhke

08 Chief: *oh! P ((name)).*
           oh! P ((name)).

In the previous example, both location ("at our house") and kin relationships ("his in-law") are in humiliative possessive construction. The speaker, L, refers to his own house and to another man's relative. Both these relationships are classified as general, nondominant, temporary, and low status. Use of an exclusive pronoun form (*aht*) in the first instance (line 03) excludes the chief from the low-status marking of "our."

Exaltive possessive construction

When speaking of something the chief or another high status individual owns, a special set of classifiers is used. Table 4.3 shows the *exaltive* classifiers I have noted in interactional data (plus one on Rehg's [1981] list, *moatoare*), along with the common language classifiers to which they correspond.

Note that *sapwellime* is used in place of both general and dominant classifiers ah and nah. Thus in exaltive speech, referring to possessions of the highest-status people, no distinction is made between items they are dominant over and those they are not, or temporary versus permanent states of possession. Sapwellime is the most frequently used exaltive classifier.

As mentioned by Rehg (1981), an exaltive possessive construction without classifiers can be formed by suffixing the possessive pronouns -*mwi* ("your") or -*ihr* ("your/his/their"[4]) to the noun representing the thing possessed, for example, *kahlapemwi*, "your body[EXAL]" and *sihlengihr*, "their (your) face[EXAL]." This

TABLE 4.3 Exaltive Possessive Classifiers

Exaltive Classifier	Common Classifier	Classifier Type
sapwellime	ah and nah	general, dominant
nillime	sapwe	land
tehnpese	ihmwe	dwellings
tehnwere	were	vehicles
moatoare	kie	things to sleep on
koanoat	kene, nime	food/drink
pwenieu	kene, nime	food/drink
sahk	kene, nime	food/drink

is similar to the common speech part–whole construction. Some of Rehg's consultants reported that nouns referring to the chiefs do not normally take possessive suffixes at all because the honorific noun itself would make clear who the possessor is. Thus the terms *kahlap* (body [EXAL]) and *sihleng* (face [EXAL]) would theoretically occur without possessive marking because these nouns are honorifically marked already (common terms being *paliwar* and *mese*, respectively). However, interactional data show that the body of the chief and other high-status participants is often expressed with both the classifier and the honorific noun.

(7) A man begins a public prayer at a feast

```
01    maing      samaht        Koht      (. . . .)
      honored one father.our(EXCL) God
      our honored father God
```

```
02→  iangaki sapwellimomwi kahlap      Isipahu,
      join.with Ps.Cl.2S[EXAL]    body[EXAL] paramount.chief
      join with your body the paramount chief
```

```
03    IsoNahnken,   Likend
      secondary.chief, paramount.chieftess
      the secondary chief, the paramount chieftess
```

In excerpt 7, instead of the predicted *kahlapihr* or kahlap, a speaker used *sapwellimomwi kahlap*. This actual speech example also suggests that more than just literal possession is being communicated. Choice may be related to issues of agency, because in suffix-possessed nouns the possessor is typically the patient or theme (see Harrison 1988), whereas agents or controllers are usually marked by the possessive article. By using the classifier *sapwellimomwi* with *kahlap*, a higher degree of agency is indicated for the possessor, in this instance God. In addition, the double honorific denotation increases the marking of the utterance as status raising of the possessor. Use of the possessive classifier, by its very redundancy, emphasizes the high status of the possessor. Note also the construction *maing samaht Koht* in line 01. The congregation's possession of God is unmarked for status; it is a common speech part–whole construction, where the possessive morpheme *-aht* ("our," exclusive) is suffixed to the noun *sahm* (father, or classificatory father). This is a highly conventionalized usage in prayer openings.

Redundant exaltive marking, as in line 02, can also be seen in a speech in excerpt 8, which a medium-ranking woman refers to two different statuses of spouses, by choice of exaltive versus humiliative classifier and by choice of exaltive versus common noun, among those in attendance at a *kamadipw en kousapw*, or a celebratory feast for a small community in November 1992:

(8) Speech by a medium-ranking woman at a feast

```
01    patpato               tikitikieng ohng eh
      LocVerb[HUM].there small.to    for   uh
      talking a little bit ((i.e., nicely)) to uh
```

02→ *sapwellimatail   werek   kan de*
      Ps.Cl.2P(INCL)[EXAL] spouse[EXAL] those or
      our high-status spouses or

03→ *atail   tungoal   pwoud kan*
      Ps.Cl.2P(INCL) Ps.Cl.[HUM] spouse those.by.you
      our low-status spouses

In line 02, the speaker uses an exaltive construction and in line 03 a humiliative one. In the exaltive, both noun and classifier are indexed for status, in the humiliative, only the classifier is indexed for status.

The exaltive nouns *tehnpas* ("dwelling," exaltive) and *tehnwahr* ("vehicle," exaltive) do appear to operate as Rehg's consultants predicted, that is, without possessive marking, because they specifically indicate the chief's possessions already. The exaltive possessive classifiers with which they could occur would be *tehnpese* (dwelling classifier) and *tehnwere* (vehicle classifier).

(9)

01 Chieftess: *ien   sidohsa,*
               there.by.you car
               there's a car,

02   *ien   tehnwaro*
               there by you vehicle[EXAL] there
               there's the chief's car

03 N: *oh   NK ((title))*
               Interj. NK ((title))
               oh, it's NK

In summary, exaltive classifiers offer more choices for categorization than humiliative classifiers, although the general classifier sapwellime is the one used most frequently. However, humiliative classifier construction can differentiate two statuses within the noun phrase. The exaltive general possessive classifier makes no distinction between control and noncontrol, whereas the humiliative classifier constitutes all relationships as temporary and noncontrolled.

Boundaries of power

A recurrent phenomenon in videorecorded interactions of oratory is the use of high-status possessive constructions for high- and low-status people together, as a collective. The following excerpt from a speech during a *kamadipw en wahu* (celebratory feast of honor) shows that in interaction, the exaltive classifier sapwellime can be used not only to refer to chiefs but surprisingly to refer to all participants present, high *and* low. For example, in line 01 (in excerpt 10), the speechmaker uses the exaltive, plural, inclusive possessive form of "our" (*sapwellimatail*), thereby including all the participants meeting together and raising the status of all. A meeting is a jointly achieved event, and this joint achievement is perhaps recognized in this use of exaltive classifier. Joining together as one they literally achieve a closeness potentially resulting in transference of power from the chief. In former times, the highest chief was kept apart from the people for this very reason; it was felt that harm could come to those who came too close (see chapter 1, in this volume), because of the potential for this transfer of power (which could maim or kill low-status persons).

(10) Speech by a high-ranking man at a feast

01→ *kumwail meleilei **sapwellimatail** tupenehn*
       you(pl)   peace   Ps.Cl.our[EXAL] meet.together.of
       you all be peaceful/be quiet so that our meeting

02 *rahnet pahn tepdahr   i pahn peki rehn*   (?)
       today will begin.already I will ask location.of (?)
       today can begin. I will ask (?)

03 *komwi   sakarada*
       you(S)[EXAL] beg.of.a.chief
       you make a speech

However, as the speech continues, notice that rather than sapwellimatail, a pronoun which raises the status of all, the pronoun *sapwellimomwi* is used (the singular second person possessive classifier), which limits the status and power through possession to God alone.

04 *keipweni[5] pahn wasa ileilei Koht, Isipahu,*
       lower myself under place elevated God,   paramount.chief
       I lower myself in the presence of high-status people under the elevated place of God, the paramount chief,

05 *Iso Nahnken, Likend   oh i pahn patohwen*
       secondary.chief, highest.chieftess and I will   [HUM]
       the secondary chief, the highest chieftess and I will

06 *kapakap maing   samaht   Koht kalahngan*
       pray   honored.one father.our(EXCL) God   merciful/thanks
       pray our honored father God merciful/thanks

07→ *iet **sapwellimomwi**   kalahngan me sansal rahnwet*
       here Ps.Cl.your(S)[EXAL] generosity   that clear   today
       here your mercy/generosity is clear today

08→ *iangaki **sapwellimomwi**   **kahlap**   Isipahu,*
       join.with Ps.Cl.your(S)[EXAL] body[EXAL] paramount.chief
       join with your body the paramount chief,

09 *Iso Nahnken, Likend   en rahnwet.*
       secondary.chief, highest.chieftess of today
       the secondary chief, the present-day chieftess

In lines 07 and 08, singular exaltive possessive pronouns are used. The possessor is the Christian God (Koht). His generosity is referenced, as well as his body. As noted earlier, ordinary part–whole relationships can be altered in honorific possession, as well as polarities of control. The speechmaker joins God's body with the bodies of the chiefs and chieftess (line 08). This literal joining across usually impermeable boundaries (bodies) is thus first achieved by constituting the different reality of honorific speech, where ordinary part–whole relationships and relationships of control are reorganized. Relations of power are indexed which alter the ordinary meaning of possession. God is asked to join his powerful, exaltive body with that of the two chiefs and paramount chieftess who are present, a joining which, according to local beliefs, would result in their sharing God's personal power, which resides in his body. Sharing in God's power is not constituted as available to all present in contrast with the earlier use of an inclusive possessive pronoun. In the first example, "meeting" together with high-status people was constituted as status raising for lower-status members. But by not including the audience in the second and third constitutions of exaltive possession (singular forms are used rather than plural), the transmission of the power of God is restricted to the two high chiefs and the paramount chieftess. Thus honorific possession can semantically and pragmatically not only constitute power relations but constitute limits on *sharability of power* across individuals as well as groups.

Productive use of classifiers: the verb "have"

Both the humiliative classifier *tungoal* and the exaltive classifier *sapwellime* can be used with an instrumental suffix to form a verb to signify possession (i.e., *tungoaleniki*, "to have[HUM]," and *sapwellimaniki*, "to have[EXAL]").

(11) From a speech

01 M: *me sansal me pein ihr **sapwellimaniki***
        that clear   that self   they have[EXAL]
        it is clear that by themselves they have

In excerpt 11, ihr (the third person form) is used as an honorific form of second person.

(12) A conversation during sakau

01 W: *pwe   lihoko   sohte kin   iang **tungoaleniki***
        because woman.those not   habitually join have[HUM]
        because those women don't usually get

02   *sent   sang hotel riau*
        money from hotel two
        money from two hotels

In the following section I show how looking closely at honorific possessive constructions can illuminate local concepts of power relations in Pohnpei. Metaphorical connections between honorific possessive classifiers and the experiential base of the human environment, particularly regarding the harvesting of food from the land, provide further insights into Pohnpeian ideologies about low status and high status.

Metaphorical connections and cognitive tracks

Work by semanticists (Bolinger 1965; G. Lakoff 1973) investigating cognitive organizational patterns shows that metaphorical extensions are significant processes at work in language (Givon 1986). Scholars in linguistics, anthropology, and psychology (e.g., Berlin and Kay 1969; G. Lakoff 1973; Rosch 1975; M. Johnson 1987) have convincingly argued that human conceptual systems grow at least partly out of bodily experience. This process involves polysemy, metaphor, and metonymy (G. Lakoff 1987), and as Quinn (1987) has demonstrated, is constituted in culturally specific ways. I am concerned in the following discussion with metaphoric and metonymic relations which are constituted in Pohnpeian honorific speech through the possessive classifiers. I look at how high and low status are constituted, not as polarities, and not necessarily as asymmetrical, but as different and yet dependent meaningful fields of relations. I argue that some of the properties of food are associated with low status whereas properties of land and distribution are associated with high status. I investigate these relationships by analyzing the semantic relationship between classifier and classified in the cases of sapwellime (the general exaltive possessive classifier) and tungoal (the humiliative possessive classifier).

I look at what I take to be significant metaphorical connections between domains as well as relevant semantic contrasts to try to understand what is a likely relationship between the domains of food and low status on the one hand and land and high status on the other. I am drawing on work in grammaticalization processes, which has shown that metaphorical associations between semantic fields is a key aspect of the development of language. Heine (1986) observes, for example, that metaphorical connections may have implications for the evolution of grammatical categories, such as turning nouns into prepositions or adverbs, for example, based on connections between "things" such as body parts, and "abstract" concepts such as relative locations in space. According to Heine, abstract phenomena are conceptualized in terms of concrete, perceptual–motor experiences: "The noun 'hand' has become a marker of *possession* in a number of African languages in accordance with the metaphorical equation 'what is in my hand belongs to me'" (Heine 1986:5).

In Pohnpeian, the honorific noun for hand/arm is *lime*, and a similar analogy is made in the case of the exaltive possessive classifier for possession of land, *nillime*, literally "at his/her hand" (ni, at; lime, hand). The general, most frequently used exaltive possessive *(sapwellime)* is a combination of "land" *(sahpw)* and "hand" *(lime)*. In contrast, the low-status possessive classifier, tungoal, is polysemous with the term for eating and food. It is this relationship between low status and food that I discuss first. I demonstrate the polysemous nature of tungoal and then discuss the semantics of the high-status classifier, sapwellime.

Tungoal and *sapwellime*

The noun for low-status food is tungoal, the verb for low-status eating is tungoal (intransitive form tungoale), and the classifier used to mark possessions of low status is tungoal. Excerpt 13 shows an example of tungoal used as a classifier and as a verb in the same speaker's utterance:

(13) Conversation during sakau

01 N: *ngehi patohwandi*   ***ei***   ***tungoal***
      I   TranVerb[HUM].downward Ps.Cl.1S Ps.Cl.[HUM]
      I take it down in my

02   *peh powe duwe me. iapw i sohte kak*
      hand above like   this. but   I not   can
      hand, above like this. but I can't

03   ***tungoale*** *mwahl i sohte kak patohwansang*
      eat[HUM]   common I not   can   TranVerb[HUM].from
      just drink[6] it any old way I can't

04   ***ei***   ***tungoal***   *pehkan   powe*
      Ps.Cl.1S Ps.Cl.[HUM] hand.those above
      take it with my hands above it

Here tungoal is used as a possessive classifier for hand and hands (lines 01 and 04), and as the verb "to eat" (line 03; "eating" is always used with sakau, which Americans classify as a drink). The polysemous tungoal thus ranges between grammatical categories within honorific contexts, often in the same speaker's utterance, creating a relation of similarity between these domains. The connection between food/eating and low-status possession suggests that the activity (eating), the entity (food), and the state (low status, possession) all described by this polysemous term share aspects in common in the Pohnpeian cognitive organizational scheme, that is, that low status possession is in some way analogous to food or eating.

Food is an important index of status on Pohnpei, as noted earlier (see also chapter 7, in this volume). Food is shared out according to rank in all eating contexts. However, in possessive constructions food is not linked to high-status possession *in general* in the same way it is linked to low-status possession in general. Although tungoal (i.e., food/eating) is used for all classes of possessives in low status, the most general and widely used classifier for high status is not semantically connected to food but entails the concepts of "land" and "hand." There is a separate possessive classifier for the food of high-status persons; it is the same term as the verb for high-status eating and the high-status noun for food. Thus, noun, verb, and classifier for food are polysemous in exaltive construction as in humiliative, but the food classifier is restricted to the domain of food and drink in the exaltive and is not extended to exaltive possession in general. The terms *koanoat*, *pwenieu*, and *sak* distinguish food, eating, and possession of food by the paramount chief, the paramount chieftess, and the secondary chief, respectively.

In suggesting that people of low status are being constructed as analogous to low-status food (through tungoal), let me offer the following evidence of the way those closest to the chief in rank are literally called high-status food. The explicit connection of persons with both food and rank can be seen with the term *koanoat*, which not only refers to the chief's food but can also be used to refer to the food of what are called koanoat titleholders (those who hold a title in line to be paramount chief). Koanoat is thus used to describe rank as well as high-status food or eating. It differentiates rank between those titleholders in the paramount chief's line and others. Such a person is often referred to as *food itself* (i.e., "koanoat," lit. high-status food) when what is meant is *koanoat titleholder* (entitled to koanoat food through rank). Excerpt 14 provides an example of the use of koanoat (the verb, noun, and classifier for high-status eating/food) to denote rank.

(14) Koanoat and rank

01 N: *mware Lepen Medewen Seu Nahleng*
     title.3S Lepen Medewen Seu Nahleng
     his title is Lepen Medewen Seu Nahleng

02   **koanoat**   *(1.5) eh title*
     food.for.paramount.chief[EXAL] (1.5) his title
     it's koanoat (1.5) his title ((in line to be chief))

Food constructs rank also through the order of serving food or sakau (considered food) and the quality and quantity of food one receives. Food belonging to the chief or chieftess is identified with the power of their office and is highly prized. If one is invited to share this food, one's portion is referred to with the term *kepin: kepin koanoat* (paramount chief's food), *kepin pwenieu* (paramount chieftess's food), and *kepin sak* (secondary chief and chieftess's food). For example, a plate of food sent to me by the paramount chieftess as I stood by the video camera filming a feast was announced to the gathering as "*Elizabet, kepin pwenieu!*" These leftovers can be thought of as shares of sacred food or sacred power and constitute rank. The term *kepin* is from *kapi* ("bottom, the lowest part of yam or taro") and the suffix meaning "of" (*-en*), so that kepin koanoat is literally the lowest part of the chief's food.

The highest-ranking person present eats first, even in casual family settings, followed in order by lower-status persons. The highest family member is served all the food, then in turn other members of the family eat what is conceptualized as the weaker part, or leftovers. At community events those with the highest rank receive the choicest and largest shares. A sense of "whole" versus "part" underlies this practice, as the chiefs must always be served, for example, an unopened box of crackers, an unopened drink, and so forth, whereas everyone else typically shares from the same plate or container. Leftovers are called *luwen*, from the adjective "weak" (*luwet*), showing the relationship of food to strength and power. In excerpt 15, speaker NE is offered some leftovers to take home, but she indicates that these high-status remains (of the chieftess) are more rightfully someone else's.

(15) Conversation at a feast

01 NK: *NE ((name)) ien   nekidala*
　　　 NE ((name)) there.by.you save.it.up
　　　 NE save the food there ((take it home))

02 NE: *ah soh komwi   men.*
　　　 but no   you(S)[EXAL] that.one.by.you.
　　　 but no that is yours.

03　　 **luwen   pwenieu   kan**
　　　 remains.of chieftess.food[EXAL] those.by.you
　　　 that is remains of the chieftess's food

Status is relevant in all eating contexts,[7] and status and food are always linked.

However, the exaltive expressions for eating and food—koanoat, pwenieu, and sak—are not used as *general* classifiers (in contrast to the humiliative term for food) but only as *specific* food classifiers or pertaining to high-status food and drink or high-status acts of eating and drinking.

(16) Pwenieu food and drink

01 NE: *Likend mwein pahn ketla   rapaki*
　　　 chieftess maybe will   LocVerb[EXAL].there find
　　　 maybe the chieftess is going to find

02　　 **pwenieu   pihl**
　　　 Ps.Cl.[EXAL].food.for.chieftess water
　　　 some water

03 M: *ser*
　　　 hey

04 NE: *ketla   ketki   **pwenieu** pihl*
　　　 LocVerb[EXAL].there take[EXAL] Ps.Cl.[EXAL] water
　　　 she went to get water

05 W: *sohte **pwenieu**   saida?*
　　　 no   Ps.Cl.[EXAL].food.for.chieftess soda?
　　　 there is no soda for the chieftess?

Pwenieu is used as a possessive classifier specifically for food and drink in excerpt 16.

Rather than relating to food, the exaltive general classifier sapwellime is semantically composed of the morphemes "land" (*sahpw*) and the exaltive form of "hand/arm" (lime). Thus most possessions of chiefs or chieftesses are categorized through this classifier as having some of the same attributes as land and hand, as well, I believe, as what is constituted by the two notions in a compound relationship (i.e., a relation of land and distribution). Though there are other specific exaltive classifiers (for vehicles, dwellings, food, land, sleeping gear, see table 4.2), by far the most frequently used classifier is sapwellime in transcripts of interactions. For example, in the transcript of a feast, sapwellime is used in over 95 percent of the cases of exaltive possession. Because this is the general classifier used most frequently for such possessives as body parts, emotions, and children, as well as small items, the link between the chief/chieftess and the land is made in almost every possessive utterance. Also, just as tungoal is used with the derivational suffix (*-niki*), which indicates to own or to have, to express low-status "having" (tungoaleniki), sapwellime is used with *-niki* to construct the high-status verb "have" (sapwellimaniki), again showing the close relation between these two terms. The link between the chief and the land is also made by members of Pohnpeian society, who attest to the chief's ownership of the entire island (at least in former times). Traditionally, the bestowing of a title carried with it rights to use a certain piece of land, thus also linking land with high rank.

Many imported items and concepts are used with sapwellime as excerpt 17 shows for the chieftess's bank book:

(17) Conversation during sakau at the chief's home

M: *nan **sapwellime**   pwuhko nan bank*
   in   Ps.Cl.3S[EXAL] book.that in   bank
   in her book in the bank ((bank book))

Thus we can look now at some of the implications of the relationships constituted through polysemy and shared semantic domains: high status is linked with the land (the source of nourishment), whereas low status is linked with food (nourishment itself), the offspring of the land. High status I believe is linked with generativity and low status with consumption. When in honorific speech different categories of the world are created from those in common speech, the status-relevant categories extend some of the properties of land analogically to the chief and some of the properties of food to the people. Properties of land on Pohnpei include sacredness, bountifulness, permanence, and a link with the spiritual world and the world of the ancestors. Some of the properties of food include perishability, sustenance, rank indexing, and obligatory networks, as well as pleasure. The humiliative expression tungoal and the exaltive expression sapwellime can also be seen in a metonymic relation—a link in terms of a relationship between land and food. Food is the offspring of land ("fruit" or agricultural produce is *wahn sahpw* in Pohnpeian, lit. the "offspring" [*wah*] "of" [*-n*] "the land" [sahpw]), and is as part to whole, where land (the chief) is whole and genitor (recall that the chief is always served an unopened box, whereas others receive parts).

The two constructed domains of low- and high-status possession, sapwellime and tungoal, can also be seen in terms of a distribution versus consumption model, with the chief as the archetypical agent (or energy source, i.e., land) and the lower-status people as the archetypical patient (consuming or receiving energy). Support for this model is provided by the morphology of the honorific verbs. Those referring to the chief and chieftesses' actions begin with the same morpheme used for the causative prefix ke- (or ka-) (e.g., ketdo, the exaltive verb for motion toward the speaker, such as come, and ketki, the exaltive verb for such transitive actions as give). Conversely, verbs for low-status peoples' same activities begin with *pa-* (e.g., patohdo for low status for movement toward the speaker, such as come, and patohwan for low-status transitive actions such as give). Low-status verbs have been linked by Fischer to *pe-* a passivizing morpheme. Fischer (1969:420) observed a relationship between exaltive verb forms with the *ket-* stem and causatives (the *ka-* prefix) as well as between humiliative verb forms with the *pato-* stem and what he calls a pseudo-passive (the *pe-* prefix) in Pohnpeian (see chapter 3 this volume).

The chief as the active energy source and the people as the passive energy goal is a formulation I believe can be useful heuristically in trying to understand the dynamics of Pohnpeian honorific speech and status relations and the place of the terms *tungoal* and *sapwellime* in constituting a universe of hierarchical relations. All possessions of low-status people which are, metaphorically, like food, depend on and flow from the original source of energy, the land (i.e., the chief). Food is ephemeral, whereas land is eternal. A relation of both nurturance and dependence is created.

This relation is further supported through practice, specifically feasting, where the connection between land and rank is developed and materialized and unified with the connection between food and rank. During feasting (which takes place at least on a weekly basis), harvested goods are brought and given to the chief, who accepts them and redistributes them (as his own) according to rank. Just-harvested food and other contributions are amassed and pooled under the authority of the chief, who symbolically and literally redistributes them to the people who consume them (see chapter 7, in this volume, for a discussion of feasting practices).

The dominance of the chief's possessions is continually construed in semantic relationships expressed by the possessive classifiers, where low-status ownership is categorized as a relationship of noncontrol and and nonpermanence (through the general, nondominant, low-status possessive classifier ah, which appears in a series with tungoal), and through feasting practices where the chief accepts as his all the fruits of the land and then redistributes them according to rank. The models provided in honorific speech create figurative relationships linking the shared experience of harvesting fruit from the land, and subsequently relinquishing control of it, with consumption and nourishment. Speakers through honorific speech generalize and humble commoners' ownership (through the use of a general classifier and a humiliative one) and contrastively particularize and elevate the chief's (through more classifiers, through the incorporation of dominant and nondominant possession in one classifier, and through the use of exaltive classifiers). Honorific language can be seen as a language of allocation through possessive constructions that classify the world in specific ways. The people are classified as consumers both symbolically in the redistribution by the chief of all the goods at feasts and by their own and others' use of the humiliative classifier tungoal, whereby they are linked to food (i.e., what is distributed and consumed). They are constituted as low-status, nondominant, and temporary (perishable).

Summary

Possession can express multiple relationships in Pohnpeian, including dominance or nondominance (degrees of control), temporal relationships, locative associations, and status as well as ownership. In status-marked speech these relationships are recategorized, as well as the usual part–whole relationships for body parts. Pohnpeian possessive classifiers not only constitute categories of rank and power relations, delimiting types, but through honorific speech dynamically reorganize or reclassify these categories.

The structure of the humiliative possessive classifier permits the placement of nouns into two contrasting informational classes about status. Rank between speaker and addressee, as well as between addressee and bystander, can be simultaneously communicated. In interaction, boundaries of power and control can be created through choices made to use inclusive or exclusive possessive pronouns; thus honorific possession can constitute not only power relations but also limits on sharability of power across individuals as well as groups.

Finally, metaphorical connections between honorific possessive classifiers and the experiential base of the human environment, particularly regarding the harvesting of food from the land, provide insights into Pohnpeian ideologies about low status and high status.

Analyzing which relationships are mapped analogically from the human experiential base to possessive indicators of status reveals how microinteractions that index status are linked to larger cultural ideologies about power and the relationships of chiefs to the people. High and low status are constituted not as polarities, and not necessarily as asymmetrical, but as different and yet dependent meaningful fields of relations.

Notes

1. See Rehg (1981) for a more detailed discussion of Pohnpeian possessive marking.
2. The basic possessive markings for person are as follows:

Singular	1st	-i	my
	2nd	-mw	your
	3rd	-0	his, her, its
Dual/plural	1st excl.	-t	ours (excl. you)
Dual	1st incl.	-ta	ours (incl. you)
	2nd	-mwa	your, two
	3rd	-ra	their, two
Plural	1st incl.	-tail	our, pl
	2nd	-mwail	your, pl
	3rd	-rail	their, pl

3. The form *ei* is a phonological variant of *ai*, the first person singular of the general classifier *ah*.

4. In Pohnpeian honorific speech, as is common in other honorific registers cross-culturally, third person plural is sometimes used to indicate the singular person of the chief (see chapter 2, in this volume).

5. *Keipweni* literally means to lower one's body in the presence of a ghost or the humans serving as intermediaries between the people and the spirits (Mauricio 1993:147).

6. The verb "eat" is used with sakau; however, in English I have translated it as "drink."

7. It is not only Pohnpeians who link concepts of status and food. A correspondence between status and food is noted in India by Brown and Levinson (1978:45), where social inequality is marked by differences in the use of familiar pronouns and in exchanges of cooked food.

Chapter 5

Women's Power Etiquette

Relationships between Gender and Honorifics

In examining the order of a social world that constructs itself hierarchically, it is important to investigate how gender participates with other symbolic systems to constitute and sustain power inequities between the sexes and between classes and individuals. Language practices create concepts of similarity as well as difference, dichotomy, and hierarchy; the relationship between these processes and their relationship to dominance are important in examining gender. Understanding the role of gender in hierarchies and in honorific speech is more than understanding some domain conceptualized as "women's activities." Women are participants in the dominant structures of meaning and practice and play an important role in the renegotiation and re-creation of that structure (cf. Moore 1986) through language practices.

It has been claimed that the secondary status of women in society "is one of the true universals, a pan-cultural fact," although the actual treatment of women and their relative power may vary enormously (Ortner 1974:67). Although this subordinate characterization seems to reflect women's experience in many societies, at the same time the judgment of who is dominant is often a factor of observing "public" roles, regardless of the fact that the very organization of social life into domestic and public spheres often represents only a male perspective. In many societies, the power of what Westerners recognize as legitimized authority may not be great (Philips 1987), for example, when sacred chiefs depend on mediators and when nearly all inhabitants claim relation to the founding ancestor/deity.

The dominant, often male point of view in the past has frequently been generalized for the whole society. As Tsing and Yanagisako (1983) point out, "politics should be seen as a system of power relationships and value hierarchies, which necessarily

includes both women and men. When male activities, groups, and ties are studied
. . . it must be recognized that these are gender-marked phenomena and do not constitute the 'human' social universe" (512). However, if women are represented as
subordinate while simultaneously maintaining considerable economic and political
power, "this is a feature of social life which requires explanation" (Moore 1988:35).
Looking at data from actual interactions, I address some of these issues in this chapter and argue that women play a crucial role in mediating, constructing, and legiti-
mizing hierarchy.

Locating gender in discourse

Because societies conceptualize men and women in culturally specific and meaningful ways, we would expect language to be a major source of gender ideologies
(Ochs 1992): "Grammar is politics by other means" (Harraway 1991:3). However,
not many features of languages directly and exclusively index gender (Ochs 1992).
Many of the language features identified as male or female can be used by, with, and
for both sexes, as careful studies of actual language use show. Direct, indexical relationships in English that index gender are limited to referential pronouns and terms
of address, in Pohnpeian to terms of address only, as one pronoun serves both genders. Forms of address signal not only gender differences but also relations of status.
This interrelatedness of gender and status makes the analysis of gender and language
strategies complex. What becomes clear in the realization that not many features of
language index gender is that it is in practice, in daily speech, in the context of particular sets of social and economic relations, that the cultural conceptions of gender
are constructed and naturalized.

Early work on language and gender in American English generally stressed differences between female and male speakers, positing gender as the most relevant
category for these differences. Men were often used as the baseline, and women were
considered from a deviance perspective. Even in these studies, however, class or status
combined with gender to produce differences. Labov, for example, in his studies in
New York City in the 1960s (see Labov 1972), determined that women use preferred,
nonstigmatized phonological variants more than men, and that women aspire to prestigious speech forms. Lower-middle-class women showed the most extreme form of
this behavior. The relation between status marking and gender marking is evident
from many studies on speech habits of white, middle-class Americans. Trudgill (1972)
suggests that women try to compensate for low status by using prestige forms of language and characterizes men as using vernacular as a "covert prestige." Status is only
one of a multiplicity of relations indexed in gendered speech, however, and the use
or nonuse of prestige forms can be analyzed as linked not to status but to self-
conscious constructions of gender differentiation. For example, Gal (1992) links
working-class vernacular to certain ideals of masculinity. Gender is a set of per-
formative acts, and the body constructs its sex in culturally located practices of
everyday life (Butler 1993).

Because not many grammatical features of language directly and explicitly
index gender, conversational strategies of turn length, interruptions, and topic con-

trol have been cited by researchers on women and language as important loci for the intersection of language and gendered practices, as well as gender and relationships to power differentials (see, for example, R. Lakoff 1973a, 1975; Zimmerman and West 1975; O'Barr and Atkins 1980; Tannen 1990). American women are reported as talking and interrupting less than men and as not maintaining topics in the same way, and this has been linked to powerlessness and the subordination of women. Other research, although it concurs that men behave conversationally in a power-oriented way, characterizes women as cooperative in discourse rather than powerless (for example, Fishman 1982; Tannen 1990).

Many of the differences first described for American men's and women's speech are actually locally specific to white middle- and upper-class groups. The early discourse about gender inequality has been criticized for failing to take into account women of color (Harraway 1991). Characterizations of women's speech cross-culturally have been found to be locally realized forms. For example, Mexicano women do not adhere to prestige norms (identified by male Mexicano speakers as a certain stress pattern and possessive constructions) (Hill 1987). Philips and Reynolds (1987) found male jurors abbreviating their talk more than women and relying on hearers to retrieve information deleted from a larger context, but Ochs (1987) found certain case markers in Samoan deleted more often by women (also reported by Shibamoto 1987 for Japanese), suggesting that in Samoa and Japan, men's speech is more syntactically complete than women's. Although R. Lakoff (1975) has argued that American women's speech is more polite than men's, and that such speech is less powerful in part because it is more polite, Keenan (1974) found in Madagascar that men are regarded as more polite than women. There, positive value is placed on speaking indirectly and avoiding open confrontation. Women's style and activities are viewed pejoratively by the men: Women bargain, haggle, reprimand children, and gossip about shameful behavior. Men dominate ceremonial speech situations and intervillage relations. In Schieffelin's (1990) study of the Kaluli of New Guinea, linguistic differences between women and men are associated solely with the activities in which they are engaged, although boys are reported to be socialized to be more aggressive in making requests. Activity-based linguistic differences have also been noted for patterns originally ascribed to women in the United States, such as baby talk. M. Goodwin (1990) describes such different organizational strategies of boys and girls in interaction.

It is obvious that it is not possible to claim that gender correlates with any one linguistic feature. In fact, social status may be a more important determinant of the occurrence of intensifiers, hedges, hesitation forms, polite forms, and other forms associated with women and powerlessness (Philips 1980). However, this too is culture specific, as Keenan's work in Madagascar shows (1974). It is not even possible to say that gender affects status which in turn affects speech. In Samoa, high-ranking men and women differ less from each other than both together differ from low-ranking men and women (Ochs 1987). Although gender affects Samoan word-order choice more than rank, rank has more of an effect than gender on other variables such as use of affect. What is clear is that both men and women participate in structures of meaning and practice which are constituted in terms of hierarchy and in terms of local ideologies of male and female categories within this structure.

Concepts of gender

Although status is often conceptualized as relational and variable according to context and culture, researchers have tended to look at gender as a single unvarying dichotomy between male and female spheres. That gender itself is a universal category should not be taken for granted. Gender categories are culturally constructed, subject to change through time, and are systematically related to other areas of cultural discourse such as the nature of persons, power, and a desirable moral order (Gal 1992:154). What counts as opposite affects the form of the differences between the sexes and the practices that naturalize a hierarchical relationship between the sexes. This includes creating cultural notions that link forms of talk to social groups.

A categorical rigidity about gender categories ethnocentrically applied cross-culturally can be counterproductive. Other cultures may not see categories as primitively as we do, as reflected in an account by Ward (1989) on transsexuality on Pohnpei:

> A young girl named Maria began exhibiting the habits of a boy as she grew into her teens. She began to go walking about at night looking for girls. The activity itself was acceptable, but a girl doing it caused consternation. Family and neighbors held a meeting to discuss the problem. Then they held a feast where they publicly declared her a boy. Her hair was cut and she was presented with male clothing. Henceforth, they announced, Maria would be Mario. I heard that Mario became a responsible citizen with a wife and children. (42)

Concepts of the individual or person are cross-culturally variable. Notions of personhood in the Pacific have been shown to be different from Western notions of personhood as morally self-contained and opposed to society (cf. White and Kirkpatrick 1985). In some areas of the Pacific, the notion of personhood often approaches what is stereotypically gendered female in the United States, where relationships have important meanings and are constantly negotiated (cf. M. Goodwin 1990). Lutz (1988) notes how inhabitants of the Micronesian island Ifaluk place a strong emphasis on perceived or desired similarities between self and other. They frequently use the pronoun "we" where Americans would use "I." Beliefs about the permeability of self and the relatedness of individuals to each other influence native notions of individual or gender-based dominance, because gender constructs are linked to concepts of self, personhood, and autonomy (Strathern 1981). Women are not only wives but sisters, daughters, and mothers; men are not only husbands but brothers, sons, and fathers. The roles of wife and sister or wife and mother can have quite different statuses. In Pacific societies particularly, the role of sister often has a greater cultural prominence than that of wife. Thus gender is constructed by speakers in relational terms and embedded in other social and cultural institutions and ideologies (cf. Borker 1980; Conkey and Gero 1991).

If the same categories that underlie cultural distinctions between the sexes are also applied to order statuses among men and among women, this indicates that gender distinctions are not unique to the domain of gender but are shared with other important domains of social life (Ortner and Whitehead 1981). The study of gender is often therefore inherently a study of relations of asymmetrical power and opportunity (Ortner and Whitehead 1981).

A patrilineal bias on the part of previous ethnographers has tended to discount the mana or sacred power of women in Oceanic societies. For example, Sahlins (1958) characterizes mana as follows: "Like the great chief in his domain, the father is in his own house a sacred figure, a man of superior *mana*, his possessions, even his food, guarded by tabus against defilement by lesser familial kinsmen. Polynesians know innately how to honor the chief, for chieftainship begins at home: the chief's due is no more than elaborate filial respect" (64). Yet manaman on Pohnpei, as mentioned in chapter 1 (in this volume), flows matrilineally to descendants within chiefly clans. Women are connected to chiefly power on Pohnpei not only through clan affiliation and marriage but also because, symbolically, the deities are in the position of mother (*ihn*) or mother's brother (*uhlap*) to members of the clan (Riesenberg 1968). Women determine the ascribed ranking of their male kinsmen (Kihleng 1996:3) and have a primary place of value in the society. In Tongan and Hawaiian societies, moreover, women regularly held the highest positions. Kirch (1984), though he generalizes a patrilineal bias, notes that women can influence rank:

> There is strong ideological bias in Polynesian societies toward patrilineage and primogeniture in the hereditary succession to high rank. Nevertheless, just as ambilateral affiliation allows for flexibility in descent group membership, there is some flexibility in succession to high office. As noted earlier, maternal linkages may be used by persons of lower rank in order to associate themselves with those of higher rank. In some chiefdoms, such as Tonga, the female role in rank determination was to become extremely important and pose potential contradictions to the political structure. (34)

Questions have been raised about the validity of descriptions emphasizing patrilineality as a structuring principle in Polynesian societies (Hanson 1982; Howard and Kirkpatrick 1989; Ortner 1981). Regarding the importance of brother–sister power relationships, it is now more widely noted, for example, that in Samoa sisters are perceived as exercising "a controlling power (mana) over their brothers, and are thus honored and served by them" (Howard and Kirkpatrick 1989:80). In Tonga, a sister outranked her brother (Gailey 1987). Hanson (1982) argues against the portrayal of women as inferior, describing them instead as conduits of sacred power, too close to the deities to be controllable by men. In Pohnpei, children born while their father is paramount chief and their mother is paramount chieftess are called *ipwin pohn warawar* (lit. "born upon the ditch" or crevice between the chief and others). These children, whether male or female, have high manaman, receive a great deal of deference, and are allowed a much wider spectrum of acceptable behavior; for example, they can ignore prescriptions of spatial status in the feast house, sit in the highest places, and walk past symbolic boundaries that are forbidden to others (i.e., they are not subject to control). Women who are *sohpeidi* (i.e., senior women in the highest-ranking matrilineages of the ruling clans and the daughters of the highest-ranking chiefs) often receive titles in their own right in recognition of their social rank and status (Kihleng 1996:128). These women keep their titles after marriage (and also assume the counterpart of their husbands' title). When a high-titled man dies, his widow is given a woman's title by the paramount chief (Kihleng 1996:129).

Locating power in discourse: Interaction 1

Participants in interaction orient to roles and identities, and these roles and identities are jointly and collaboratively achieved. As discussed in previous chapters, lower-status speakers are the ones who construct status inequalities through language. Status negotiations include complicity, accommodation, and indirection, as well as resistance, contestation, and conflict. Domination and power are rarely uncontested.

In the following interaction, a transcript of a videotape of evening sakau at the home of the Nanmwarki of Madolenihmw, the use of directives to move participants in sakau to appropriate positions shows the significant role women can play in constructing status asymmetries and sustaining the existing social order. In the strip of interaction I discuss here, the porch at the chief's residence becomes a field for the operation of power. The participants are engaged in structuring the small porch area to constitute what they feel is the appropriate distribution of space. Using honorific speech, they direct the movements of the chief and chieftess and collaboratively achieve a relative position/place for all. The symbolic hierarchizing of space on the porch can be followed step by step through turns at talk. The structured ordering of space along ranked lines redefines the porch area. It requires negotiation and collaboration to achieve. Verbal status indicators (i.e., honorific verbs), together with nonverbal signals such as gestures, map onto the physical environment a hierarchy of status among participants.

As discussed in chapter 3 (in this volume), distribution of space is an important way to make concrete symbolic asymmetries. The woman's role as distributor of space is noted in the following discussion. Her role can be viewed both as empowering her to structure the space (her high degree of personal agency within traditional structure) and/or her complicity with constructing an asymmetrical relation which will leave her in a lower position than the people she is directing. This is not a distinction easily made, as evidenced by the chief's resistance to her directives. Each step in the process is negotiated.

A sequence of positioning and repositioning of the chief and chieftess is engendered by a question posed by the chief's adopted daughter (adopted when the chief was married to his previous wife, and before he became paramount chief) to the already-seated participants: "*Ah i pahn pato ia wasa*" ("but where will I sit"). Figure 5.1, frame 1 shows what the daughter sees as she poses her question.

(1)

((first video frame action occurs here))

Daughter:	*ah I pahn pato*		*ia*	*wasa?*
	but I will	LocVerb[HUM]	where	place?
→	but where will I sit?			

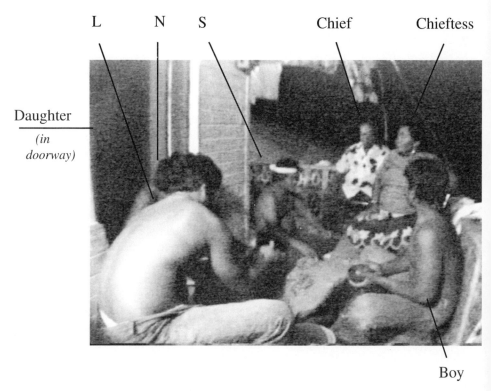

Figure 5.1 Video Frame 1

Chieftess: *ie*   ((signals downward, in front of her))
              here.by.me
              here

Sou: *pohn   takaio.*
              on   rock.there
              on the rock.

As she looks around the porch area, she clearly does not see a suitable place to sit. By choosing a question format, she invites others to collaborate on solving the problem. The question is directed to no one in particular; the polysemous humiliative pato "be (at a location)" is used for her own act of sitting, the humiliative verb for being in one place. Although the chieftess invites the chief's daughter to sit below her, another participant, S, indicates that there is not enough room by joking that the daughter should sit on the sakau stone. This would be unthinkable because this is where the sakau is prepared. After S finishes speaking, the chief scoots his chair a few inches to his right. However, as the chief finishes moving, his daughter uses honorific speech to direct him to move further. She begins a series of directives to rearrange the positions of the chief, chieftess, and herself to appropriately order the space not only for herself but for everyone.

(2)

01 Daughter: *men*   ***omwi.***   ***omw***   ***ket***
               there.by.you you(S)[EXAL] you(S)[EXAL] LocVerb[EXAL]
               there by you. you be

02   *men*   *ah iet*
               there.by.you but here
               there but here

03 Chieftess: *sohte lipilipil*
               not   choosy
               it doesn't matter

In excerpt 2, the daughter directs the chief. Her hand is pointed straight out toward the chief and chieftess. She uses the exaltive verb "ket" and the exaltive pronoun "omwi." The chief's person and his movements are indexed as exaltive.

The chieftess resists the directives by saying it does not matter where they sit (line 03). It is customary for Pohnpeians to exhibit modesty by resisting taking a high position. The practice of resisting symbolic elevation, which both chieftess and chief engage in, places the burden of power and responsibility on lower-status members of the community to enforce asymmetries, ensuring that hierarchy is built from below. The chief's daughter in one sense becomes the chieftess's advocate and negotiates her position into a higher one. The daughter herself is not of high status (she takes the complimentary title to her husband) but is claiming a high-status position for another. The chieftess and the chief are already differentiated from the others because they are sitting on metal chairs, whereas everyone else sits on the floor or on small cement blocks. Vertical hierarchy, however, is just one component of spatial asymmetry. The other is horizontal (i.e., relative position on the floor). The chief sits at the back of the porch and the lowest-status participants closest to the front (in this case closest to the camera). The chieftess should share the highest place next to the chief.

The daughter then issues a series of directives, commanding removal of an ice chest and the movement of the chief, the chieftess, and finally herself. She uses the verb forms appropriate to the status of each: patohsang for the ice chest and ketla for the chief. In referring to the chieftess, she uses the honorific pronoun "komwi" without a verb. She does not use a questioning intonation, nor does she modify the force of her directives. In excerpt 3, note the difference between her directive to S (a man participating in the sakau preparations) about the ice chest and the chief's indirect question to S about the ice chest.

(3)

            ((second video frame action occurs here; see figure 5.2, frame 2))

01 Daughter: *S pwe   ma ice boxo   pato-*
               S because if ice box.there.afy&m LocVerb[HUM]
               S ((name)) move the ice chest out of there

Daughter   S   Chief   Chieftess

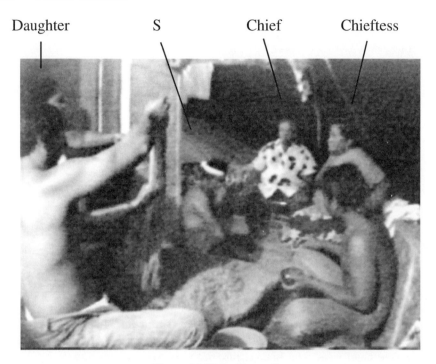

Figure 5.2 Video Frame 2

02   *ice chest en patohsang   mwo*
                ice chest to LocVerb[HUM].from there.afy&m
→   move the ice chest from there

03   *eri   Mwohnsapw*
                so then chief
                so then the chief

04   *ketla   mwo ah komwi*
                LocVerb[EXAL].there there and you(S)[EXAL]
                moves there and you

                [   ]

05 Chief: *ke   kak   pwekada ice boxen?*
    ((to S))   you(S) can   lift.up   ice box.there.by.you
→   can you lift up the ice box?

06 Daughter: *ah ngehi*
                and me
                and me

07 Chief: *ke   kak pwekada ice boxen?*
                you(S) can lift.up   ice box.there.by.you
                can you lift up the ice box?

The chief's attempt to influence the activity at hand is far more indirect than his daughter's. He asks S a question: whether he is able to move the ice chest. Indirect speech acts can mean more than they say, and interpretation is left up to the listener. More room is available for negotiation and the possibility of noncompliance, as a negative answer to a question is not necessarily a direct refusal of a directive. Questions from high- to low-status persons often are understood as embedded imperatives (Ervin-Tripp 1977), merely because of status roles and not because of any linguistic evidence.

In her first directive about the chief's movement, the chief's daughter uses the status-raising verb "ketla" for the chief's action. In her repeat of her directive to move the chief, she chooses a more specific locative suffix for his movement (-*wei*, "there toward you") than in her first directive:

(4)

01 Daughter: *eri Mohnsapw* **ketwei**
            so   chief   LocVerb[EXAL].there.toward.you
            then the chief goes there

02   *ah* **komwi**   *ah ngehi*
            and you(S)[EXAL] and me
            and you ((chieftess)) and me

            ((third video frame action occurs here; see figure 5.3, frame 3))

Daughter   S   Chief

Figure 5.3 Video Frame 3

S   Chieftess

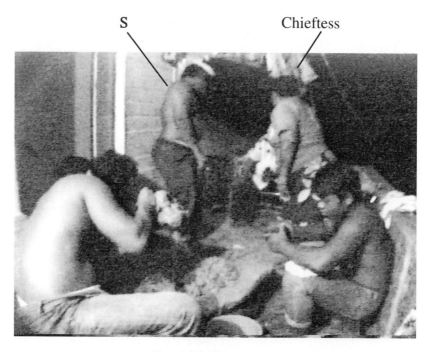

Figure 5.4 Video Frame 4

(5)

01 Daughter: *ke sou ketwei*   *kis*
                          you not LocVerb[EXAL].there.toward.you a.little
                          can't you move a little

02   *ah Likend   me ah*
                and chieftess here and
                and the chieftess here and

                ((fourth video frame action occurs here; see figure 5.4, frame 4))

All the directives are delivered with status-raising forms of the locative verb. It is not only the daughter who uses strong directives with status-raising honorifics to the chief or chieftess. As seen in excerpt 6, her husband and a teenage boy also participate in verbally directing them and assigning their positions. They also use the status-raising verbs appropriate for movements of the chief and chieftess (those with *ket* root):

(6)

01 Daughter's Husband: *io   Likend pahn **ketwei***
                                there Likend will LocVerb[EXAL].there.toward.you
→   there Likend will move toward you

02		*mwo*
		there away from you and me
		there

03 Daughter:		*na re* **ketwei**		*mwo*
		so they LocVerb[EXAL].there.toward.you there
		so they ((you, the chief)) move toward you there

04		*ah Likend me*
		and chieftess here.by.me
		and the chieftess here

(7) Boy		((talking to chieftess))

01		*komw*	**ketdo**		*me*
		you(S)[EXAL] LocVerb[EXAL].here here.by.me
		come here by me

02 Chieftess:		*ia?*
		where?

The use of directives from lower-status participants to the chief is also evident in the ritual formula for leave taking when in the presence of a chief or other high-status person. The lower-status person who wishes to leave will say to the high-status person, "*komw ketda*" (you[EXAL] stand[EXAL] up), so that leave taking may be done without having to raise one's head higher than the chief. The chief does not stand, actually (cf. McGarry ms), but acknowledges the respect, an example of language making explicit an organization of meaning that transcends the visual sphere. Komw ketda as leave taking in a directive form literally insists on self-lowering, building the status hierarchy through the actions of those below. Using honorific speech for directives appears to both modify the coerciveness of the directive and at the same time empower lower-status persons to direct chiefly behavior. The fact that the chief does not stand up indicates, however, that the illocutionary force of such directives may be of greater symbolic than literal import. Nonetheless, symbolic systems are crucial in the creation and maintenance of artificial differences between social actors.

To turn now to the chief's directives, as mentioned in previous chapters, the chief does not use honorific speech but common speech in addressing his subordinates. In the previous interaction, his directives are, however, surprisingly indirect, given what we know about his high status. For example, in excerpt 8, when talking about the need for more light, the chief makes a request beginning with "if" (*ma*), which marks his utterance as conditional, and *dene*, which is a reported speech marker (i.e., as if the speech or request of others is conveyed by the chief). Dene can denote two general meanings, that the events spoken about were not directly observed or experienced by the speaker or that the speaker obtained the information from another source (Mauricio 1993:435). The chief also uses a questioning intonation.

(8)

01 Chief: *ma dene   ehu dengki mihmi me?*
            if   they say one light   stay   here.by.me?
            they say one light can also be here?

The chief appears to be using strategies designed to achieve collaboration and shared decision making. His hedges invite cooperation, as does his question, in answer to which another's opinion is warranted. The differences in tone, modality, and directness between the chief and his daughter are not what might have been predicted given the authority and prestige of the chief and the often-described lower status of women.

It is important to look at the uptake of directives, to note their interactional import. The chief's albeit indirect wishes are carried out almost immediately, whereas his daughter repeats her directive three times, upgrading it in specificity. Although her directives do heavily influence the structuring of the social space, the chief evidences several strategies for resisting. His resources for challenging her claims to verbal authority over space include ignoring her (hence her repeated directive), questions, other-initiated repair (correction), framing a response as a proverb, and humor. Nonverbally he executes actions of his own initiative. Excerpt 9 provides some examples.

First, the chief frames his resistance in a proverbial style:

(9)

01 Chief: *ah i mwahuer   me*
            but I good.already here.by.me
            but I'm okay here

02 →   *sohte me kin   kasauada sohpeidi*
            not   that habitually move   those.who.face.down
            no one can move the sohpeidi ((high-status members of the chief's clan))

((group laughter))

This strategy does not directly confront his daughter but uses the indirect form of many Pohnpeian proverbs. The sentence has a generalized subject and habitual aspect, followed by a dispreferred action and preceded by negation. Several other Pohnpeian proverbs are listed here for comparison:

Sohte ohl kin sansara mwahl
No man habitually opens his mouth uselessly

Sohte ohl kin masak lih
No man is habitually afraid of a woman

Sohte ohl kin mwuskihla mehkot ahpw pwurehng kangala
No man habitually vomits something up and then eats it again
(a man should not go back on his word)

Sohte me kin padok emen ohl
No one habitually plants another man
(no one should continuously put another man in an embarrassing position)

(Proverbs from McGarry ms)

Thus the relationship of the chief's statement "*sohte me kin kasauada sohpeidi*" to the structures of the proverbs can be seen, particularly in the beginning formula *sohte me kin* followed by the disapproved action.

By using proverbial structure, the chief does not invoke his own authority but cites the authority of tradition to legitimize his resistance, as well as his point of view, because he draws attention to his role as "sohpeidi," a term that refers not only to relative position but to the highest of statuses (sohte me kin kasauada sohpeidi). Sohpeidi (lit. "face downward") are those who sit on the feast house platform and look down and out over their subjects. They are high titleholders of the same clan as the paramount chief. It is interesting to note the difference between the customarily appropriate behavior cited by the chief in the proverbial expression ("no one tells a chief where to sit") and what really goes on. Nevertheless, when consultants are asked about behavior, they often cite proverbs and ideal behavior, showing the importance of such repositories of knowledge as handy cues for patterns of dominance and/or subordination and other appropriate forms of behavior.

In a second strategy, the chief questions his daughter's directives. Questions are often used to initiate repair (i.e.. self- or other-correction). Sometimes a simple repeat of another's directive has the interactional effect of beginning an error correction or modification sequence.

(10)

01 Chief: *ah ah ohlo   pahn da?*
               but but man.there will   what?
               what will that man[1] do ((where will he sit))?

02 Daughter: *soh mwo [i pahn pato   mwo ah*
               no   there I   will   LocVerb[HUM] there but
               no there, I will stay there but

                       [

03 Chief: *eh,*
                       eh,

04 Daughter: *ia   mwohmwen.*
               what appearance.that by you
               how does that look.

In excerpt 10, the chief queries his daughter on what the man (S) will do. This is after the daughter's third directive. The chief then moves himself (see the difference in his seating positions in figure 5.5, frames 5 and 6), directing his own actions out loud ("I will walk here") and transforming her directive into a self-directive. But she

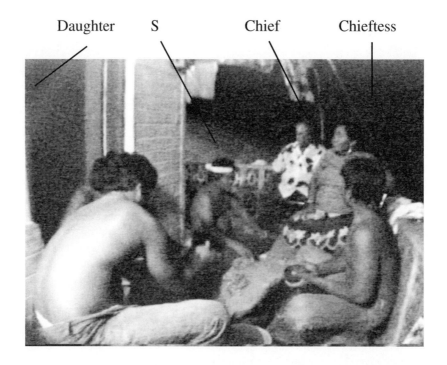

Figure 5.5 Video Frames 5 and 6

then questions his self-directive, perhaps based on clarification of his intentions because of his use of the verb *keidi* (to walk) and the fact that he is heading toward the stairs and exit (i.e., perhaps leaving), and at the same time she challenges his renegotiation of the situation.

When everyone is finally seated, including the daughter, who takes up her position as server of sakau to the chieftess, it is clear that the daughter has had a commanding role in shaping the nature of the interaction to follow, by indexing relative status in a more complex way than honorific speech is able to do. That is, whereas honorific speech constructs two distinct oppositions between high and low, nonverbal, spatial signs are able to categorize more finely and sharply between individuals sitting next to each other and sharing and exchanging similar speech patterns. That this renegotiation of space enhances her own prestige and that of the chieftess is clear. Before her instructions, the chieftess was sitting closer than the chief to the camera, a position relatively lower. At the end of the reconfiguration, the chieftess is sitting in a position of much higher authority, as is the chief's daughter.

Although the spatial symbolism reflecting the status hierarchy on the island— with the chief and chieftess at the top—was constructed, the authoritative voices in the decision making necessary to achieve this ordering and distribution of social space were those of the lower-status participants. Indeed, the chief and chieftess appear to resist the reordering of space to reflect hierarchical symbolism.

Gender and conceptions of reality: Interaction 2

Gal (1991) observes that power is more than an authoritative voice in decision making, and that "its strongest form may well be the ability to define social reality, to impose visions of the world" (197). In the previous interaction I showed a woman's influence on the structuring of the symbolic hierarchy of social space. In another interaction I recorded on Pohnpei over a year earlier, another woman plays the role of public cultural critic, commentator, tease, and authority, this time in the presence of the second-ranking chief of Madolenihmw, the Nahnken (this interaction was also discussed in chapter 2, in this volume).

In some of the studies quoted earlier, on gender differences in language use, dominance was quantified by means of interruptions, tag questions, silences, length of utterance, and number of utterances. These methods can illuminate patterns but can also oversimplify and fail to capture the situated social construction of reality. It is the construction of multiple or different versions of reality I would like to address here, and one particular woman's public role in this construction on Pohnpei.

The interaction described took place in the feast house of the second-ranking chief of the district of Madolenihmw. Four people are the primary speakers in the interaction: the chief, the menindei (who is the master of ceremonies in the sakau), one of the sakau pounders, and the wife of the adopted son of the chief. The chief and the menindei are urging others to join in pounding the sakau; these others are resisting because of the presence of the video camera. The woman is a bystander; she herself cannot volunteer to pound sakau, as only men traditionally do the pounding. As shown, however, the woman participates extensively in other ways.

Were I to describe the interaction quantitatively by gender and utterance, as in some of the previous American studies on language and gender, the following patterns emerge: The participant who speaks the most utterances is the menindei. His utterances in the strip of interaction before the actual pounding begins number twenty-two. This is not surprising, as he is the master of ceremonies and directs the activity. The woman's utterances number eighteen, the chief's fifteen, and the pounder's ten. Looking at word length of utterances, the woman's are the longest, averaging 6.4 words, the chief is next with 5.2, the menindei averages 4.1, and the pounder 3.5. The woman has the longest utterance (eighteen words), and the largest number of utterances over ten words (five). The chief has one utterance over ten words, the menindei two, the pounder none.

Although these numbers are interesting, ethnographic evidence suggests that conclusions drawn on their basis would be misleading for a number of reasons. First, as noted by Duranti (1981, 1994) for Samoa, the allocation of space is often a more salient guide to relations of relative status than speech in Pacific societies. On Pohnpei of course, not only space is important but also relative height. In the interaction described, the chief is the only participant on the feast house platform, all others are standing on the dirt floor, or sitting (lower than the chief) around the kava stone located on the dirt. The woman occupies a peripheral position at the edge of the feast house. Also, chiefs often speak through others, increasing the symbolic distance between themselves and their constituents and husbanding their authority (cf. Duranti 1981; Marcus 1984). Thus the lack of speech cannot necessarily be correlated with a lack of authority or status. The institution of a spokesperson or mediator allows the chief greater flexibility in accepting or declining responsibility and in maintaining public displays of elite status.

Interruptions and overlaps have also been a focus of gender and language studies in the United States. In the Pohnpeian interaction, five overlaps are noted; in three (60 percent), the woman is the overlapper; that is, she begins to speak before another speaker has completed his utterance. Other overlappers are the pounder and the menindei. In excerpt 11, the woman speaks while the chief is speaking. She draws attention to the fact that a possible participant is escaping into the bush. This interpretation is confirmed by the response of the menindei, who then calls to the man. She is playing an active, albeit offstage, role in helping to gather male participants.

(11)

01 Chief: *mwekid pil   lokaia pahn pil mie*
              moving   also talk   will also is
              there will also be moving and talking

                     [   ]

02 Woman: *ekei!   Ander!*
              (exclamation) Ander
              what! Ander!

(1.0)

03 Menindei: *uh uh uh nahn kohdo*
                uh uh uh buddy come.here.towards.me
                uh uh uh buddy come here

In another instance, the woman speaks at the same time as the chief. They are both giving directives to the pounders, who have finally arrived. The chief instructs them to come pound, the woman to take their shirts off. Here she constructs the reality of movie making rather than sakau pounding. Rather than citing tradition as the reason the shirts must be off, she cites the video: "So your skin will show in the movie."

(12)

01 Chief: *kumwa kohdo   mah iang sukedi*
        you(D) come here first join pound.down
        you guys come here first and join the pounding

        [   ]

02 Woman: *kumwa kihsang mah ahmwa seht kan*
        you(D) take.from first your(D) shirt those.by.you
        you two first take off your shirts

03 *pwe   kilimwa   kan   en iang pwarada*
        because skin.your(D) those.by.you to join show.up
        so that your skin shows

04 *nan kasdo*
        in   movie
        in the movie

The overlaps of the chief and the woman can be seen as supportive simultaneous speech, an urgent signal that a potential participant is exiting the area (excerpt 11). In excerpt 12, when the chief and the woman speak together, both are giving directives (not contradictory) to participants who have been finally persuaded to join. Contextual factors seem to place a value on speed and cooperation in this interaction, and it is important to note that the Pohnpeian speakers are attempting to organize an activity. Goal-directed activities often alter conversational preference structures. However, they are rich sites for the construction of power relations. Analyzing the part that each gender plays in organizing the activity and constructing meaning from that activity can be instructive for understanding gender as an important delimiter of status or power.

In the interaction being discussed, the woman uses no honorific forms, which seems rather remarkable, but no one uses them (this is discussed in chapter 3). At the point in the interaction that a switch to honorific forms is initiated by the menindei, she drops out of the conversation. A different reality is contextualized by the menindei with the use of honorifics, in which a strict sequence of actions will be followed, and during which space is assigned a different meaning. The position of mediator is institutionalized in several ways in Pohnpeian social structure and it is a position with power, especially for recontextualization. In this interaction, it appears that the woman is also acting as a type of mediator or commentator on the activity in progress. In American culture, a commentator is a mediator who distills information for the audience and draws attention to issues of importance. In this interaction, the Pohnpeian woman publicly comments on the action and continually constitutes the reality of the video recording. In excerpt 13 she recontextualizes the chief's directive about sakau in terms of the movie:

(13)

01 Chief: *en kohdo*   *iang sukusuk.*
             to come.here.toward.me join pounding
             tell him[2] to come and pound.

02 Woman: *en kohdo*   *en iang kilele.*
             to come.here.toward.me to join picture.this.by.me
→   tell him to come and join this movie.

03 Chief: *en kohdo*   *iang* (?)
             to come.here.toward.me join   (?)
             to come and join (?)

                         [   ]
04 Pounder: *KOHDO MAH KITA IANG SUK SAKAU*
                    come   first we(D) join   pound sakau.
                    come here let's pound sakau first

                             [
05 Woman: ((laughter))

Only one other speaker references the movie: A pounder says, "If it's really moving I'll join," and the chief replies, "It's really moving." This dialogue both challenges and validates the woman's construction of reality.

I would like to analyze the interaction from the point of view of what the woman is "doing" with her utterances to see the interaction as a series of social acts. In her comments, much cultural information is being communicated through teasing, humor, accounts, and commentary. This is in distinction to the male speakers, who mainly issue directives and ask questions. In describing more specifically the woman's use of language, I focus on teasing, cultural commentary, and construction of an authoritative stance.

The woman's two questions are delivered in a teasing or mocking manner ("Is that the sakau? Make a pretty face" and "Are these the actors?"):

(14)

01 Woman: *ih sakauen   met, wiada ahmw*
             it sakau.that.by.you now, make   your(S)
             is that the sakau, make a

02   *mahsamwahuen*
             face.good.there.by.you
             pretty face

In both instances she refers to the making of a video about sakau. Teasing can serve as a way to construct alternate realities and as a challenge to legitimacy. Ervin-Tripp (1992) found increased use of aggressive humor by women in mixed-sex groups in the United States compared to same-sex groups. In U.S. institutional settings, it is noted widely that joking is the prerogative of those in higher-status positions. In the following utterance, the woman teases the men about taking off their shirts:

(15)

02 Woman: *kumwa kihsang mah ahmwa seht kan*
             you(D) take.from first your(D) shirt those.by.you
             you two first take off your shirts

03   *pwe   kilimwa   kan   en iang pwarada*
             because skin.your(D) those.by.you to join show.up
             so that your skin shows

04   *nan kasdo*
             in   movie
             in the movie

A focus of the teasing is the appearance of the naked body; it could be a comment on American movies' predilection for showing nakedness (Pohnpeians watch American videos) and an effort to embarrass the men. Pohnpeians value modesty and are also sensitive to the possibility of humiliation from inappropriate behavior, because shaming is an important form of social control. Sakau is pounded with at least part of the men's attire still traditional—the absence of clothing above the waist.

In excerpt 6, the woman gives an authoritative account of why it is so difficult to get participants. However, getting sakau pounders is a recurrent problem; hence, in casual sakau preparation it is commonplace to see only two men doing the work.

(16)

01 Woman: *kilele   me   kalewedahr*
             picture.this.by.me the.one scare.already
             this picture taking is what has scared away

02   *sounsakaukan*
             experts.at.sakau.those.by.you
             those sakau experts

The woman makes several comments on Pohnpeian culture during the interaction. The chief says, "Tell them to come and pound, they don't have to drink it"—a reference possibly to the age of the boys he is trying to recruit, or possibly to religious affiliation (many Protestants do not drink sakau). In response to this directive, the woman states: "So this is a movie about paradise, it's not a movie about parasites."

(17)

01 Woman: *ah kasdohn paradise me,*
ah movie.of Paradise this.one.by.me,
oh! this is a movie about Paradise,

02   *kaidehn kasdohn parasite*
not   movie.of parasite
it's not a movie about parasites

This is a sophisticated comment on Pohnpeian culture and sakau practices. Sakau preparation is time-consuming and energy intensive. Sakau drinking is very popular. People remark on the "ability" of some to arrive just as the sakau is ready to drink without having to do any of the work, and tradition dictates that no one can be refused a drink. The idea of having people pound who do not want to drink is equated with paradise, whereas people who drink who did not pound are referred to as parasites. Both words ("paradise" and "parasite") are English-language concepts which are heavily value laden. The first, paradise, reflects the imported Christian notion of paradise, a place where one goes for reward after maintaining high moral standards and hard work on earth. The second, parasite, has many negative connotations, including disease. The evocation by the woman of imported Western concepts during my film making with an imported camera raises interesting symmetries. Western technology is evidencing the same potential for sweeping cultural change on Pohnpei that Western religion did centuries earlier; religion is evoked by the use of the term "paradise." The notion of Western science is evoked by the use of the term "parasite"—Western health practices have resulted in many changes as well. Perhaps the anthropologist (myself) can also be viewed as a parasite. Saying that the film is about paradise also suggests that it will not capture the real Pohnpei and is somewhat of a fantasy, which is in some measure accurate, as every film represents certain choices on the part of the film maker.

The difference between the words "paradise" and "parasite" is in fact only one letter; this suggests that the difference between the two in reality is tenuous on an island where a careful balance of reciprocities is required to ensure that each member of the society has a share in leisure time. In fact, one word is almost a metathesis[3] (transposition of two phonemes in a word) of the other, especially as in some earlier spelling systems, no distinction was made between the sound now represented by the letter *d* and the sound represented by *t*, although they are different phonemes (Rehg 1981). The utterance is delivered with a certain artistry—each clause contains exactly the same number of syllables, and there is a play on the similarity between the two English words, which rhyme slightly and are placed at the end of each clause. The word *kasdoh* (movie) is repeated in each clause to create a balanced effect: *Ah kasdohn paradise me, kaidehn kasdohn parasite.*

In another utterance, the woman responds to the menindei's call for participants by saying "D (personal name) will take my place." This is another joke and cultural comment because, of course, as a woman, she cannot pound sakau in a formal setting (though women sometimes pound in informal settings). In Pohnpeian cultural terms, she does not have a place at the sakau stone to give away; her comment brings this to everyone's attention. This utterance can also be interpreted as her claim for a place and a strategy for constructing equality. Place is of course an important symbol for status in Pohnpei and other Pacific cultures.

(18)

Woman: *D ((name)) me   pahn wilialie.*
          D ((name)) the.one will   change.me
          D is the one who will take my place

The woman constitutes an authoritative stance through her speech. In excerpt 19, she chastises those who are trying to avoid participation by saying, "I told you so." She casts herself in the role of expert as well as in control of events.

(19)

01 Woman: *ke   les   pwe   ke   pahn udahn mih*
          you(S) comeuppance because you(S) will   really   stay
          you had it coming because you will really be in it
          ((see I told you that you would be in the movie))

02   *loale kahpw ((ke   ahpw)) sou les?*
          inside   you(S) but   not comeuppance?
          but didn't you have it coming?

In excerpt 20, the woman tells them it is not up to them to decide whether to participate; their wishes are not important in contrast to the wishes of the others who want to see the film made. She represents herself as one who knows the order of command:

(20)

01 Woman: *mwahu ma kumwa sohte inangih*
          good   if   you(D) not   desire
          it doesn't matter if you two desire it or not

In excerpt 21, the woman laughs at W's attempts to escape, tells him he cannot avoid participating, and suggests that if he were to appear suddenly out of hiding it would confuse viewers:

(21) Woman speaking ((laughing voice))

01 *W ((name)) keido   mahs pwe   kasdo*
   W ((name)) move.here.toward.me please because movie
   W move here toward me please because this movie

02 *me   nannanti. ah e de rukuruk*
   this.one.by.me trying.hard but he lest hiding
   is trying hard to happen. lest you are hiding

03 *oh mie la   towe   ah pa   pwerida heh heh*
   and be   there occupant he suddenly appears   heh heh
   and then suddenly appear as a participant heh heh

The woman continually constitutes the reality of the movie and then acts as director, assigning roles for the men to play ("you guys pretend to be the villains"), much as the menindei is assigning roles for the sakau, and she singles out one of the participants for a starring role:

(22)

01 Woman: *kumwail en wiada mwohmen   kaun en pwihn*
           you(P)   to make   appearance.of leader of group
           you all pretend to be that bad group ((villains))

02   *suwedo kowe A ((name)). heh heh heh heh*
           bad.there you(S) A ((name))   heh heh heh heh
           especially you A. heh heh heh heh

She also contextualizes the event in terms of movie making when she uses the presence of the ethnographer and the institution of the film-making enterprise as an account to give weight to her directives:

(23)

01 Woman: *kumwa pahn kihsang ahmwa seht   kan*
           you(D) will   take   from   your(D) shirt those by you
           you will take your shirts off

02   *pwe   lihe   pahn wiada kasdo*
           because woman.this.by.me will   make   movie
           because this woman will make a movie

Here the woman perhaps draws on other layers of significance in this interaction. The movie is being made by a woman (myself), which gives me some authority and also casts me in the role of director, yet I have no voice as my grasp of Pohnpeian was rudimentary at the date of this interaction, during my first trip to Pohnpei in the summer of 1990. By recontextualizing the event in terms of my video, the woman adds voice to my authority and position.

In the previous excerpts it becomes clear that though the woman does not have an official place in the formal sakau (tradition dictates the pounders must be men with their shirts off), she actively participates and comments on the action. She constitutes an authoritative stance by constantly redefining the activity in terms of movie making (only one other mention is made of the movie and no one else mentions the movie maker) rather than sakau. That she is not part of sakau in no way makes her participation less public. The practice of kava or sakau reconstitutes a hierarchy from those present (see chapter 1, in this volume). If hierarchy is being constituted here it is not without significant input from at least one female participant, even to the point of constructing a place for herself to voluntarily (and appropriately within the Pohnpeian modesty practice) give up to someone (often one who is actually lower in status). In Pohnpei and elsewhere, modesty can serve to elevate or confirm one's own status. The previous interaction shows the Pohnpeian woman's strong voice in defining the reality of the movie making and linking it to other Pohnpeian cultural realities. Though women on Pohnpei may be excluded from pounding sakau, this should not be assumed to mean that they are excluded from negotiating the significance of such exclusion.

Linking the first interaction to the second, each woman takes a strong role in assigning meaning to the interaction: One using directives in honorific speech; the other constitutes herself as an authority and critic. The bystander status of the woman in the second interaction can be seen as a position of strength and security, as she can be aggressive in her humor and assign comeuppances without fearing her own, because women do not pound sakau for chiefs. This conservation of power is a theme running throughout Pohnpeian interactions and may in fact be a key component in the fact that chiefs do not use honorific speech, a fact that gives them automatically a comparative position of both strength and immunity from mistakes and the resultant shame.

Each chief in each interaction uses strategies of indirection and collaboration. In the second interaction, the second-ranking chief does not tell those running away to come; he tells others to tell them. He also tells others to tell them to take their shirts off. He uses collaboratively worded utterances, such as "join the pounding," and moderates the force of his urging with encouragement: "just come and pound, you don't have to drink it." In this way chiefs can conserve their power and limit risk of defiance. The chief's voice has been multiplied through the collaboration and cooperation of other voices, often quite literally, as in the second interaction where the woman, the menindei, and the pounder all issue commands at the behest of the chief. The participants are thus empowered by the delegation of directives at the same time their delivering of them (the chief's words) enhances his power and status.

Likend's (the Paramount Chieftess) speech: Interaction 3

The importance of building power from below can be seen in a speech by the paramount chieftess at a large community-wide feast, shown in excerpt 25. The speech is a response to a high-titled man, N, who complained that the women of the *pwihn* (a group of communities) had not worked hard enough in preparing the feast. The event is a *kamadipw en wahu*, or feast of honor. These feasts are held at the beginning of the yam harvest to show honor and pay tribute to the chiefs and the chieftesses. The significance of the chieftess's speech can be understood given the importance of public displays of service and demonstrations of honor through behavior and prestations to chiefs (discussed in more detail in chapter 7). If the women's service is publicly labeled as deficient (as is claimed by the man), this is humiliating and dishonoring to them as well as to the chiefs and chieftesses. Because rises in status through the title system are dependent on public performances of honor and the tangible results of hard work, such a negative characterization can have serious future consequences.

The menindei, or master of ceremonies, introduces the chieftess's speech after she notifies him that she wishes to speak to the gathering. It is part of his job to see that participants in the feast event are notified of the sequence of rituals and of the wishes of the high-status people. He introduces the chieftess's speech as one that will give advice to the women. The chieftess, however, recontextualizes her speech as one that will not give advice. The text of the menindei's introduction is shown in excerpt 24:

(24) Menindei's introduction

01   *na kumwail lihakan   kumwail menlau*
     so you(P)   women.those.by.you you(P)   thanks/please
     so all you women you all please

02   **patohdo**   *ansouwet Likend pahn* **mahsen**.
     LocVerb[HUM].here now   chieftess will speak[EXAL]
     come here now the chieftess is going to speak

03   *kumwail menlau*   **patohdo.**   *kumwail*
     you(P)   thanks/please LocVerb[HUM].here you(P)
     you all please come here toward me you all

04   **tungoalenki** *kaweid, pahn sang Likend.*
     have[HUM]   advice,   will from chieftess
     will have advice from the chieftess

He uses an other-lowering verb to refer to the women's action of coming to hear the speech (patohdo, "come"), but he modifies it with the addition of an offer of gratitude for their compliance (*menlau*, "thanks") in line 01. The chieftess's speech is referred to as *mahsen*, the other-raising or exaltive word for the speech of high-status persons. Thus he indexes two different status levels of women. As illustrated shortly, the chieftess in contrast links herself with the lower-status women in a strategy to empower them (share power) and join with them as their representative in refuting N's claim.

That the menindei singles out only women as the addressees of the chieftess's remarks is interesting. It is possible that he has misunderstood the reason for her wishing to speak, or that he has assumed that because of N's remarks about the deficiencies of the women, she is going to lecture the women. The chieftess immediately contradicts his interpretation; her first words are "no advice." Rather she says the women give her advice. She then performs the formulaic and ritual apology that accompanies all public speeches delivered in the presence of the paramount chief or secondary chief, those by women as well as men: *keipweni*. Keipweni is literally to lower one's body in the presence of a spirit or the humans serving as intermediaries between the people and the spirits (Mauricio 1993:147). It is translated by some as an apology for unworthiness. The chieftess publicly acknowledges the chiefs, another high-titled man, and specifically gives honor (*wahuniki*) to the heads of the communities and any other royalty present and the royal children.

(25) The chieftess's speech:

01 *sohte kaweid. irail me   pahn kaweid ie*
    not   advice   they   the.ones will   advise   me
    not advice. they are the ones who will advise me

02 *keipweni*
    lower myself
    I ask forgiveness for my unworthiness

03 *pahn kupwuren*   *Isipahu, Iso Nahnken, Luhk*
    under desires/thoughts[EXAL].of chief   second.chief   Luhk
    in the presence of/under the protection of the highest chief, secondary chief, and Luhk
    ((title))

04 *oh wahuniki (?) oh koarosie Soumas akan*
    and honor.about (?) and all.here   Soumas   those.by.you
    and honor (?) and all the Heads of communities

05 *nan   pwihn keieu, oloiso   kan   ma pil*
    inside section first   royalty[EXAL] those.by.you if   also
    of Section One, the royalty, and also if

06 mie   serihso.
    there.are   royal.children[EXAL]
    any royal children are present.

Many speechmakers begin by humbling themselves with a self-lowering verb, but in the chieftess's speech, after the required formulaic *keipweni*, which prescriptively precedes all speeches, the next three honorific words are exaltive words. It is a very skillful version of a formulaic opening, placing her speech in the context of tradition and under the auspices of the most powerful members of society. After paying honor, she announces the reason for her talk. She says it is to give praise (as she has just done), but also it is to respond to N's remarks. She in fact makes N responsible, the *cause* of her standing up. This contextualizes her remarks not as pertaining just to women but to men and a result of the actions of a man.

    She raises herself, not only physically but by referring to her standing up, not with a humiliative verb but with a common one (*uhda*). The humiliative form is usually chosen in these instances, especially when one is standing in the presence of the chief. She, however, does not construct her act of standing to be of low status.

07 *rahnwet i*
    today   I
    today I

08 *pil pekida ei ansou pwe   i en iang*
also request my time   because I to join
also request some time in order to join in

09 *pateng   kapinga ahpw mehlel N ((title))*
be.together to praise   but   really   N ((title))
giving praise/thanks but really N

10 *me   kareieng ei uhda,*
the one cause.to   my standing.up
is the one who caused me to stand up

Then she uses reported speech (dene is the reported speech marker) to criticize N. The reproach is made in a humorous manner and elicits laughter. She repeats N's criticism of the women and repeats it as the cause of her "standing up" in a position of authority.

In the following section the words *tungtungoalehla* and *sak* are used. They are humiliative and exaltive forms of eating, respectively. That the chieftess uses the word *sak* is significant. She thus includes very high-status women in N's criticism of those who are just eating but not helping. Sak is the word for eating of the second-ranking chief and chieftess. Food for the chieftess herself is *pwenieu*, for the paramount chief and certain titles of his clan *koanoat*.

11 *pweki e kasalehda me. dene*
because he showed   this it.is.said
because he showed this. It is said

12 *pwopwoud mwahl*   ((group laughter))
marriage   useless
spouses are useless

13 *iang **tungtungoalehla** de **sak**   ahpw*
join   eating up[HUM]   or eat[EXAL] but
they just join the eating, but

14 *sohte katepe. ih karepen ei **patohda**   uhda.*
no   worth.   it cause of my LocVerb[HUM].upward stand
don't provide anything. this is the cause of my standing up

The chieftess's second use of the term for "stand" is preceded by a humiliative verb of motion. This time she modifies her action of standing and indexes low status. In the next section, the chieftess invokes the past and so frames her response to N's criticism as knowledgeable and authoritative, based on her history of interacting with the women he is criticizing. She incorporates the women as instrumental in her own rise in status to the paramount chieftess; they have continuously given her help in addition to honor and love.

15 *I tamataman mwohn pahr ehu de riau samwalahr*
I remember   before year one or two gone.already
I remember one or two years ago

16 *me i* **patohda**   *mwohn kumwail pwihn keiehu*
    that I LocVerb[HUM].upward before you(P)   group first
    that I stood up before you all in Section One

17 *Areu nan kousapw Areu ahpw nan   lepidi*
    Areu inside community Areu but   inside section.down
    Areu, in the community of Areu but in Section

18 *keiehu.(?)ih sohla   itar   mwohmwod*
    first   (?) it no.longer enough sitting
    One. it is no longer enough for me to sit

19 *i direkihla   uwen ei kaping pweki   sang ni*
    I plentiful.give size.of my praise   because from at
    I give fully the amount of my praise/thanks because from

20 *ei kesepwilsang   Likend saikinte alehdi*
    my change.of.status.from chieftess not.yet   take.down
    my rise in status to chieftess I have not yet finished

21 *soahngen mwohmwen sansalamwahu de mwohmwen*
    the.kind.of appearance of show.good   or appearance.of
    getting the kind of good demonstration or appearance of

22 *limpoak mehlel. kaiden pil   wahu te,*
    love   truly.   not   also honor only
    true love. not only honor

23 *wahu iangaki limpoak me i*
    honor join.with love   that I
    honor joined with love that I

24 *alehdi sang kumwail lihen   lepidiwet*
    get   from you(P)   women.of section.this
    have gotten from all you women of this section

After invoking memories of love and help and appealing to emotion, the chieftess eliminates the men from her praise. Thus she turns the criticism around and calls the *men's* behavior into question. They, by implication, have not honored, loved, and helped her enough. Right after she implies this, and laughs, she humbles herself with the use of a self-lowering form of have.

25 *mwein kaiden ohlakan,   mwein*
    maybe   not   men.those.by.you maybe
    maybe not those men, maybe

26 *kumwail lihakan.   ((small laughter))*
    you(P)   women.those.by.you
    all you women.

Next, she says that she is going to plant a yam to symbolize the cooperation of the women. By using yams, the chieftess links her recognition of the women to a traditional and prestigious symbol of status and achievement. Yams are the symbol of procreative and productive power on Pohnpei (see chapter 7), and are the focus of prestige competitions (see Kihleng 1996 for a discussion of women's exhange practices).

The chieftess praises the women for their help. She states that she has only been the paramount chieftess for two years and is used to serving rather than being responsible for their welfare. This captures well the responsibility the Pohnpeian chiefs and chieftesses feel for their constituents. By using the adjective "young," and by referring to a child, the chieftess asks for the kind of help young people need: guidance and nurturing. She thus reverses the usual roles of chieftess and subordinate and raises the status of the women as knowledgeable caregivers.

27 *rahnwet, i pil **tungoaleniki***
    today   I also have[HUM]
    today I also have

28 *ehu kaping kalangan. nin duwen dahme*
    one praise thanks.   according.to what
    another praise and thanks. according to what

29 *sansalada **sapwellimomwail** wahu rahnwet*
    clear.become your(P)[EXAL]   honor today
    has become clear by your honor today

30 *me   pil kisin doropwe pwe   duwen*
    this.one.by.me also small paper   because about
    here is also an envelope because this is the way

31 *i kin   koasokoasone ei **tungoal**   program*
    I always organize   my Ps.Cl.[HUM] program
    I always organize my humble program

32 *ma i pahn alesang wasakis   kutohr   riau*
    if   I will   take.from some place small yam (lit. egg) two
    I will get from someplace two small yams

33 *i pahn kapwuredieng   wasahu lihen   wasahu*
    I will   put.back.down.toward place.one woman.of place.one
    I will put back/leave one of them to the women of this place

34 *ehu pwe   i tamataman   dahme i kasalehda*
    one because I.am.remembering what   I showed
    one because I remember what I showed ((have said before))

35 *kitail lihakan   en miniminpene,   oh kumwail*
    we(P) women.those.by.you to cooperate.together and you(P)
    we women must cooperate together and you all

36 *saweseie pwe   inenen pwulopwul i seri*
    help.me because really young   I child
    help me because I am really young, I'm a child

37 *nan dohkwet i mah paliwaret sounpahren*
   in   work.this I old   body.this   year.of
   in this work I am old, my body is many years old

38 *tohto ahpw ei   lemelem pwulopwul   pweki*
   many but   my thinking young   because
   but my thinking is young because

39 *i   sahn   ih me   i   ahn*
   I   not.accustomed.to   that's.it   I   accustomed.to
   I'm not accustomed to—that's it—I'm accustomed to

40 *pahpah i   sahn*
   serving   I   not.accustomed.to
   serving I'm not accustomed to

41 *kohwaki   de apwali   aramasakan.*
   trusteeship.about   or   take.care.of   people.those.by.you
   the trusteeship or the taking care of people.

42 *i peki remwail   pahrkei*
   i ask   location.of.you(P)   years.some
   I asked you all some years

43 *samwalaro   kumwail en seweseie oh utungie pwe*
   already.gone.there   you(P)   to help.me   and prop.me because
   ago you all to help me and prop me up because

44 *ma i   pahn ale utuht ei kupworoporki me i   kak koahiek*
   if   I   will   take prop   I   hope.about   that i   can   capable
   if I take your propping up I hope that I can be capable

45 *pwehki kumwail ah ma   soh ah   ih pahn mwohmwen*
   because you(P)   but if   no   then it will   appearance.of
   because of you all, but if not then it will show

The chieftess links her ability to be the chieftess to the women's ability to "prop her up" and then links this back to N's criticism. Without the women's help, she herself would just be sitting and filling her stomach and not doing anything (just what N has criticized the women for). Then she thanks N, adding before his name a high-status pronoun, *komwi*. She thanks him for giving her an opportunity to take action. Thus his negative action is recontextualized as positive. She then directly links her thanks with a redistribution of the tribute that has been given to her in the form of cash. She constructs the women as inheritors of wealth and helpers of men in the future.

46 *me I pahn mwohmote wia audaude kapedeie   me soh*
   that I will   sit.only   do   filling   stomach.my   that not
   that I will only sit filling my stomach that

47 *katepe ieu. eri ((laughs)) kalangan en **komwi**   N*
   worth   one   so   thanks   to you(S)[EXAL]   N
   is worthless. so ((laughs)) thank you N (man's title)

48 **komwi**   *me*   *kamwekmwekidier rahnwet. oh*
   you(S)[EXAL] the.one cause.me.move.already today   and
   you are the one who caused me to take action today, and

   ((laughs))

49 *pwehki e sohte mehkot me i kak* **patohwan**   *mehn*
   because it not   something that I can TranVerb[HUM] thing.to
   because there is nothing that I can say that

50 *kak kaitar*   *de wia kaweid ohng lihen*
   can cause.enough or do   advice for   women.those.by.you
   can be enough or that will give advice for the women of

51 *pwihn keieu ah ei kaping mihmi ni kisin*
   section first but my praise stays at small
   Section One but my praise is in a small

52 *daropwekis me i iang alehdi rahnwet*
   paper.small that I join get   today
   envelope that I got today

53 *i pil men kitail koaros en* **sapwellimankipene**
   I also want us(P) all   to have[EXAL].together
   I want us all to have together ((share))

54 *de* **tungoalenkipene** *ei* **tungoal**   *talate*   *eisek,*
   or have[HUM].together my Ps.Cl.[HUM] dollar.only ten
   or humbly have together. I have only ten dollars

   ((laughs))

55 *eh soh. kamwan met.* **komw**   *lih*   *kaun en pwihn*
   eh no. joke   now. you(S)[EXAL] woman leader of section
   eh no. I'm joking now. you, the woman head of the section

56 **komw**   **patoda**!   *oh ale oh nehk   ohng*
   you(S)[EXAL] LocVerb[HUM].up and take and distribute to
   you come up! carry this and distribute it to

57 *lih   soumas en kousapw pwihn- kousapw weneu. kitail*
   woman leader of community section- community six.   we
   the women leaders of Section Six. We all also can

58 *en pil kak sohsoki oh sowaseki ohlakan   ehu ansou*
   to also can inherit   and help.with men.those.by.you one time
   inherit with and help with these men in a time

59 *me pahn kohdo. kalangan en* **kupwuromwail.**
   that will   come. thanks   to   feelings/heart[EXAL]you(P)
   that will come. thank you.

   The chieftess recontextualizes criticism of the women as an opportunity for her to praise them. She uses her response to characterize the actions of women as cooperative and helpful to herself as well as to men. She links her own power and success to them. She formulates her criticism with honorific vocabulary and established norms for giving honor while standing in a position of authority and making a speech. The chieftess acknowledges all those who contribute to her own success, even N's contribution to the opportunity to showcase her abilities and knowledge and to refute his claims. She restructures the success of the feast of honor event as dependent on women.

Asymmetrical relationships are constituted through her honorific speech. Her own status is high, but not without proper humility. She builds the status of women through her own status and links the status that accrues from their good service to future recognition. The chieftess continually uses such words as "cooperation" and "propping up" to stress the connection between the other women and herself. She invokes the authority of the past as she challenges and renegotiates N's view of reality.

The chieftess's speech shows a Pohnpeian woman's strong voice in contesting and redefining the reality of women's contribution to society and linking it to other Pohnpeian cultural realities. The chieftess takes a strong role in assigning meaning to the interaction using honorific speech, as social meanings are indexed within the message. Hers is a position of strength and security; she uses honorific speech and collaboratively worded utterances to construct a discourse that showcases and multiplies the contributions and strength of the women and joins them with her own high status as royalty. She links past, present, and future. All this is in contrast to N's attempt to differentiate women from men in terms of social worth. Attempts to categorize are, of course, controlling acts. Through honorific speech, the chieftess constructs a socially mediated response to this categorization.

Summary

In many societies, the control of representations of reality and of the means by which they are communicated and reproduced is a source of social power which becomes genderized and, thus, unequally valued. On Pohnpei, all social actors have access to honorific speech, and female members of the community can take an active role by invoking positional identities and guarding the representations of women in their constituency. The use of honorific language not only reifies existing status differences but can be used as a creative force to challenge authority, because it accords prestige to the user, referent, and addressee.

The role of language in producing, reproducing, and transforming notions of reality (Vygotsky 1962, 1978; Giddens 1984) and constructing the sociocultural practices of a community is well established. It is in practice, in daily speech, in the context of particular social and economic relations that women collaborate in the construction of cultural ideologies and representations. Specific structural characteristics of the Pohnpeian polity and honorific vocabulary provide tools for both men and women to legitimize their contestation of entitlement or accrued prestige.

Language is a creative force in these interactions. In verbal transactions, whether in honorific or common speech, in the presence of high chiefs, these women constitute a discourse about representation, one from within the group, one from without, and one from the perspective of the highest rank, that transcends the activity at hand and links it to a larger symbolic scheme.

Notes

1. The chief refers here to one of the other participants.
2. Nda, "to say" is understood to be implied here.
3. The fact that this is almost a metathesis was pointed out to me by Sandro Duranti in an earlier draft.

Chapter 6

Positioned Knowledge

Constructing Asymmetrical Epistemologies

In the Introduction, I described the salient domains for honorific speech forms as bodily location in space, possession, food, and the mental predicates "know" (with "see" as a metaphorical construct for "know") and "say." In previous chapters I discussed Pohnpeian locative verbs as well as possessive constructions. In this chapter I discuss how Pohnpeians status-mark knowledge in honorific speech as well as references to acts of speaking.

Knowledge on Pohnpei is not seen as value neutral but as both life giving and life threatening. Having knowledge increases an individual's manaman or power, and the transmission of knowledge (which can decrease power), like the transmission of manaman, is highly elaborated. In Pohnpei, information is embodied and truth valued by reference to its source, often the spiritual world. The collaborative construction of meaning and reality is stratified as speakers choose humiliative or exaltive marking for their own or others claims to knowledge, references to speech, or acts of seeing. The control of the articulation of knowledge in Pohnpeian society[1] is a focus of this chapter, as the verbs "say," "know," and "see" can each be described as concerned with epistemology (the nature and source of knowledge). I discuss how references to the acts of speaking and knowing are status-marked in honorific speech and how this influences speaker strategies and the organization of information.

Pohnpeian information management is linked to issues of status not only through honorific speech but through modesty practices: "[T]he Ponapean pattern of modesty actually requires that a curer deny his skill" (Riesenberg 1948:406), and "prevents a Ponapean from admitting his skill at anything" (407). As demonstrated in previous chapters, modesty plays an important part in negotiations of status on

Pohnpei and ensures that recognition of status comes from others. Concealment, or as I prefer to call it *conservation* of information, which is discussed in this chapter, includes denial and disclaimers of truth. The term "conservation," I feel, reflects the link between knowledge and manaman and the idea of the explicit management of fragile and potentially diminishing resources. Given Pohnpeian ideologies about the relationship between knowledge and power, the choice of certain conservation strategies has consequences for shaping the nature of events to maximize status.

Language is a crucial tool in the social construction of knowledge functioning not simply as a device for reporting experience but also as a way of defining experience for its speakers (Sapir 1929). Language mediates between individuals and between individuals and the environment (Vygotsky 1962, 1978). The importance of language is both recognized and constituted in Pohnpei by the status marking of verbs of speaking. As Silverstein (1987) notes, verbs of speaking are metapragmatic verbs in that they describe the event of communication with language. Thus it is significant that Pohnpeians status-mark such metacommunicative moments. The event of speaking itself plays a crucial role in our awareness of participant roles, as a sort of prototype act for assessing the "naturalness" or psychological salience of how various referents are coded into agents or patients in language (Silverstein quoted in Lucy 1992).

As shown in this chapter, Pohnpeian knowledge is viewed as socially distributed (i.e., possessed differently by different individuals and different types of individuals), and truth is constantly negotiated. One of the ways knowledge is differentiated is according to status, which conditions epistemological stance; this has consequences for the collaborative construction of knowledge and the negotiation of truth and information:

> Truth, at least in those cases in which we find people busy at defining it or searching for it, is typically a social matter, something that people must reckon with together. This is so not simply because conventions and public criteria are needed for the assessment of truth, but because truth itself becomes an instrument, a mediating concept living in particular practices, through which important social work gets done. (Duranti 1993:218)

In the Solomon Islands, the Kwaterae people describe mana as encompassing not only power but truth (Karen Watson-Gegeo, personal communication), linking truth with social position or status.

The Pohnpeian theory of the subject includes conceptualizing each individual as a container that accumulates and stores knowledge. The sense of the body as a container is common across cultures and derives from human experience (G. Lakoff and M. Johnson 1980). Falgout (1984) reports this container idea on Pohnpei expressed as a basket; baskets are predominantly made and used for holding food. Words in fact are metaphorically like food; they enter the body and are a transforming energy. The metaphoric relationship between words and food can be seen in the proverb *Sohte ohl kin mwuskihla mehkot ahpw pwurehng kangala,* or "No man vomits something up and then eats it again" (a man does not go back on his word) (McGarry ms).

Pohnpeian ideologies of knowledge are thus "embodied" (cf. Falgout 1984), in contrast to Western ideas of knowledge as "disembodied" or external, existing out in the world. The act of knowing on Pohnpei is status-marked according to its bodily location (in a particular person). The phrase "the chief knows" is expressed as "the exalted body knows." There is no noun for "knowledge" in Pohnpeian. Instead, there are knowledgeable persons (those who are *audapan*, "knowledgeable"; *eritik*, "knowledgeable about many things," or "thoroughly knowledgeable"; *eripit, kupwurekeng* [EXAL], or *loalekeng*, "wise, knowledgeable"). Besides these adjectives (which can also be described as verbs because they describe states) is the verb form of "know."

One cannot simultaneously have knowledge and provide it (like food or energy, it is a diminishing and perishable force). Unlike food on Pohnpei, which is abundant, however, knowledge is viewed as a scarce resource. The mysteries of human cognition are linked in important ways to the supernatural on Pohnpei. The link of certain types of knowledge to manaman (supernatural power) is instantiated in the belief that the ultimate source of knowledge is the ancestral spirits, who transfer knowledge rights to individuals in dreams (cf. Falgout 1984). Each Pohnpeian is thus a potential mediator between the spirit world and the everyday "containerized" world of the body. Spirits retain proprietary rights to knowledge and become angered if knowledge is shared with other humans. Thus knowledge is typically not a commodity of exchange and does not increase in value in the manner of other exchange goods, which are expected to be returned at a higher value (see chapter 7, in this volume). Knowledge of medicine, for example, is often not transmitted to a chosen junior family member until the death of the senior is imminent and loss of power no longer relevant (cf. Gewertz and F. Errington 1991).

Sharing knowledge decreases manaman and can prove life threatening. Thus, whereas in American culture you can give someone information without losing it or diminishing your own mastery, in the Pohnpeian conceptual scheme transferring information can result in a loss of life force from the giver and a gain in life force for the receiver. Knowing is expressed in humiliative speech as a transitive act (i.e., with a goal or receiver of the action) and including a transformation of some kind. In transitive clauses, the effects of the action pass over from one participant (the agent) to another. The low-status verb form of "know" is the same as the transitive verb for such acts as "bring," and "take." Speaking is recognized as an important conduit of knowledge. Information is organized, however, to conserve power and to limit sharing it. Petersen (1993) discusses an institutionalized pattern of concealment of information and feelings on Pohnpei (by not speaking), expressed by consultants as *kanengemah*, an idealized character trait of restraint. Concealment of truth or true feelings is also prescribed for Trobriand Islanders as proper behavior (Weiner 1984) to avoid open conflict and by Brison (1992) for the Kwanga of Papua New Guinea. I feel that this restraint, though it may function to avoid interpersonal conflict (cf. Weiner 1984; Brison 1992; Petersen 1993), is also crucially linked to hierarchy, power conservation, the distributed nature of information and knowledge, and views of humans as complicit partners (with the deities) in the engineering of the universe, including procreation and death. Words and truth have dangerous properties and potentials like mana and must be carefully controlled, but they also have great efficacy such as in incantations to bring rain. Speech is action and talk is a causative force.

Validity claims are regularly hedged in an attempt to conserve knowledge and to constrain the exchange of certain information. An important strategy of limiting the transfer of knowledge involves the use of a formulaic phrase to negate the factivity of one's previous stretch of talk. Providing partial or incorrect information is an acceptable strategy to thwart listeners' attempts to obtain and share a speaker's exclusive knowledge (i.e., to limit manaman transfer/power sharing). In an interaction to be discussed shortly, even at the prompting of other Pohnpeian participants, a male participant elects a strategy of conservation of knowledge and invokes the phrase *pirakih me i pwapwa* ("what I am saying is twisted") for his past and future remarks. This is an approved and traditionally authorized strategy of conservation, and the formulaic phrase is regularly used as a closing for narratives of oral histories. Tellers indicate that they have purposely made the story "twisted" to mislead listeners. The following quotes are from Luelen Bernart's written account of Pohnpeian oral history (Fischer, Riesenberg, and Whiting 1977):

> What I am saying is twisted. Let those who know it set it straight (142).
>   Now this is not the direct story, for what I say has glanced off it, but let those who know hear later and set this story straight (154).

These statements suggest an inherent contestability to knowledge, and place responsibility on the audience for discerning truth. Knowledge is presented not as authority but as the first part of a dialogue with other voices. Truth is socially distributed and highly contested. There is a great deal of creative freedom to constitute new "twists" to engage in social interaction yet conserve power.

Status-marked speaking, knowing, seeing

A tension between retaining power by not speaking of one's knowledge, expertise, and thoughts and the necessity to constitute authority through social interaction is mediated in part by modesty practices and other conservation of knowledge strategies and in part by social stratification of acts of speaking and knowing (including seeing) in language. Thus what the chief knows does not have to be revealed or demonstrated to be constituted as powerful. In Oceanic societies there is a precedence for the highest in authority to be in the background and conserve knowledge (A. Strathern 1982). In contrast, if a low-status individual uses the verb "know" in the presence of high-status individuals, his or her power and knowledge is quite literally diminished through language itself. Ongoing processes of thinking, which do not propose a definite epistemic stance, however, are more regularly status-marked for high-status people than for low-status people.

In humiliative speech, a single term is used for the concepts "know", "say" and "see," whereas in exaltive speech finer semantic distinctions are available (following a pattern noted in other domains; see chapters 3 and 4, in this volume), and there is a verb that pertains particularly to the paramount chief's speech, identifying him as the only possible source of an utterance. Table 6.1 shows verb choice from interactional data.

There is some discrepancy between interactional data and traditional sources about the exaltive forms. In two different texts written by Pohnpeians (Cantero ms) and a manuscript containing information about oral history as well as information

TABLE 6.1   Differences between Humiliative and Exaltive Verbs

Humiliative	Exaltive	Paramount Chief Only	Translation
patohwan	mwahngih		know
patohwan	mahsan, -ih	poahngok, -ih	say
patohwan	mahsanih		see

on honorific speech, given to me by consultants on Pohnpei, the verb *ereki* is listed as an exaltive form of "know" together with *mwahngih*, and quite a few verbs are listed as exaltive forms of "see"—*udial* (stare, watch), *sahkih* (glance), and *idawarih* (brighten eyes). For the paramount chief only, the verbs are reported as *langih* (become seen) and *ninlangih* (see). *Idawarih* is reportedly used for both say and see (like *mahsanih* linking say and see for high-status individuals). This does not mean that these lexical items are not in use in some contexts, but in my data I find a smaller set. "Say" and "see" are typically combined as one exaltive term (mahsanih).

The humiliative patohwan is quite polysemous, used as know, say, and see, as seen in excerpts 1 through 3. This verb is the same one used in transitive actions involving movement of objects (see chapter 3). Because of the polysemous nature of patohwan, I translate it in the interlinear gloss as "TranVerb," for transitive verb:

(1) Low-status "knowing"

01 LA: *ma i **patohwante**   i pahn wiada ei tungoal*
         if   I TranVerb[HUM].only I   will   do.up   my   Ps.Cl.[HUM]
         if I had only known I would have fixed my

02   *moange*
         hair this.by.me
         hair

(2) Low-status "saying"

01 L: *eri ngehi- ih **patopatohwanongie** me*
         so   I   he   TranVerb[HUM].to.me   that
         so he was telling me that

02   *re lel mwo*
         they reach there
         they reached there

(3) Low-status "seeing"

01 N: *ma mehn   America pahn **patohwan***
         if   people.of America   will   TranVerb[HUM]
         if Americans are going to watch

02   *kasdohn*
         movie that.by.you
         that movie

Though the humiliative expression patohwan is polysemous for know, say, and see, the chief's state of knowledge is always explicitly expressed and clearly differentiated from the acts of speaking and seeing. The verb *mwahngih* is used for know, whereas the verbs *mahsanih* and *poahngokih* are used for say. Excerpts 4 and 5 refer to the highest chief's knowing. In excerpt 4 he is present; in excerpt 5 he is not. The chief is referred to by the exaltive noun for "body," *kahlap* (i.e., "the exalted body knows"); knowledge is construed as embodied or located within a specific individual.

(4) High-status "knowing" (the chief is present)

01 L: *soahng mwo pil   mwahuer   pwe*
       type   there also good.already because
       that is good because

02   *kahlap   en **mwahngih** me*
       body[EXAL] to know[EXAL] this
       his body ((the chief)) will know this

03 N: *e   mwahngih   me*
       he knows[EXAL] this
       he knows this

04   *kahlap   ketin   **mwahngih***
       body[EXAL] [EXAL] knows[EXAL]
       his body knows

(5) High-status "knowing" (the chief is not present)

01 N: *lahpen ih   paid   pahn kokohla Kolonia?*
       person him/her who.else will go.there Kolonia
       he/she and who else will go to Kolonia?

02 L: *ohle   me   ketin   **mwahngih***
       man.this.by.me the.one [EXAL] knows[EXAL]
       this man ((the chief)) is the one who knows

There is a distinct verb to mark the paramount chief's speaking, *poahngok* (transitive form *poahngokih*).

(6) Paramount chief's "speaking"

01 N: *Mwohnsapw- Mwohnsapw **poahngokih** en wiawi keneine*
       chief-   chief   says[EXAL] to doing careful
       the chief- the chief says to do it carefully

Thus it is possible to identify speech as coming from the highest chief and no one else. The term *mahsanih* is used for the secondary chief's speech and also for other high-status persons, for example, the second-ranking chiefs.

(7) Secondary chief's "speaking"

01 Menindei: *ohlen   nek **mahsanih**onguhk dahme pwungen*
           man.by.you could tell.to.you(S)   what   correct.of
           that man ((the chief)) could tell you the

02   *ahmw pahn mwohd*
           your(S) will   sit
           correct way for you to sit

Mahsen is the nominalized form of the exaltive word for speech, and pato (i.e., with no suffix) is sometimes used as a nominalized form of patohwan (i.e., speech).

In regard to the polysemous humiliative verb "patohwan," patterns emerge that suggest that speakers have strategies to resolve ambiguity, and speakers can choose when to constitute status as a relevant part of epistemological stance. Transcripts of actual speech (discussed later) show that it is in fact important for Pohnpeian speakers to distinguish what is known from what is said. In interactions with the paramount chief and chieftess, common speech verbs are often used to distinguish knowledge from speaking, even though humiliative speech prescribes the same term for both, and even though in interactions where these two activities (speaking and knowing) do not co-occur they are always status-marked with the polysemous term. There also appears to be a relationship between status marking and metacommentary in casual narratives.

Polysemy and patohwan

Speakers cross-culturally construe a metaphorical relationship between the bodily experience of seeing and the more abstract notion of knowing (see G. Lakoff and M. Johnson 1980; Sweetser 1990, 1992); for example, in English the adjective "clear" is often used to refer to a property of knowledge as well as of sight; similarly someone who is "in the dark" (cannot see) does not know. On Pohnpei, this same link of light and knowledge is conveyed with the use of *rotorot* (lit. "dark" reduplicated) for a person lacking knowledge. Many forms of knowledge can be gained through observation, and knowledge can be visually *displayed* through prestations at feasts.

Know, see, and say as concepts are also related, especially when talking in the past sense, where a past act of seeing or saying (i.e., reported speech) is now an act of knowing. Speaking is often expressed metaphorically as an exchange of objects (see Reddy 1979; G. Lakoff and M. Johnson 1980) and vocabulary from the domains of physical motion, object manipulation, and location is often transferred to the "less physical" domains of speaking and thinking (Sweetser 1992:5). In Pohnpeian humiliative speech, the humiliative form of the transitive verb used for moving objects ("bring," "carry," "give") is used for say, know, and see. In exaltive speech, however, see and say can be joined by one polysemous verb (mahsanih), but know is expressed separately (mwahngih), so that real-world sight is not metaphorically mapped onto the cognitive domain of chiefs and deities, perhaps suggesting a more salient connection between the spirit world and knowledge than between the physical world and knowledge.

Although in Pohnpeian low-status speaking is linked to knowing through the polysemy of patohwan, there appears to be a better mapping between see and know than between say and know. This construal is consistent with earlier remarks on the purposeful "twisting" of the truth in speech, so that one's knowledge is explicitly separated from what is transmitted/exhibited in speech. In the following sections I describe how speakers disambiguate speaking from knowing but not seeing from knowing in low-status marking.

The English verbs "see" and "know" can serve equally well as translations for the polysemous patohwan. In excerpt 8, a high-ranking woman relates a narrative to the chieftess. Patohwan is used with the suffix -da, used with verbs of perception or thinking to indicate that something suddenly enters into one's consciousness.

(8)

01 Woman: *ansou me i pahn duduo*?
        time   that I will   bathe
        when I was going to bathe?

02   *ah   i **patohwanda**   me mie*
        then I TranVerb[HUM].suddenly that there.is
        then I suddenly realized/knew/saw that there is

03   *mehkot   nan pwungara.*
        something in   between.them.
        something between them.

This utterance can encompass the meaning "suddenly saw" as well as "suddenly realized." This difference is not crucial for the communication of this information, because an interpretation of what the speaker saw (and the assumed shared cultural knowledge of what it "meant") is provided. What is significant is that the speaker constructs her own knowledge/powers of perception as low status.

In excerpt 9, the same woman also refers to knowledge that comes from witnessing behavior between people. The knower is an idealized member of the community ("no one" in "it is said no one knows"), whose status is also constructed as low.

(9)

01 Woman: *dene   sohte me **patohwan**   dahme*
        it is said no.one that TranVerb[HUM] what
        it is said no one knows/sees what you two are

02   *kumwa wiwia?*
        you(D) doing
        doing?

In excerpt 10 as well, seeing and knowing are equally relevant, because N is talking about my wishing to video-record the sakau ceremony. "Seeing" how it is done is the same as "knowing" how it is done in Pohnpeian contexts of learning, as Pohnpeians regularly cite "watching" as the way to acquire skill (see also Ochs 1988 for Samoa).

(10)

01 N: *apweda   pwe   e   men   **patohwan***
     and.what.else   because   she   wants   TranVerb[HUM]
     and what else because she wants to know/see

02   *wiepe*
     doing about
     how it's done

Although know and see are congruent concepts, using patohwan for both know and say poses problems of ambiguity for speakers. The following excerpts show instances of the actions of speaking and knowing in the same utterance. Speakers typically solve the problem of ambiguity by choosing honorific form for *only one* of the terms, either speaking or knowing. Speakers typically status-mark the first activity in a sequence (whether speaking or knowing) and do not status-mark the second, different activity to more precisely distinguish between these two activities, that is, while they should be using patohwan for both activities, according to prescriptions for honorific speech behavior and according to instances in which the verbs do not co-occur in recorded speech data.

In excerpt 11, the speaker N status-marks the verb of speaking but not the verb of knowing. The humiliative verb pato used for "talk" is the verb uttered first, followed by the common (unmarked for status) form of "don't know" (*sese*). N and L also use *patopatohwan* ("talking"), the reduplicated form of patohwan. What is status-marked is LA's talking, not her knowing. Typically in honorific register sese (lit. soh "not" + ese "know") would become *sohte patohwan*. In this example, however, the speaker uses sese, common speech. The addressee, LA's "not knowing" is *not* characterized as humiliative, which modifies somewhat the force of the remark ("don't join talking [marked for low status], you don't know what I'm talking [marked for low status] about"), and also clearly differentiates what is known from what is said.

(11)

01 LA: *oatilikamw*
     mouth.lying
     lying mouth

02 N: *ke   dehr iang **pato**   ke   sese*
     you(S) don't join   TranVerb[HUM] you(S) don't.know
     don't join in the talking since you don't know

03   *dahme i **patopatohwan***
     what   I TranVerb[HUM]
     what I'm talking about

04 LA: *soh me i patopatohwan*
      no   that I TranVerb[HUM]
      no this is what I'm saying

In excerpt 12, the opposite is found. All the verbs referring to the act of know-ing are expressed in humiliative form and all the verbs referring to the act of saying are in common speech, even though, as mentioned earlier, these activities are regu-larly status-marked when they do not co-occur. The *first* status-marked verb is "know" (in the previous case, the *first* status-marked verb is "say"). Excerpt 12 is a narrative about marital infidelity or improper social relations. N, a woman, relates what she tells to E, a woman who she is describing as engaging in improper behavior. N con-stitutes her own epistemic stance as well as that of an idealized other as humble through status marking the verb "know" although she uses common speech for describing her own and E's acts of speaking. N says in line 03 *ngehi idek* ("I ask"), and in line 04, *e nda* ("she says"), and in line 06 *i ndang* ("I say to"); these are all common verbs. Knowledge is expressed as patohwan (line 08).

(12)

01 NE: *ansou me i pahn duduo?*
      time   that I will   bathe
      when I was going to bathe?

02   *ah i patohwanda*   *me mie*
      then I TranVerb[HUM].suddenly that there
      then I suddenly realized that there is

03   *mehkot   nan pwungara. ngehi idek: ke   pahn*
      something in.between.them I   ask   you(S) will
      something between them. then I asked her "when will

04   *pwurala   iahd? ah e   nda i pahn kohla*
      return.there when   and she say I will   LocVerb.there
      you go back" and she said "I will go to

05   *Lohd*
      Lohd" ((place))

(. . .)

06 NE: *ah i ndang: E ((name)) dene*
      and I say to   E ((name)) it is said
      and I said "E it is said

07   *ihs me ke   pahn pitih.*
      who that you(S) will   cheat
      who do you think you're going to cheat."

08   *E* ((*change in voice pitch*)) *"pwekida"?*
      E   why?
      E said "why?"

09   *dene   sohte   me **patohwan**   dahme kumwa*
      it is said no.one that TranVerb[HUM] what   you(D)
      it is said no one knows what you two

10   *wiwiahn?*
      doing.already
      have been doing?

In both exaltive and humiliative speech, then, a separation between knowing and saying is observed. In the case of exaltive speech, this is done with different honorific verbs; in the case of humiliative speech, where the same verb is used for both, speakers can override honorific prescriptions and use common speech in honorific contexts to make this distinction. The patterns of both exaltive and humiliative thus converge and are coherent with cultural practices of conserving knowledge in speech, so that what is said is not the same as what is known.

Processes of thinking are not humbled in the same way as knowledge states for low-status persons; a low-status person's act of thinking does not propose a definite epistemic stance or involve knowledge transmission. In English the use of a nonfactive predicator such as "think" commits the speaker to neither the truth nor the falsity of the proposition expressed by its complement clause (Lyons 1977: 793). Ongoing thinking processes rather than states of knowledge are often expressed in *common* speech for lower-status persons but are always expressed in exaltive for high-status persons. For example, in excerpt 13, a speechmaker uses as equivalent terms (joined by the conjunction *de*, "or"), the exaltive term for "think" and the common term for "think." The term *kupwur* means think, feel, know, and anything that is inside the body of an honored person, especially a chief, but here the meaning is suggested by the use of the specific common verb used as its equivalent (*medemedewe*) in the phrase.

(13) First young male speaker

25 → *rahnwet kitail en tepda **kupwukupwure** de medemedewe*
      today   we(P) to start   thinking[EXAL]   or thinking
      today let's start thinking or thinking

26   *mahsen   kaperen wet de mahsen   kesempwal wet*
      word[EXAL].of happy   this or word[EXAL] important   this
      about language that is happy or language that is important

In another instance, the common verb *lemelemengki* is used for "thinking about" in a narrative where "knowing" has been consistently expressed as the humiliative *patohwan*.

(14)

01 N: *eri ih me re   lemelemengki me*
        so it that they thinking.about that
        so that's why they think that

In one case in my data, where the humiliative term "patohwan" *is* used for thinking, it is an insult (potentially threatening), preceded by the form of the verb *kadehde*, "to witness with certainty," tying the use of patohwan to the act of seeing and to epistemic stance. L is relating an insult that another person has delivered at an earlier occasion:

(15)

01 L: *dene   ke   **patohwan***
     it is said you(S) TranVerb[HUM]
     it is said you know

02   *dahme I kadekadekuhkih*
     what   I witnessing.with.certainty.you.about
     why I am staring at you

03   *eh nahn? da? kaidehn I 'lel kin   uhk*
     eh friend? what? not   I beauty habitually you(S)
     eh friend? what? not that I'm attracted to your beauty

04   *I **patopatohwan** ma aramas emen kowe*
     I TranVerb[HUM] if person one you(S)
     I'm wondering whether you are a person

05   *de pwise en pwihk io*
     or shit of pig   there
     or a pig shit

Here epistemic stance is in process ("I am wondering"), but it is tied to an act of seeing ("witnessing with certainty"). The potentially antagonistic nature of the utterance may also influence the speaker's choice of humiliative verb for her process of wondering, as seen in chapter 3 (in this volume).

Information management and status

Given that information and the act of conveying information can be status marked in honorific speech, and given the Pohnpeian ideologies about the relationship between knowledge and power, the choice of certain conservation strategies has consequences for shaping the nature of events to maximize status.

Conserving information: Socialization practices

In excerpt 16, a young boy is explicitly socialized not to reveal an incident during which he has injured himself and has therefore shown a lack of skill or personal power. The young boy is telling how he cut his foot when he stepped on his knife (i.e., machete). The man directs the boy not to talk about the incident because it is shameful (showing lack of mastery with a knife). The man uses a status-neutral verb for speaking (*koasoia*) for the talk of the boy. He then switches from the common pronoun ke to the exaltive pronoun komwi to criticize the action he believes showed lack of mastery.

(16)

01 Boy: *i kauwada nei naipo ngehi doakedahng*
          I raise.up   my knife   I   touch.up.to
          I stood my machete up as I reached up

02   *nan keleuko   ngehi tenekihda kiam en kehp*
           in   hibiscus.those I   tie.up   basket of yam
           in the hibiscus bushes to tie up a basket of yams

03   *nan keleuko*
           in   hibiscus.those
           in the hibiscus

04 Man: *oh ke   dehr koasoia pwe   kanamenek*
          oh you(S) don't tell   because cause.shame
          oh don't talk about it because it's embarrassing

           (3.0)

05   *ei? mehnda komwi   en kauwada*
           eh? why   you(S)[EXAL] to raise.up
           eh? why did you stand it up

The boy's narrative retelling is censored and recontextualized into a shameful experience (*kanamenek*, "cause shame"). One of the consequences of not concealing lack of skill is teasing and nicknames that permanently fix embarrassing incidents as labels (cf. Leiber 1984). In fact, the use of komwi (not appropriate in reference to boys) in the last line (05) was interpreted by one consultant to mean that the man was making fun of the boy's talkativeness and drawing attention to the boy's self-raising or boasting. Power comes from the mastery of language and knowledge; examples of a person's lack of mastery should be concealed.

Conservation of knowledge in oral history narratives

The close relationship between status and knowledge can be seen in the following excerpts from a discussion between two men (two bystanders and myself listen) about the history of the island. Status and skill are explicitly linked when competitive banter about skill in making sakau turns into a heated argument about which discussant's family is of high enough status to be chief. The utterance that links information conservation and status is "we're not going to talk about it because we're the ones going to be the paramount chief." Disputes about legitimacy to rule are not uncommon, as noted by Riesenberg (1968) describing the royal succession in the chiefdom of Uh (N's chiefdom):

It is especially in the foregoing description of affairs in Uh that it becomes clear that statements by natives that such-and-such a subclan constitutes the only legitimate royal [paramount chief or Nanmwarki] or noble class [in line for Nahnken, secondary chief] are to be discounted as idealizations, based perhaps on knowledge of a limited period of history or a nostalgic harking back to things as they are supposed once to have been, and sometimes on personal interests. (37)

In Uh, one subclan of clan 2, the Sounpeinkon, formerly furnished the chiefs of the A-line [paramount chief or Nanmwarki]. One day all the men of this line went fishing and during their absence another subclan of the same clan, the Sounpasedo, held a war feast and laid their strategy. When fishermen return from fishing they carry their catch to the community house to be distributed and receive in exchange land produce from the other people who have assembled to await their coming. When the Sounpeinkon arrived at the community house they found that the Sounpasedo had taken all the places of honor on the main platform and had crowned themselves with royal wreaths. The Sounpeinkon were few in number and retired without a fight . . . (38)

Historically, the first Nanmwarki (paramount chief) of Uh was the son of the Nanmwarki of Madolenihmw (as the son would have taken the clan of his mother, the ruling clans of Madolenihmw and Uh are thus different). This links the two chiefdoms under discussion in the argument in important ways.

According to oral historians' accounts, which have now been written down in several places (Hambruch 1936; Fischer, Riesenberg, and Whiting 1977; Hanlon 1988; Mauricio 1993), the first clan to arrive on Pohnpei was the Dipwenmen clan. Following them was the Dipwenwai (L's clan in the following discussion) and the Ledek (S's clan). The Lasialap clan and the Dipwenluhk (N's clan) according to historians are descended from divine beings on the island itself (Hanlon 1988:7). In excerpt 17, two men (L and S) argue about the political charter of the chiefdom of Madolenihmw and which clans are rightful heirs to the throne (or garland). N is from the chiefdom of Uh, whereas L is from the chiefdom of Madolenihmw. N's clan is Dipwenluhk, the clan for which he is claiming highest honors in the discussion. L is disputing this claim. L claims the right to be Nanmwarki for the participants, excluding N (with the use of an exclusive pronoun). But L himself is not of the clan that theoretically ascends to the position of Nanmwarki in Madolenihmw. Only the young boy is of this clan.

As the discussion begins, N boasts that only people like himself from the Uh chiefdom are qualified (in skill and knowledge) to demonstrate sakau making in a movie. N is not behaving according to avowed modesty practices concerning skill and knowledge but is elevating his own status. L counters that N (from Uh) *is* in the video making the sakau (i.e., there is no problem).

(17)

01 N: *mehn   Uh te   mehn kak wia   kasdohn suk   sakau*
　　　people.of Uh only people can doing movie   pound sakau
　　　only people from Uh can make this movie about pounding sakau

(3.0)

02 B: ((laughs))

03 L: *ah ahmw wiahn*
    but your(S) do.already
    but you're doing it already

This does not end the discussion, however, because the boy then restates N's claim to superior knowledge, explicitly characterizing Madolenihmw residents as having lesser skill. Repeating another's assertion can have the effect of beginning an error-correction sequence in American English (Schegloff, Jefferson, and Sacks 1977), but N does not correct or modify his claim. Rather he adds a further challenge: The people of Uh are not cowards. L contests this, reframing a lack of cowardice as boastfulness. N restates his claim of exclusive skill ("we [not you] do it so nothing is wrong/we do it exactly right"). There are no honorific words in this sequence; at the same time, no honorific substitutions would be required given the choice of vocabulary by the speakers. Although *mwohd* ("sit") is sometimes expressed by *patohdi* (Loc-Verb[HUM]-downward), it more often is not in interactional data. The only other verb, *wia*, does not have an honorific equivalent.

(18)

01 Boy: *mehn   Uh te   me   mwahu en wia kasdo*
      people.of Uh only the ones good   to make movie
      only people from Uh are good at making a movie

02 N: *pwe   re   me   nan kapehd tikitik*
    because they the.ones in   stomach small
    because they are the ones with a small stomach
    ((could mean either strong willed or not big bellied))

03 L: *kaidehn nan kapehd tikitik. kala.*
    not   in   stomach small boastful
    not small in the stomach, but boastful.

04 N: *re   kin   kak wia kilikilepw ah*
    they habitually can do   alone   but all
    they always can do it alone and

05   *koaros mwohd (?)*
      all   sit   (?)
      everyone sits (?)

06 L: *mmm?*

07 N: *koaros   mwohmwod ah kiht   (?kilikilepwki)*
    everyone sitting   but we(EXCL) (?alone.with)
    everyone is sitting but we (not you) alone

08   *sohte (?) sapwung*
      nothing (?) wrong
      are not wrong (we do it exactly right)

In excerpt 19, L counters with: "We are not going to talk about it because we (excluding N) are the ones who are going to be chief." Rather than ending the discussion, however, this begins a heated argument about whose knowledge is correct about which clan can provide the rightful heir to the chief. The argument thus shifts from a contest of skill in sakau making to a dispute about legitimacy of authority and knowledge as well as links to sacred power. At the end of the argument, L again uses a conservation strategy, this time the phrase *pirakih me i pwapwa* ("what I'm saying is twisted"), which will cast into doubt everything he has revealed. Thus L is able to both demonstrate his knowledge and conserve it.

When L initially attempts a conservation strategy, he switches to honorific register for the verb "talk" or "say" ("we're not going to talk about it"). He first uses the pronoun *kitail* (inclusive), then corrects himself and switches to *se* (exclusive), excluding his addressee, N.

(19)

01 L: *dahme kita   pahn wia- kitail   pahn- se*
     what   we(D) will   do-   we(P.INCL) will-   we (EXCL)
     what we two will do- we all will- we (not you, N)

02   *sohte pahn **patohwan**   pwe   ih kiht   me*
     not   will   TranVerb[HUM] because it us(EXCL) that
     are not going to talk about it because we're the ones

03   *pahn Nanmwarki*
     will   paramount.chief
     (not you) going to be the chief

N counters this claim and follows it with a remark inferring that L and the others are commoners, rather than chiefly (i.e., equal to everyone else) (*pahrekieng aramas koaros*).

(20)

01 N: *ma sohte Dipwenluhk kumwail sohte pahn Nanmwarki.*
     if   not   Dipwenluhk you(P)   not   will   chief
     if not Dipwenluhk clan, you cannot become chief

02   *kumwa kak pahrekieng aramas koaros*
     you(D) can equal.to   people   all
     you two are like everybody else (commoners)

03 L: ((laughs))

Being equal to everyone else is insulting to Pohnpeians.

N and L then enter into a dispute about the origins of the political charter of the chief of Madolenihmw. The discussion is elliptical and vague with unclear allusions to times and events. Even the two disputants often ask for clarification of each other's remarks. When we translated this discussion, my consultant described it as follows:

"like they're talking about secret knowledge, not really telling." Toward the end of the discussion, L identifies what he feels is the point of their disagreement and makes reference to what others (from a nearby community) have told him. N challenges L's validity claim and judges L's claim to be "a complete lie."

(21)

01 L: *ih men me sohte dehde*
    that's.it that not   clear
    that's what is not clear

(. . . .)

02   *soh kaidehn kumwail kelepw kin   nda me ah*
    no not   you(P)   alone habitually say this but
    it's not only you all who always say this but

(. . .)

03   *pwe   mehn   Wapar me koasokoasoi ie*
    because people.of Wapar that talking   me
    people of Wapar told me

04   *me irail me*
    that they that
    that they

05 N: *dah?*
    what?

06 L: *mwo. ihwasa me Nanmwarki kesepwilda*
    there. it.place that chief   change.status.up
    the place that the chief was crowned

07   *ie*
    there

08 N: *likamw tohr*
    lie   plain
    a plain lie

Two verbs of speaking (line 02 and 03) used in the segment are not in honorific form. The subjects of the verbs are generalized others ("not only you" and "people of Wapar"). By not using honorific verbs of speaking, L neither elevates nor humbles his description of his sources' speech acts and does not status-mark his epistemic stance. N terms L's knowledge of the place the chief was crowned as "a plain lie." This segment shows the contested nature of historical events and genealogies of power on Pohnpei. Sources of knowledge are named as individuals: the chief at one point and residents of Wapar (a neighboring community) at another. Each speaker conserves information by inferring rather than stating stores of meanings and understandings.

N and the boy begin to talk to each other in low voices and L asks whether they are criticizing the discussion as forbidden. The young boy (the only one theoretically in line to be chief) says "no." The young boy then surprisingly acts as an advocate for ethnography, in order to have the oral history "for the record." He claims that the discussion will help my research about customs of Pohnpei. L then uses the phrase *pirakih me i pwapwa* ("what I am saying is twisted," i.e., inaccurate) to negate the factivity of the information he has just given, marking it as invalid, insincere, and nonauthentic.

(22)

01 L: *da   wia?   e keinepwih?*
       what doing? it prohibited?
       what's wrong? is it prohibited/forbidden?

02 Boy: *soh.*
       no.

       (2.0)

03 Boy: *ih soahng me lihen   anane*
       it type   that woman.this needs
       that's the kind of information this woman needs

04→ L: *pirakih   me I pwapwa*
       crooked/twisted that I saying
       it's crooked what I'm saying

Pwapwa is an archaic form of the verb "to speak," which survives in this formulaic utterance, in proverbs, and in an emphatic marker *pwa*. In excerpt 23, N and the boy try to persuade L to discuss history. N uses humiliative speech to say, "Let's not talk in a way that is not correct." L, however, declines ("you can explain it, but as for me, I'll do my own will").

(23)

01 N: *kaidehn kitail   en **patpato** ni sohte pwung*
       not   we(INCL) to talking at not   correct
       let's not talk in a way that is not correct

02 Boy: *lihen   anane meing.   koaros me wahu*
       woman.this needs   high language all   that honor
       this woman needs to understand high language and all that is honorable

03 L: *ah mwahu wia en wehwe ohng kumwail ah*
       but good   do to explain for   you(P)   but
       it's good for you to explain it but

04   *ngehi (.5) I pahn wia insenei*
       me   I will   do will my
       as for me, I'll do my own will

05 S: ((bowing toward where the Nanmwarki will soon appear))
　　　'leliah
　　　greeting

　　　(7.0)　　　((The chief enters and sits down))

06 N: ***komw***　　　***pato***　　　　*pahn* ***kupwur***　　　*S*
　　　you(S)[EXAL] LocVerb[HUM]　under　command[EXAL] S
　　　you move under the chief's command S ((title))

((S, who has been standing, sits down))

Excerpts 19–23 imply a lack of institutionalized control over meaning and, in fact, a striving away from institutionalized history making. Sources of power compete, and the modes or articulation of knowledge are framed as counterfeit in their most institutionalized transmission, as historical narratives.

In oratory, however, the transmission of institutional meanings is controlled and legitimated under the auspices of the chief, as is discussed shortly. It appears that evidential standards for oratory differ from those for oral histories.

Oratory and embodied knowledge

The nature of Pohnpeian oratory is shaped to maximize the status of the chief and the deities. It is a discourse of chiefly authority wherein all speakers' words are metaphorically situated below the heart of the chief and the deities. Speakers first request permission of the chief to speak and then preface their speech with keipweni, which literally means to lower one's body in the presence of a ghost or the humans serving as intermediaries between the people and the spirits (Mauricio 1993:147). Evidentials for a public claim seem to differ from those for private belief as expressed in the above section regarding the genealogy/historical legitimation of the reigning chief.

Permission to speak is symbolically requested of the chief (it is a formality, not a direct request) with the term *sakarada* (sometimes expressed as *sakaradan*, i.e., with the *suffix -en* for "of"), translated as "to beg of a chief" or "to confess." It usually occurs in a nominalized form, as in excerpt 24, where sakarada is used as a synonym for oratory. The chief speaks of the sakarada, or speeches, that have preceded his.

(24) The paramount chief's speech

01 *ni duwen ara* **sakarada** *de sansaleng ohng Isipahu*
　　at about　their speech　or clear.to　for　the chief
　　according to their speeches or what they showed clearly to the chief

That public speech is synonymous with begging or requesting authority from a chief frames public speech as authorized by him.

Keipweni is followed by the phrase *pahn kupwur* (see line 03 in excerpt 25), which is difficult to accurately translate into English. Kupwur means such concepts as "wish, intention, plan, decision, desire, heart" (Rehg and Sohl 1979) pertaining to the paramount chief or deities. Pahn kupwur can mean literally the chest (i.e., upper torso) of the chief, but also can mean something that in English might be expressed as "under the command of the paramount chief" or "under the authority of" or "under the desires of." In oratory, this phrase situates one's words as under (within) the authority of those of the highest rank, including God, the chiefs and chieftesses, and others specifically named, as shown in excerpt 25 in a speech by a young girl, who uses sakarada.

(25) Serepein in Ononleng

01 *mwohn i pahn patohwen doul- doula ei   tungoal*
   before I will [HUM]   go- go on my Ps.Cl.[HUM]
   before I go on with my

02 **sakaradan** *wahu* **keipweni**
   speech.of   honor lower myself
   speech of honor I lower myself

03 **pahn kupwuren**   *samatail Koht*
   under heart/desires.of father.our God
   under the heart/desire of God our father

04 *wahuniki soumwourou kan,   lapalap kan*
   honor.about high.priests   those, large   those
   honoring the traditional high priests, the high people,

05 *pahpa kan,   nohno kan*
   father those, mother those
   fathers, mothers

The speech of a boy (at a Catholic youth gathering) is also situated under God's authority, as well as that of the chieftess and the traditional high priests.

(26) First young male speaker

01 *mwohn i pahn patohwen doula i pahn patohwen*
   before I will [HUM]   go.on I will [HUM]
   before I go on I

02 *doula i pahn wia   tungoal*   **sakaradan**
   go.on I will make Ps.Cl.[HUM] permission.to.speak.of
   go on I will make my request to speak

03 **keipweni**   **pahn kupwuren** *samatail Koht,*
   lower myself under heart/desire father.our God
   lower myself under the heart of our father God

04 *wahuniki erekisohn   Pohnpei ieu. sapwellimahr*
   honor.about body[EXAL].of Pohnpei one their[EXAL](P)
   honor for the body/people of Pohnpei their

05 *likend   koa, oh soumwourou koa me sansal*
    chieftesses those, and high priests   those that show
    chieftesses and high priests that show

Even the chief does not assume rights to speak in oratory without keipweni. Excerpt 27, a speech by the paramount chief of Madolenihmw, shows that he, too, modifies his authority to speak. He situates himself as under the authority of all those in the traditional hierarchy, just as any person would. This is consistent with prescriptions for modesty for all including the chiefs.

(27) Speech by the paramount chief

01 *mwohn ei pahn patohlang   ni ei tungoal   sawas ieu*
    before I will LocVerb[HUM].to at my Ps.Cl.[HUM] help   one
    before I go on with my help

02 *ohng rahn kesempwal en rahnwet. i men*
    for   day important of today.   I want
    for this important day. I want to

03 *wia ei tungoal   **keipweni pahn kupwuren***
    do my Ps.Cl.[HUM] lower myself under feelings[EXAL]
    lower myself under the authority of

04 *samatail koht, Iso Nahnken, Likend,*
    our.father God, secondary chief, paramount chieftess,
    our father God, the secondary chief, the paramount chieftess,

05 *Noahs, oh Ounsouna*
    Noahs, and Ounsouna

(. . .)

06 *i men **patohwan** ong pwihn, eh- kaun en pwihn e sohte*
    I want say[HUM] to group, uh- leader of group he not
    I want to say to the section, uh to the leader of the section, he doesn't

07 *doadoak laud sohte e pwukoa laud, ihte!*
    work   hard not e duty   big, only!
    work hard, that's not his largest obligation really!

(. . .)

In this speech, the chief also uses the verb *patohwan* for his own act of speaking (line 06). Having humbled his words to the level of his audience with an initial patohwan, he later, however, raises himself and the whole group with the use of the inclusive plural pronoun *kitail* (we inclusive plural) plus the exaltive term for the verb "know" (see excerpt 28, line 02). He raises the status of the audience's act of knowing how to show honor to chiefs. However, the modifier *ele* ("perhaps") occurs before this statement, making the groups' knowledge not certain. Cognitive validity is contingent on some display of skill (i.e., prestations) and proper behavior to the chief.

(28) knowing

01   *oh ih me ei tungoal   pato lel   rahnwet. wahu!*
      and it this my Ps.Cl.[HUM] speech reaching today.   honor!
      and this is what my speech reaches today. honor!

02→ *ele   kitail koaros **ketin   mwahngih**. wahu samatail*
      perhaps we(P) all   [EXAL] know[EXAL] honor father.our
      perhaps all of us know. Honor that our ancestors

03   *ko   me   ketin   wiada*
      those the.one [EXAL] make.completed
      made

Rights to speak are also linked to chiefly authority and status at certain points during the sakau ceremony. Specifically, no one is supposed to talk during the interval when the first four cups of sakau are served, which instantiate the power hierarchy of the island. In Madolenihmw, the paramount chief is served first, the secondary chief next, the paramount chieftess next, and finally the paramount chief again. I never observed the rule against talking in literal force; rather, at large events where the chiefs were present, this rule appeared to be interpreted to mean quiet talking rather than loud talking. In excerpt 29, N tells LA and another not to talk because it is not yet the fourth cup of sakau (*sapw*). LA has been telling the story of how she and her companions met some people on the road who tried to dissuade them from coming to drink sakau.

(29)

01 LA: *se   kahngete. kapwkapwuriei   kiht.*
        we(EXCL) refuse.just cause.return.outward us
        we just refused. he tried to turn us back.

02   *se   kahngete.*
        we(EXCL) refuse.just
        we just refused

03 N: *kumwa dehr **pato**   pwe   wie   koanoat*
        you(D) don't talk[HUM] because make chief's.food
        don't talk because we are making sakau for the chief

04→   *saik   sapw*
        not.yet fourth.cup.of.sakau
        and it is not yet the fourth cup

The directive by N not to talk resulted in the participants continuing to talk in a very low volume.

Summary

It is through speech that assertions are made about particular propositions, known or believed. These propositions can be modified by English speakers and Pohnpeian speakers by choice of verb. In English the verbs "know" and "believe" describe different commitments of truth (Lyons 1977:793), "know" being the stronger commitment, claiming an unassailability or well-groundedness. As shown in the formulaic "what I'm saying is twisted," in discussing oral histories Pohnpeian speakers regularly commit themselves not to the truth of their remarks but to the falsity. As another example, the English equivalent of the adverb "apparently" (lit. "open to view, clear, manifest") (i.e., indicating probable truth) is translated in Pohnpeian as *likamw* ("lie") or *likamwete* (lit. "lie + just/only"), indicating the proposition is probably not to be believed.

The metacommunicative act of referring to the activity of speaking as well as knowledge claims are subsumed under the legitimacy of the power hierarchy of the island. The verbs "know," "say," and "see" are routinely status-marked in contexts in which honorific speech is appropriate, constituting a stratified ideology of knowledge, including visual perception, and authorship. Though the same polysemous verb is prescribed for these activities in humiliative speech, speakers show the importance of differentiating between knowing and saying by dropping out of honorific register into casual speech. This resonates well with cultural beliefs about speech transmitting only partial knowledge or inaccurate information. Pohnpeians constitute positioned knowledges. The ritual phrase *pirakih me i pwapwa* allows speakers to both demonstrate knowledge and conserve it. The management of information in Pohnpei is related to power management and conservation, as well as to limiting sharability of power.

Note

1. For a more complete discussion of Pohnpeian practices surrounding knowledge, see Falgout 1984.

Chapter 7

Valuing Stratification

Honor in Oratory and Feasting Practices

Throughout this book I have been looking closely at how social stratification is constructed through "practical activity" (Bourdieu 1977). As Bourdieu (1977) states: "Practice always implies a cognitive operation, a practical operation of construction which sets to work, by reference to practical functions, systems of classification (taxonomies) which organize perception and structure practice" (97). As shown in previous chapters, Pohnpeians constitute status as an important organizing principle, both verbally and visually. Honorific speech is an important tool in this process. In this chapter, I discuss more broadly the concept of honor in Pohnpeian society as it is expressed in a public discourse about honor at honor feasts (*kamadipw en wahu*). In oratory, honor is topicalized, and it is classified as sharing properties with other socially valued cultural ideas and ideals. At public feasts, self-depletion (figuratively through language and literally through resources) is classified as its opposite (accrual).

I argue in this chapter that honor should be reconsidered by social scientists as a set of practices whereby community members are socialized to associate positive attitudes with stratification and dominance (see also Abu-Lughod 1986 for a discussion of the morality of hierarchy in Bedouin society). I propose that honor in Pohnpei and perhaps elsewhere fundamentally and essentially organizes embodied attitudes (including affective displays) about individual social difference. Honor practices particularly (1) positively value and rationalize acts of self- and other-subordination (part of this practice involves discursively construing literal subordination/depletion/humiliation as its opposite, i.e., symbolic elevation), and (2) positively value structural hierarchy, including gender hierarchies. Linguistic forms and feasting practices in Pohnpei contribute to the creation of a homology between getting honor and giving honor, between honor and humiliation/abasement. In Pohnpeian interactions discussed in previous chapters, status is negotiated through modesty and so-called honorific speech (which is actually humiliative and self-subordinating in the majority of instances). How self-subordination becomes praiseworthy and elevated is a focus of this chapter.

In much of the anthropological discourse on honor (cf. Campbell 1964; Herzfeld 1987; Peristiany 1966; Pitt-Rivers 1977), honor is discussed not as it is constituted in interaction but as an intangible moral force guiding participants' actions. Bourdieu (1990), for example, recognizes the processual nature of honor as learned over multiple transactions but describes honor as a diffuse and generalized *sense*: "[T]he sense of honor as a feel for that particular game, the game of honor" (22). My view is that honor is perceived by consultants and ethnographers as a "sense" or "feel" because of socialization practices that link an individual's voluntary participation in social stratification with certain attitudes and emotion states and with the body. Honor thus may be more profitably analyzed as a socialization practice that models positive feelings about stratification and dominance, from the perspective of low status as well as high status. Linking subordination with positive embodied experience is a key to the effectiveness of honorific practices in achieving voluntary social stratification, or self-lowering, building the hierarchy from below, and with the persistence and self-regulation of such systems. Rosaldo (1983) also links feelings with hierarchy when discussing shame in Illongot society. She links shame not with control of the self but "with a set of feelings that relate to the conflicting claims of hierarchy and 'sameness' or autonomy, in Ilongot social life" (139).

In the following sections I show examples of honor as a topic in the oratory of Pohnpeian men and women. Throughout I discuss the construction of a homology between giving honor and getting honor.

Honor and stratification

Previous anthropological discussions of honor centered primarily on societies bordering the Mediterranean.[1] Yet a number of these authors note the relationship of honor to stratification. Abu-Lughod (1986) shows how the code of honor among the Bedouins of the Egyptian Western Desert structures individual behavior to maintain hierarchy. Pitt-Rivers (1966) states that honor is problematic between equals because it "derives from the domination of persons" (60). Bourdieu (1965) similarly sees honor and equality as mutually exclusive: "The ethos of honour is fundamentally *opposed* to a universal and formal morality which affirms the *equality* in dignity of all men and consequently the *equality* of their rights and duties" (228 [emphasis added]). Davis (1977) argues perhaps most strongly that honor is a function of (economic) stratification.

> The essential characteristics of honor are first that it is a system of stratification: it describes the distribution of wealth in a social idiom, and prescribes appropriate behavior for people at the various points in the hierarchy; it entails acceptance of superordination and subordination. Second, it is an absolute system . . . each competitor

> occupies a unique position in the hierarchy. One of the weapons in such discrimination is the distinction between honor–virtue and honor–status . . . third, it does seem to be characteristic of honor that it is associated with integrity: the whole man is contemplated. What a whole man is, though, varies from society to society." (98)

The explicit distinction between "honor–virtue" and "honor–status" mentioned by Davis is a recurrent theme in studies of honor. For Pohnpei (and possibly elsewhere), the link of honor with virtue[2] is a key to the naturalization, embodiment, and reproduction of the types of behaviors Davis calls "honor–status," or those that construct hierarchy.

Though the relation between honor and stratification is widely recognized, most authors (with the exception of Davis) reject stratification as *the* organizing principle behind honor practices (as I am arguing). They claim, for example, that seeing honor as primarily linked to stratification practices fails to account for what is called the "egalitarian" (Stewart 1994:12) construal of honor. This egalitarian notion constructs the "self as a sacred object" or each member of society as possessing honor to the same degree (Stewart 1994:12); that is, honor is described as essentially "individual will" (Peristiany and Pitt-Rivers 1992:222), personal integrity (Davis 1977), a potential or actual moral worth available *equally* to all. The differentiation between self and society is common in this and other definitions of honor. Stewart (1994), for example, refers to "honor in the public sense and honor in the private sense" (12), and Pitt-Rivers (1966) refers to honor as esteem in one's own eyes and the eyes of society (503). But this construal depends on a culturally relative notion of the self as something that can exist apart from society and, in fact, may be an artifact of a particular culture area's construal of "self" rather than a question of deep differences in what "honor" is. For example, the Western model of self sees the individual and the social as opposed, whereas Oceania gives evidence for other views. As Lutz (1985) describes for Ifaluk atoll (Micronesia), what Westerners would call individual attitudes are conceptualized as shared. People of Ifaluk talk of "our insides," not those of a solitary person. As White and Kirkpatrick (1985) explain about the Pacific: "'[T]he person' may not map culturally valued units so much as points of potential disjuncture from such units" (11). Ito (1985) remarks that for Hawaiians, the self "is a socially interactive concept tied to correct social behavior (*hana pono*) between Self and Other" (320), and White (1985) says of A'ara speakers in the Solomon Islands: "A'ara descriptions of personal behavioral traits are basically about *interpersonal* process rather than the characteristics of individuals as social isolates" (341). In Pacific cultures there is no sharp divide between self and society. If, as White (1985) suggests, the individual person maps onto points of social *dis*juncture—one would not expect a notion of personal honor apart from society (but one would expect a notion of personal shame).

If a notion of individual honor covaries with notions of the individual, the "paradox" of honor experienced as both an individual/egalitarian concept and a societal/hierarchical concept can perhaps be resolved. Honor as an aspect of the self (opposed to society) can be viewed as constitutive of a culturally specific relation of self to society and not in conflict with what I am proposing is the more basic underlying relation between honor and stratification or hierarchy.

Honor and sentiment

I have made the claim that honor is a set of practices whereby social stratification is not only naturalized and habituated (e.g., in language and bodily position) but valued. A significant part of this process in Pohnpei involves organizing positive feelings around honor (which is principally shown through subordination). A link between feeling and honor has in fact been noted for honor practices cross-culturally, and most authors include in discussions of honor the notion of sentiment (Pitt-Rivers 1968; Abu-Lughod 1986). In fact, Pitt-Rivers (1968) analyzes honor in terms of "a sentiment, a manifestation of this sentiment in conduct, and the evaluation of this conduct by others" (503). What I would like to discuss here is the relation between sentiment, stratification, and honor—the role of affect or sentiment in embodying and naturalizing stratification through linking honorific practices with shared positive attitudes or emotion. As Foucault suggests, emotions can be "the place in which the most minute and local social practices are linked up with the large scale organization of power" (Dreyfus and Rabinow 1983:xxvi). Friederich (1972:280) shows how grammaticalized honor is linked with affective responses in a discussion of choice of status-marked pronouns in Russian, which can have social as well as affective purposes.

Emotions or sentiments are, of course, cultural rather than natural categories, and cultural beliefs about emotion are linked to broader cultural beliefs about the person (Levy 1984; Harre 1986; Lutz 1988:82). The Western discourse about emotion is distinct from the discourse about emotion in the Pacific (Lutz 1985, 1988; Gerber 1985), for example. Wittgenstein observed that Westerners see emotions as internal events because of a practice of "perceptual introspectionism" (Coulter 1986). In contrast to Westerners, Pacific Islanders offer very few descriptions of internal sensation but, rather, direct their attention externally into the social world (Gerber 1985:137; see also Lutz 1988). Thus I am not claiming to know what Pohnpeians or others are feeling when they practice honor; I am interested in what feeling categories (or perhaps embodied sensory experiences) are linked with honor in discourse. When Pohnpeians link a discourse about honor with a discourse about positively valued affect, specifically *limpoak*, "love" (which I will talk about shortly), the love Pohnpeians talk about is constructed differently from American notions about love. Yet in both cases the term describes a *positive and valued relation between people*. Lutz (1988) compares American and Ifaluk Islanders' (Micronesia) concepts of love:

> Both emotions entail the desire to see the other person's needs satisfied, although those needs are culturally defined in somewhat different ways. Americans focus primarily on the explicit goal of "making the other happy," while the Ifaluk focus on the needs for health, food, and kinship, needs whose fulfilment is not spoken of as having the primary goal of creating happiness. Both are emotions of strength in that the person who experiences them is empowered; that is, each sees him- or herself as capable of fulfilling the other's need. (146)

It is just because emotion is culturally constructed that links between the body and the social world can be drawn (Lyon and Barbalet 1994:48) and the embodiment of social values can be recognized and analyzed. As I have discussed in more detail in chapters 3 and 5, posture and body position in space are significant ways that Pohnpeian honor practices are embodied.

A common site for the organization of positive embodied attitudes about self-depletion is in the oratorical and tribute practices at public feasts. In Pohnpeian oratory where honor itself is the topic, honor is objectified and celebrated as an essential ingredient to the continuance of life, as something that comes from a specific place in the heart and is joined with love. Honor is characterized as something that can be made, shown, and even quantified. In the following data segments I illustrate how grammaticalized honor (described in previous chapters) works together with a metadiscourse about honor to construct (1) an embodied notion of honor linked to positive affect and a valued relation between people, and (2) a homologous relation between status depletion and status elevation, or the giving and receiving of honor.

In the speech by the paramount chief of Madolenihmw (excerpt 1), *wahu* ("honor") is located within the physical body of each individual. Honor comes "not from the arm, not from the leg, but from only one place in the heart." Honor is the very core or life center of the body, in contrast with legs and arms which are peripheral. One can live without an arm or a leg but not without part of one's heart. The source of honor is inside the body, where feelings and thoughts reside. As mentioned in the previous chapter, Pohnpeians see the body as a vessel or container for thoughts and feelings; feelings and thoughts are not resident in the head but in the whole body and must be shown outwardly to be known by others.

(1) The paramount chief's speech

01 *wahu sohte kohsang ni pehn aramas*
    honor not   come.from at arm.of person
    honor does not come from the arm of a person

02 *wahu sohte kohsang ni nehn aramas.*
    honor not   come.from at leg.of person
    honor does not come from the leg of a person.

03 *wahu kohsang   wasatekis   ni mohngiong.*
    honor comes.from place.only.small at heart.
    honor comes from only one place in the heart.

Honor is thus represented as emanating from the heart and also as part of the human body, something inherent and inherited; wahu has a definite location in the body of each individual. The linking of specific affective states with specific body organs is common in Pacific societies and elsewhere (cf. Besnier 1990).

In the next two excerpts, honor is joined with love by the use of a serial verb construction (4:04–05), by the verb "join" (3:03) and by defining the two words "love" and "honor" as "the most important things in existence" (4:04–06). In excerpt 2, a speech by the chieftess, honor (wahu) is explicitly joined with (*iangaki*) love (limpoak).

(2) The parmount chieftess's speech

01 *soahngen mwohmwen sansala mwahu de mwohmwen*
    type of   appearance of show   good   or appearance of
    the type of displays and good shows or displays of

02 *limpoak mehlel. kaiden pil wahute,*
    love   truly.   not   also honor only
    true love. not only honor,

03 *wahu iangaki limpoak me   i*
    honor join with love   the one I
    honor joined with love is what I

04 *alehdi   sang kumwail lihen   lepidiwet*
    take down from you(P)   women of section this
    have gotten from all you women of this section

In excerpt 3, a speech by the section head of a community (a man), love and honor are again discussed together and are characterized as the most important things necessary to continued existence. The suffix *-pene* is used serially both with love and with honor. Pene is one of the directional suffixes for verbs and means "toward each other," often translated by consultants as "together." The speaker states that "loving together/toward each other" (*limpoakpene*) and honoring "toward each other/ together" (*wahupene*) are the "most important things" in the continuance of "being alive." The speaker repeats the phrase "most important" (*keiehu kesempwal*) at the beginning of this short section and at the end. Thus two things are first—love and honor. The serial construction *limpoakpene wahupene* (lines 04 and 05) links love with honor.

(3) Speech by the section chief of local community

01 *dahme keiehu kesempwal ni duwen   atail   pahn*
    what   first   important   according.to our(INCL) will
    what is most important according to our future

02 *ketin   ieias,   kupwkupwure*
    [EXAL] being.alive[EXAL] desiring/feeling[EXAL]
    existence, is desiring/feeling

03 *de roson   en*
    or strength/health of
    or the strength of

04 *sapwellimatail limpoakpene*
    our[EXAL](p)   love.together/toward.each.other
    our love together

05 *wahupene   me   pahn*
    honor.together/toward.each.other the.one will
    honor together that is what will be

06 *keiehu kesempwal.*
    first   important.
    most important.

The speaker uses the honorific (exaltive) term *ieias* for "being alive/living," linking low- and high-status persons' existence together. The exaltive possessive pronoun "our" (sapwellimatail), which modifies love and honor, similarly links low- and high-status persons' loving together and honoring together. The suffix -pene suggests symmetry—an egalitarian flow of love and honor of high and low status toward each other; an equality of reciprocity is constructed about love and honor. However, as the speaker continues (excerpt 4), the arousal of feelings—as in love, desire (*inangih*)—and togetherness is linked to service (*pahpah*) to the chiefs. Subordination (to the chief's desires *kupwur*) is thus specifically linked to feelings of love and desire.

(4)

01 *pein kiht   kamelele oh men*
    self   we(EXCL) believe   and want
    by ourselves we believe and want

02 *patehng niduwen   aht   inangih*
    join.to   according.to our(EXCL) arouse.feeling/desire
    to join according to our arousal of feelings/desires

03 *pahpah **kupwur**   en Isipahu   Isonahnken*
    serve   desire[EXAL] of highest.chief secondary.chief
    to serve the desires of the highest chief, the secondary chief

Whereas in the previous part of the speech (excerpt 4) the speaker uses exaltive forms for both the chiefs and the people together, just before talking about the arousal of feelings and service to the chiefs, he disjoins low-status persons from high-status persons by the use of the exclusive form of the pronoun "we" (*kiht*), line 01, and "our" (*aht*), line 02. The chiefs and chieftesses are thus excluded from the linking of love/desire and *service*. Low and high status are also disjoined when the aroused feelings of the people are expressed in status-unmarked form (inangih), whereas the feelings of the chiefs are expressed in exaltive form (kupwur). Previously in the same speech (excerpt 3), the chiefs and lower-status persons were joined with a single exaltive verb and possessive pronoun. Here, however, exclusive and low-status forms construct hierarchy, linking positive feelings of only low-status persons with subordination or service to the chiefs and chieftesses.

    In excerpt 5, by another speaker on a different date, togetherness (*-pene*) recurs as an important word connected with wahu *(kitail ketkipene wahu,* "we (P) bring toward each other honor"). This phrase is repeated on two different occasions during this speech. The source of honor is located by this speaker, an older woman of medium rank, as inside the family (again the source of life). Honor is thus tied to family values: kin relationships, nurturance, intimacy, sharing, obligation.

(5) Speech by a titled woman at a community feast to prepare fish for presentation to the paramount chief, involving special cutting and specially woven presentation baskets

01 *kitail ketkipene*   *wahu oh dahme*
   we(P) TranVerb[EXAL].with.toward.each.other wahu and what
   we bring together honor and what

02 *mwomw   pwukat wiada ohng Pohnpei oh kitail*
   mwomw.fish these   make   for   Pohnpei and we(P)
   these fish make for Pohnpei and we are

03 *peneinei.*
   family
   family.

(. . .)

06 *ihme keiehu peki kitail en*
   it.that first   ask   we(P) to
   what is most important to ask is that we

07 *ketkipene*   *wahu sang nan*
   TranVerb[EXAL].with.toward.each.other honor from inside
   bring together honor from in

08 *peneinei nan   tehnpaskan*   *oh*
   family   inside feast.houses[EXAL].those.by.you and
   the family, from in the chief's feast houses

09 *lelehng   nan kousapw.*
   reaching.to inside community
   and reaching out into the community.

Honor flows from the family, from the high-status feast houses and reaches out into the community. In excerpt 3 and 7, as well as other speeches, possessive pronouns referencing acts of honor by low-status persons are expressed in exaltive form (e.g., sapwellimatail), thus literally elevating the status of those whose status is diminished through the process of giving honor to chiefs.

    The concept of togetherness or honoring toward each other initially constructs a reciprocity and symmetry that would seem to be antithetic to stratification and subordination, but, as discussed in chapter 2 (in this volume), intimacy and solidarity are part of the construction of hierarchy in Pohnpei. In excerpt 7, the chief specifically states that "we are all the same":

(6) The paramount chief

   ahpw maingkoa   kitail duwepenehte.
   but   honored.people we(pl) same.together.just
   but honored people we are just the same.

Honor is objectified in these speeches as something that is shown, made, and made clear. Words such as *mwohmwen* ("appearance of") and *sansal* ("evident," as in showing clearly) reappear continuously with wahu, as excerpt 7 shows:

(7) The paramount chieftess

01 *ehu kaping kalangan. nin duwen dahme*
    one praise thanks   according.to what
    another praise and thanks. according to what

02 *sansalada   sapwellimomwail wahu rahnwet*
    clear.become your(P)[EXAL]   honor day.this
    has been shown by your honor today

In excerpt 8, a speech by the chief, wahu is "made" (*wiada*). The suffix—*da*, "upward" on the verb *wia* ("to do, make")—signifies that an action has been carried through to its logical conclusion.

(8) The paramount chief

01 *kousapw en pwihn keisuh rahnwet. doadoak riau wet de*
    kousapw of group seventh today   work   two these or
    kousapw of Section Seven today. two works or

02 *mwekid riau wet patpene   oh wiada rahnwet,*
    move   two here be.together and make today
    two activities together are going on today.

03 *me wiada wahu rahnwet.*
    that make honor today
    that [are] making honor today.

The chief describes how shows of honor can be deficient or "not enough." Deficiency is the opposite of goodness. The word *iou* (excerpt 9, line 01) can also be used to mean "sweet, tasty, delicious."

(9) The paramount chief

01 *mwomw   iou wahu*
    appearance/tradition good honor
    honor is a good tradition

02 *maingko   i sohte men pilada*
    honored.people I not   want choose
    honored people I don't want to choose

03 *menia wahu me   mwahu oh menia wahu*
    which honor the.one good   and which honor
    which honor is the one that is good and which honor

04 *me   sohte itar*
   the.one not   enough
   is the one that is not enough

Although I do not have any data on word etymology, there is an obvious relation between the Pohnpeian adjective for "good" (*mwahu*) and the word for honor (*wahu*) (see excerpt 9, line 03). Good news is *rongamwahu*; having a good reputation is *adamwahu*.

In summary, the source of honor is embodied in a specific organ. Honor is linked with positive feelings—love and togetherness, desire, and life itself, as well as such family values as kin relationships, nurturance, intimacy, sharing, and obligation. Desire is linked to service to the chiefs and honor constructed as something shown through acts of subordination.

Chiefs and chieftesses reward wahu through praise, material goods, and promotions to new, higher titles. In excerpt 10, the chieftess links her gift of money to the honor she has received (see Irvine 1989 for a discussion of linguistic elements as goods and services exchangeable against other goods and services, including cash).

(10) The paramount chieftess

01 *ehu kaping kalangan. nin duwen dahme*
   one praise   thanks   according.to what
   another praise and thanks. according to what

02 *sansalada **sapwellimomwail** wahu rahnwet*
   clear.become your(P)[EXAL]   honor today
   has been shown by your honor today

03 *me pil kisin doropwe pwe   duwen i*
   that also small paper   because about   I
   there is also an envelope because the way I

04 *kin   koasokoasone ai **tungoal** program*
   always organizing   my [HUM]   program
   always organize my program

((the envelope contains cash—later this envelope is specifically given to the woman who is head of the section, see excerpt 11))

Honorific speech plays an important role in this exchange—constructing a balance of reciprocity that at the same time entails hierarchy. The exaltive possessive pronoun sapwellimomwail, "your (P)," is used for the people's showing of honor, raising the status of the honor they have given the chieftess, whereas the humiliative possessive pronoun *ai tungoal* is used for the chieftess's "program" or her gifts to the people to show her praise. This choice of pronouns (*sapwellimomwail wahu* vs. *ai tungoal program*) can be seen as lowering the status of the chieftess's program, that is, what she gives back to the people in exchange for their honor (which she exalts). This constructs inequilibrium out of the exchange. Her use of the humiliative for her return gift is self-lowering but also lowers the value of the people's reward. What remains high in the balance is the honor given to the chieftess. As discussed in previous chapters, modesty constructs an interactive process whereby status raising comes from others. The peoples' giving of honor is reconstrued as something that *raises* their status rather than lowering it.

Excerpt 11 shows the chieftess instructing the women's head of the section to come up and take the envelope of money and to distribute it to the women community (kousapw) leaders (a section or pwihn is a group of kousapws).

(11) The paramount chieftess, continued

01 **komw**   lih   kaun en pwihn, komw
you(S)[EXAL] woman leader of section you(S)[EXAL]
you, the woman head of the section, you

02 **patohda!**   oh ale oh nehk   ohng
Loc.Verb[HUM].upward and take and distribute to
come up! and take this and distribute it to

03 lih   soumas en kousapw pwihn— kousapw weneu.
woman leader   of community section— community six
the woman leaders of the community of Section—community six

Excerpt 12 is from a speech in which the chief rewards a man's past tributes at honor feasts by bestowing a title on him (this is discussed in more detail later). The chief links honor with rank and hierarchy—the giving of high titles (*lengileng*), lines 03–04. Stratification is linked not only with honor, but with institutionalized history.

(12) The paramount chief

01 eri e sansal me rahnwet kitail ket
so it evident that today   we(P) LocVerb[EXAL]
so it is evident that today we are all involved

02 nan mwekid riau ehu wahu oh ehu lengileng
inside moving two one honor and one high.title
in two activities: one honor and one title giving

03 koarosien kin   ketin   mwahngih lengileng. lengileng
all here   always [EXAL] know[EXAL] high.title   high.title
all of us know about high titles. A high title

04 mehkot   me kesempwal (. . .)
something that important   (. . .)
is something that is important (. . .)

05 e pil sangete ni keilahn   aio.
it also from only at other.side.of yesterday
it also comes from long ago

05 *kitail pil ketin   kadakadaudote*
   we(P) also [EXAL] recalling.past.history.just
   we all are just tracing ancestry/recalling past history

Feasts or contests of honor: How losing is construed as winning

At all Pohnpeian feasts (kamadipw), whether funerals, harvest feasts, honor feasts, or section feasts, participants compete to show the most honor to the chief through prestations of food.[3] Goldman (1970:497) characterizes such competitive exchanges in ranked societies as "honorific exchanges." Skill and prowess in agriculture and animal husbandry (as well as access to imported goods and cash)—that is, economic capital—are converted to "symbolic capital" (Bourdieu 1977) or status, which is appropriated and redistributed by the chief. Honor and prestige accrue to the producers *and* the chiefs and chieftesses.

Competition for prestige at these feasts on Pohnpei is elaborated to the degree that Bascom (1948) referred to them as part of a separate "prestige economy" in his discussion of Pohnpeian commercial and subsistence resources. Bascom (1948) remarked on a categorical separation between food for consumption and food for giving honor to the chiefs and chieftesses: "[N]ot infrequently families go hungry at home when they have large yams in their farms ready for harvest. Only small yams are used at home for subsistence purposes; prize yams are saved for feasts" (212). That prestige foods are categorically not for nourishment but for display resonates well with the nature of prestige and its relationship to distinction and surplus wealth.

In excerpt 13, at a title giving (the same one described earlier), the chief links his giving of a high title to a man's prestations to the chief. The chief's thanks are expressed in the form of a very high title, a sohpeidi title. Luhk (one of the wealthiest business men on the island, known for his generosity) is now sohpeidi, a member of the chief's clan, and entitled to sit in a position similar to chiefs and chieftesses—facing the people. The chief praises the title recipient's (Luhk) hard work (*doadoak inenen laud mehlel*, "working very big truly"). The modifiers "very" (*inenen*), "big" (*laud*), and "truly" (*mehlel*) redundantly praise Luhk's contribution. Luhk's rise in status is directly linked to his previous work, especially his *kanaiehngete*, or caretaking (of the chief), by giving large amounts of goods at feasts. Even though Luhk is already a rich man (*soahngen pai me komw sapwellimanki*, "the type of wealth you have"), he still works for the chief (*komw nahnnantiengete oh lel rahnwet*, "you are trying hard [even] until today"). Throughout, pronominal reference to Luhk is in exaltive form (komw, komwi, owmi), elevating Luhk. The chief uses humiliatives for himself, thus raising Luhk's status above his own. Luhk's work in previous honor feasts and in the present context has resulted in the chief raising him to the highest of statuses. This high position carries with it increased responsibility to show honor to the chief through giving agricultural and other goods, and in thanks Luhk reportedly gave the chief U.S. $1,000.

(13) The paramount chief

01 *ie   ih duwen rahnwet*
   here it about   today
   here is what it is about today

02 *pwihn keiehu kalangan en Luhk.* **omwi**   *doadoak*
   group first   thanks   to Luhk your(S)[EXAL] work
   section one thanks Luhk. your work

03 *inenen laud mehlel. e kanaiehngete*
   very   big   truly   it takes.care.still
   is really very great. it still takes care

04 **komwi**   (*?*) *aio*   **omwi**   *doadoak pwe*
   you(S)[EXAL] (?) yesterday your(S)[EXAL] work   because
   you (?) yesterday your work because

05 *soahngen pai*   *me komw*   **sapwellimanki.**
   type.of   wealth/fortunate that you(S)[EXAL] own[EXAL]
   you are fortunate/wealthy in what you own.

06 **komw**   *kakehr   soupeiwei   iang*
   you(S)[EXAL] can.already face.there.toward.you join
   you can already face there toward you ((take a high-status position spatially)) and

07 **sapwellimatail** *pai.   ah soh* **komw**   *nahnantiengete oh*
   our[EXAL](P)   wealth but no you(S)[EXAL] try.hard.still   and
   join our luck/wealth but no you still keep trying hard

08 *lel   rahnwet. eri i met ni oarolap oh mwotomwot*
   reach today   so I here at summary and short
   until today. so here I summarize briefly

09 *me i men wia ei* **tungoal** *kaping kalangan ohng*
   that I want make my [HUM]   praise thanks   for
   that I want to give my praiseful thanks to

10 *Luhk rahnwet.*
   Luhk today
   Luhk today.

After goods brought as tribute to the chief have been amassed and displayed (sometimes the stack of sakau plants reaches to the roof and hundreds of pigs lie tied to poles in the yard) and each contribution is compared, the goods are redistributed according to rank, the highest-ranking individuals taking the choicest and largest amounts. One shows honor and "wins" prestige therefore by "losing" goods. As Petersen (1986) describes: "A real Pohnpei, I am told, is expected to *luhs laud*, to 'lose big'" (86) at feasts. Depleting ones' personal and familial resources, a positively valued act, increases the resources of the highest-status members of the community, just as in honorific speech diminishing oneself raises the status of others. However, this depletion is interpreted as the reverse in oratory and in the praise that accompanies "superior" acts of self-depletion (as in Luhk's case discussed previously).

Prestige competitions in Pohnpei at first appear counter to local ideologies of the preeminence of birth in determining status as well as prescriptions on modesty, including concealing expertise (see chapter 6) and sanctions against self-promotion. In fact, pressing forward one's claims for renown and personal skill at farming are inherent in prestige competitions and in specific strategies such as withholding one's contribution in order to present it at a dramatic moment in the event. At the same time, those members of the community most likely to have the wealth and power to marshall large amounts of agricultural goods are those whose birth rank entitles them to the choicest lands. Thus an elaborate public system of achievement through skill and an asymmetry constituted around agroforestry and animal husbandry in fact will most certainly reify existing social stratification, and add practical, publicly achieved value to the ideology of rank ascription by birth. Structure (ascribed rank) is in a recursive relation to practice (achieved rank). These are complex events in which pride and vanity are appropriate and approved; what is celebrated and honored is one's prowess in subordination to the chief (i.e., laboring to bring prestations which honor the chief). Prestige contests are in fact honor contests which *appear* to allow structural mobility but in fact reconstitute existing structures of stratification. Pohnpeians sometimes complain about the strain of feasts on their resources and the fact that "the high [titled] people" take the largest share. At the same time, making honor is socially valued and construed as necessary to existence. Both men and women in Pohnpei are active participants in this process.

To read much of the anthropological literature, however, is to observe that honor is generally regarded as the domain of men. Bourdieu (1965), for example, describes honor among the (male) Kabyle as a game of "challenge and riposte"—the acquisition, maintenance, or loss of public honor. Abu-Lughod (1986) in her study of Bedouin culture similarly genders honor as male but claims for women a genderized portion of the honor game with her recharacterization of shame into modesty. Modesty is the "honor of women and the weak" in Bedouin culture (Abu-Lughod 1986:276). In Pohnpei, women are partners with men in coconstructing and socializing honor, because it is clear that as wives, sisters, and mothers, as well as autonomous social actors, they can be effective agents in negotiating honor through language and participating in feasting events. Women have important roles in determining reputation; indeed, this is one of the reasons women's conversational networks and gossip are widely feared. In the Madagascar community studied by Keenan (1974), women discuss "in detail the shameful behavior of others in daily gossip" and "steal honor away from the family" (139). Honor is gained through compliance with acceptable norms of behavior, and can even connote an *exceptional* compliance with institutionalized patterns or ideals (Abou-Zeid 1966). Reliance on consultants' idealizations about honor, however, has overemphasized the male role in constituting honor, although field observations can contradict such idealizations (Wikan 1984; Herzfeld 1987).

In Abu-Lughod's discussion of Bedouin veiling, modesty or what she terms "women's honor" serves as an interactional communication of status. Women, for example, do not veil for men who are of a lower status than their husbands: "[T]he system is flexible, leaving room for women to make judgements about relative status and even to negotiate status" (Abu-Lughod 1986:163). Thus women practice modesty through veiling not to all men, only those of higher status; conversely, attachment of shame is related to failure to observe this hierarchy. By veiling, women subordinate themselves (literally making themselves less visible). In not veiling, they subordinate others. By constructing the appropriate hierarchy, they gain self and other approbation/esteem. It is clear that honor emerges in interaction among and between men and women.

In excerpt 14, the paramount chieftess publicly complains that the women are not receiving a share of the prestige goods (ascribed honor) at a feast. She indicates the role high-status women in Pohnpei can play in negotiating honor and status.

(14)

Chieftess: *lihaka   sohte kak iang*
woman.these not   can join
can't these women join in

kepin   koanoat?
leftovers.of food[EXAL]?
the distribution of the chief's leftovers?

Kepin koanoat are not only high-status remains (as discussed in chapter 4, in this volume) but are gifts of food the paramount chief gives to the people in acknowledgement of their service. The phrase can also refer to "any form of recognition" by the paramount chief (e.g., titles and chiefly consent, as well as settlement of disputes) (Kihleng 1996:155). Paramount chieftesses have the authority to order that certain of these feast foods, particularly pigs, be reserved for distribution by and for women (Kihleng 1996:241). This distribution is called *medehde en lih* ("coconut.leaves.on. which.feast.food.is.distributed of woman").

Pohnpeian consultants as well as most ethnographers report that prestige or honor contests are male oriented; that is, the most attention is given at prestige competitions to products that are gendered male. The most important prestige goods are all agricultural products raised by men: "Yams, pigs, and *sakau* are given the highest statuses in terms of the social value, called 'honor' (*wahu*), in their respective categories" (Shimizu 1987b:132). Ortner (1981) notes: "Simply put, the other-than-gender prestige hierarchies of most societies are, by and large, male games" (19). Yet women have important roles at Pohnpeian prestige events and contribute such items as cloth, sugar cane (certain varieties of which are referred to as female sakau), canned goods, soaps, head wreaths, and perfumed oil with which to anoint title holders. In addition, women compete with each other using yams, pigs, and sakau at women-only exchange events (see Kihleng 1996). Leaving women out of prestige contests overlooks the enormous prestige that accrues to women in many societies from bearing children. Agricultural prowess, the source of male prestige in Pohnpei, is related to manaman and fecundity, just as the main source of women's prestige is fecundity. Women's prestige items in Pohnpei are notable for including imported "convenience" foods, which are symbolically just as "surplus" as the men's yams not grown for consumption. Imported food is pervious to new and innovative symbolic meanings; that is, it is easily categorized as different from traditional sustenance foods, an important factor in prestige competitions. Use of imported convenience foods also facilitates stockpiling in advance, similar to the way men inventory sakau and yam plants with an eye to prestige displays.

Homologies

Looking at Pohnpeian honorific language, it can be seen that grammatically "honor" consists of *both* superordination (status-raising speech is honorific) and subordination (status-lowering speech is honorific). Honor, therefore, is constructed as two different acts, both called honoring. The term "honor" acts metonymically as part for whole, describing both honor and humiliative practices. Calling *both* of these processes honorific (in language) and construing both as honor making creates a homologous relation out of two opposite acts, a practice I believe helps to construct the perception that in honoring others one gains honor.

classification:	HONOR	
practice:	+ honor	- honor (humiliation)

The reciprocally construed nature of honor in status-marked language, in oratory, and in feasting practice helps to organize certain perceptions of subordination or depletion (such as the use of humiliatives in language) as having a significant relation to superordination. In Pohnpeian oratory, strategic linguistic choices by orators use the status-marking feature of the language to reciprocally construct honor for the givers of honor. Orators linguistically elevate the status through language of those who have depleted themselves. Uses of status-elevating language to refer to those of low status, for example, in acts of praise for their honor giving, explicitly connect the ideas of giving honor with receiving honor. Feasting practices similarly build honor out of self-depletion; subordination is interpreted as superordination. Assigning positive affect to self-subordination and depletion or devitalization and reinterpreting subordination as superiority are crucial elements in the practice of honor in Pohnpei.

The fact that honor practices in Pohnpei are essentially made up of subordinating, humiliative and self-depleting behaviors is occluded in language ideology, with a term that is related only to half of a pair of opposite operations, and in rhetoric where the specific behavior of humiliation is valorized through explicit praise and through inverting in language the structural status relation between chief and chieftess and the rest of the society. The "taxonomy" and practice of honor organize interactional behavior (including language and food distribution) so that subordination is perceived as having a homologous relation to superordination. Status depletion and status elevation, or the giving and receiving of honor, are similar in structure and function and construed as contained in the same idea.

194   POWER SHARING

Summary

In this chapter I have shown how humiliative behavior is classified as positively valued and natural (i.e., necessary to life) behavior by both men and women in oratory. In addition, in prestige competitions, losing (depletion) is construed as winning. Individuals are symbolically depleted in honorific humiliative language, and resources are literally depleted in prestige competitions. Assigning positive affect to self-subordination and depletion or devitalization is a crucial element in the success of a hierarchy that depends on the support of lower-status members, who in this case build the hierarchy from below.

Prestige competitions in Pohnpei are important sites in the constitution and negotiation of hierarchy and honor and in publicly ratifying structures of stratification. Prestige competitions or competitive exchanges in ranked societies are important links in the rational organization of hierarchy and honor.

The specific practices called "honorable" (i.e., attached to positive affect values) are of course represented and evaluated differently in different societies as any cross-cultural reading will affirm (cf. Rosaldo 1983). These differences can lead to the conclusion that honor resists exact definition (Herzfeld 1987:15). I propose instead that these differences can lead us into the productive realm of analyzing and comparing, not the abstract idealized concepts of honor and shame but the organization of interactive resources of dominance and subordination.

Notes

1. See, for example, Campbell 1964; Bourdieu 1965, 1990; Peristiany 1966; Peristiany and Pitt-Rivers, 1992; Pitt-Rivers 1966; Davis 1977; Blok 1981; Wikan 1984; Abu-Lughod 1986; Brandes 1987; Gilmore 1987; Herzfeld 1987; Stewart 1994.

2. See Abu-Lughod 1986.

3. For a more complete discussion of Pohnpeian feasts, see Shimizu 1982, 1987b; Kihleng 1996; Petersen 1977, 1982, 1986.

Conclusion

This study has shown how the analysis of sequential interactional data together with ethnography can call into question widely held theories about the nature of social stratification, including women's roles in the constitution of hierarchy. Power relations are often represented as categories of powerful versus powerless, but interactional data reveal an ongoing, active negotiation about power and status relationships among peers as well as among subordinates and superordinates. I have used the phrase "power sharing" to describe the process in Pohnpei by which all members of the community participate in the everyday process of constructing and negotiating social stratification.

The fact that Pohnpeians' use of status-marked forms is not as regularized as native speakers imply or as theories would predict suggests that asymmetries of status may be context specific in ways not revealed by generalized descriptions of a society's social organization. Situational and contextual factors, as well as topic and stance (e.g., confrontational and epistemic), can influence choice of honorific register, and participant identity or role is not always a reliable guide. Further study about which types of interactions are relevant for building hierarchical relations is needed.

I have argued that the conventional notions of power and solidarity are far more interrelated than social theorists have suggested. Interactional data show that an important first step to constructing hierarchy in Pohnpei is constructing solidarity. This suggests that solidarity and hierarchy are not opposites but related in important ways. In Pohnpei and perhaps other areas in the Pacific, a ranked hierarchy can be intimate in ways Westerners do not usually recognize—similar to a family model, where there is a high degree of responsibility and caregiving from high- to low-status individuals and a great deal of affection and valued dependency from lower-status persons to higher-status ones. This dependency, I believe, creates a situation of intimacy rather than social distance. Honorific speech provides an etiquette of power relations that allows agents to share in power and negotiate a status hierarchy. Solidarity indicates shared values, a necessary first step toward constituting a social order, especially in constructing systems of social inequality, such as a hierarchical one in which power is built from below through honorific speech and modesty practices.

The close analysis of status-marked speech also reveals that status hierarchies are constructed in two ways in Pohnpei: (1) as a relation, for example, low status is the converse of high status; and (2) equally important, as separate meaningful domains, for example, high status is not just a different "level" of status but rather is culturally construed as a different meaningful domain. For example, Pohnpeian humiliatives and exaltives are deployed in different ways and are organized structurally (e.g., morphologically and semantically) in different ways. There is a greater reduction in the range of vocabulary items to index those terms that refer to low-status than to those that index high-status individuals and groups (this is also found in other honorific systems), and high-status markers are used invariantly, whereas low-status markers vary according to topic, context, and other pragmatic considerations. High status and low status are not just constituted as polarities but as states with differing degrees of agency and/or causality. Not all semantic domains are status-marked. The important fields for status marking in Pohnpei are body location in space, possession, knowledge, food, and references to speech itself.

As shown in the discussion on honorific possession, moving from common speech (unmarked for status) to honorific speech entails a re-creation of social relations and systems of relations, which are embodied in lived experiences. Looking at how the honorific possessive classifiers organize relationships into different categories shows how experience can be meaningfully and culturally structured through metaphorical and metonymic associations. Analyzing which metaphorical relationships are mapped from the human experiential base to grammar can reveal how microinteractions that index status are linked to cultural ideologies about power and the relationships of chiefs and chieftessses to the people. Honorific possessive classifiers instantiate a relationship between the chief as the land or genitor and the people as the offspring or fruit of the land. A link can be made between shares of power and shares of food; food and rank are connected in many ways on Pohnpei, including through the consumption of sakau.

Information management is linked through language in interaction to issues of status and power sharing in Pohnpei. Sharing knowledge decreases personal power, and information is organized to conserve power. In casual speech this is done through strategies of epistemic uncertainty, as well as by employing a formulaic phrase negating the factivity of what was previously said. In oratory, all speech is framed under the authority and power of the chief. Pohnpeians constitute positioned knowledges, and the source location of knowledge is tied to legitimacy. Metapragmatic verbs of speaking (talking about speech) are status-marked, as well as the verbs "know" and "see."

A reliance on consultants' idealizations about "honor" in anthropological studies has overemphasized the male role in constituting honor. As I have shown, women as well as men participate in honor practices and constitute a discourse about honor. I have argued that honor in Pohnpei organizes positive embodied attitudes about social stratification. Acts of self- and other-subordination are positively valued in oratory and in feasting practices. Part of this practice involves the construction of a homology between getting honor and giving honor, between honor and abasement. In honor and prestige competitions, lower-status participants "win" by "losing," depleting their resources or their status and increasing those of the highest-status members of the community.

Throughout this book I have shown how power relationships indexed in language in interaction can have far-reaching consequences for the constitution, reproduction, and naturalization of asymmetry across events, across space, and across time. I have discussed how status is mapped through language onto the spatial environment. The spatial hierarchy can more finely discern each person's status relationship, so that whereas language primarily differentiates between two statuses, high and low, and children are grouped with titled women and men using the same low-status verb, the spatial map of status can communicate individual distinctions (i.e., that one is higher on the rank hierarchy than another). However, through language a participant's activities can be constituted by different speakers to have two different status levels. This is not possible in spatial arrangements, indicating the importance of language as well as the contestable nature of status in language.

Language is a creative force in the construction of the sociocultural practices of a community. Looking at specific interactions between members of a community can show how social stratification is organized and reorganized through language and how linguistic forms are an essential tool in the collaborative construction of meaningful social relations.

Bibliography

Abou-Zeid, Ahmed. 1966. Honour and Shame among the Bedouins of Egypt. In *Honour and Shame*, ed. John G. Peristiany, pp. 243–259. Chicago: University of Chicago Press.

Abu-Lughod, Lila. 1986. *Veiled Sentiments*. Berkeley: University of California Press.

Agha, Asif. 1993. Grammatical and Indexical Convention in Honorific Discourse. *Journal of Linguistic Anthropology* 3(2):131–63.

————. 1994. Honorification. *Annual Review of Anthropology* 23:277–301.

————. ms. Honorific Register and Systems of Deference in Lhasa Tibetan.

Atkinson, John M., and John Heritage, eds. 1984. *Structures of Social Action*. Cambridge: Cambridge University Press.

Austin, John L. 1962. *How to Do Things with Words*. Oxford: Oxford University Press.

Bakhtin, Mikhail. 1981. *The Dialogic Imagination*. Austin: University of Texas Press.

Bascom, William R. 1948. Ponapean Prestige Economy. *Southwestern Journal of Anthropology* 4:211–21.

————. 1965. Ponape: A Pacific Economy in Transition. *Anthropological Records*, vol. 22. Berkeley: University of California Press.

Bauman, Richard, and Joel Sherzer. 1974. *Explorations in the Ethnography of Speaking*. London: Cambridge University Press.

Bean, Susan. 1978. *Symbolic and Pragmatic Semantics: A Kannada System of Address*. Chicago: University of Chicago Press.

Becker, J. A. 1986. Bossy and Nice Requests: Children's Interpretation and Production. *Merrill Palmer Quarterly* 32:393–413.

Beeman, William O. 1986. *Language, Status, and Power in Iran*. Bloomington, IN: Indiana University Press.

Berlin, Brent, and Paul Kay. 1969. *Basic Color Terms: Their Universality and Evolution*. Berkeley: University of California Press.

Besnier, Niko. 1990. Language and Affect. *Annual Review of Anthropology* 19:419–51.

Blok, Anton. 1981. Rams and Billy-Goats: A Key to the Mediterranean Code of Honor. *Man* (n.s.) 16:427–40.

Bolinger, Dwight. 1965. The Atomization of Meaning. *Language* 41:555–73.

Bonvillain, Nancy. 1997. *Language, Culture, and Communication.* Upper Saddle River, NJ: Prentice-Hall.

Borker, Ruth. 1980. Anthropology. In *Women and Language in Literature and Society,* ed. Sally McConnel-Ginet, Ruth Borker, and Nelly Furman, pp. 26–44. New York: Praeger.

Bott, Elizabeth. 1972. Psychoanalysis and Ceremony. In *Interpretation of Ritual,* ed. J. S. LaFontaine, pp. 121–53. London: Tavistock.

Bourdieu, Pierre. 1965. The Sentiment of Honour in Kabyle Society. In *Honour and Shame,* ed. J. Peristiany, pp. 191–241. Chicago: University of Chicago Press.

———. 1977. *Outline of a Theory of Practice.* Cambridge: Cambridge University Press.

———. 1984. *Distinction: A Social Critique of the Judgment of Taste.* Cambridge, MA: Harvard University Press.

———. 1990. *In Other Words.* Stanford: Stanford University Press.

Brandes, Stanley. 1987. Reflections on Honor and Shame in the Mediterranean. In *Honor and Shame and the Unity of the Mediterranean,* ed. David Gilmore, pp. 121–34. Washington, DC: American Anthropological Association.

Brenneis, Donald L., and Fred R. Myers, eds. 1984. *Dangerous Words: Language and Politics in the Pacific.* New York: New York University Press.

Brison, Karen. 1992. *Just Talk.* Berkeley: University of California Press.

Brown, Penelope, and Stephen Levinson. 1978. *Politeness.* Cambridge: Cambridge University Press.

Brown, Roger, and Albert Gilman. 1960. The Pronouns of Power and Solidarity. In *Style in Language,* ed. Thomas A. Sebeok, pp. 253–76. Cambridge: MIT Press.

Brown, Roger, and M. Ford. 1961. Address in American English. *Journal of Abnormal and Social Psychology* 62:375–85.

Butler, Judith. 1993. *Bodies That Matter: On the Discursive Limits of "Sex."* New York/London: Routledge.

Campbell, John. 1964. *Honour, Family, and Patronage.* Oxford: Oxford University Press.

Cantero, P. Paulino, S. J. ms. Kisin Diksineri en Meing 500, ni Mahsen en Pohnpei.

Christian, F. W. 1899. *The Caroline Islands: Travel in the Sea of Little Islands.* London: Methuen.

Cicourel, Aaron. 1980. Three Models of Discourse Analysis. *Discourse Processes* 3(2): 101–31.

Cole, Michael. 1985. The Zone of Proximal Development: Where Culture and Cognition Create Each Other. In *Culture, Communication, and Cognition: Vygotskian Perspectives,* ed.. James Wertsch, pp. 146–61. Cambridge: Cambridge University Press.

Comrie, Bernard. 1976. Linguistic Politeness Axes: Speaker-Addressee, Speaker-Reference, Speaker-Bystander. *Pragmatics Microfiche,* 1.7, A3–B1.

Conkey, Margaret, and Joan Gero. 1991. *Engendering Archaeology.* Oxford: Basil Blackwell.

Coulter, Jeff. 1986. Affect and Social Context: Emotion Definition as a Social Task. In *The Social Construction of Emotions,* ed. Rom Harre, pp. 121–50. New York: Basil Blackwell.

Craig, Collette. 1986. *Noun Classes and Categorization.* Philadelphia: John Benjamins.

Davis, John. 1977. *People of the Mediterranean.* London: Routledge & Kegan Paul.

———. 1986. The Semantic Role of Noun Classifiers. In *Noun Classes and Categorization,* ed. Collete Craig, pp. 297–308. Philadelphia: John Benjamins.

Dixon, Robert M. W. 1971. A Method of Semantic Description. In *Semantics: An Interdisciplinary Reader in Philosophy, Linguistics, and Psychology,* ed. Danny Steinberg and Leon Jakobovits, pp. 436–71. Cambridge: Cambridge University Press.

Douglas, Bronwen. 1979. Rank, Power and Authority: A Reassessment of Traditional Leadership in South Pacific Societies. *Journal of Pacific History* 14:2–27.

Drew, Paul, and John Heritage. 1993. *Talk at Work*. Cambridge: Cambridge University Press.

Dreyfus, Hubert, and Paul Rabinow. 1983. *Michel Foucault: Beyond Structuralism and Hermeneutics*. Chicago: University of Chicago Press.

Dunn, Cynthia. 1996. Style and Genre in Japanese Women's Discourse (Ph.D. diss., University of Texas, Austin).

Duranti, Alessandro. 1981. Speechmaking and the Organization of Discourse in a Samoan fono. *Journal of the Polynesian Society* 90:357–400.

———. 1988. Intentions, Language and Social Action in a Samoan Context. *Journal of Pragmatics* 12:13–33.

———. 1992. Language in Context and Language as Context: The Samoan Respect Vocabulary. In *Rethinking Context*, ed. Alessandro Duranti and Charles Goodwin, pp. 77–99. Cambridge: Cambridge University Press.

———. 1993. Truth and Intentionality: An Ethnographic Critique. *Cultural Anthropology* 8(2):214–45.

———. 1994. *From Grammar to Politics*. Berkeley: University of California Press.

———. 1997. *Linguistic Anthropology*. Cambridge: Cambridge University Press.

Duranti, Alessandro, and Charles Goodwin. 1992. *Rethinking Context: Language as an Interactive Process*. Cambridge: Cambridge University Press.

Duranti, Alessandro, and Elinor Ochs. 1990. Genitive Constructions and Agency in Samoan Discourse. *Studies in Language* 14-1:1–23.

Earle, Timothy. 1977. A Reappraisal of Redistribution: Complex Hawaiian Chiefdoms. In *Exchange Systems in Prehistory*, ed. Timothy Earle, pp. 213–29. New York: Academic Press.

———. 1987. Chiefdoms in Archaelogical and Ethnohistorical Perspective. *Annual Reviews in Anthropology* 16:279–308.

———. 1991. ed. *Chiefdoms: Power, Economy, and Ideology*. Cambridge: Cambridge University Press.

Errington, J. Joseph. 1988. *Structure and Style in Javanese: A Semiotic View of Linguistic Etiquette*. Philadelphia: University of Pennsylvania Press.

Errington, Shelley. 1990. Recasting Sex, Gender, and Power. In *Power and Difference*, ed. Jane Atkinson and Shelley Errington, pp. 1–58. Stanford, CA: Stanford University Press.

Ervin-Tripp, Susan. 1977. Wait for Me Roller Skate! In *Child Discourse*, ed. Susan Ervin-Tripp and Claudia Mitchell-Kernan, pp. 291–314. New York: Academic Press.

———. ms. The Learning of Social Style Marking and of Honorifics.

Ervin-Tripp, Susan, and Martin O. Lampert. 1992. Gender Differences in the Construction of Humorous Talk. Proceedings of the Berkeley Women and Language Conference, pp. 108–17.

Falgout, Suzanne. 1984. Persons and Knowledge in Ponape (Ph.D. diss. Department of Anthropology, University of Oregon).

Ferguson, Charles A. 1964. Baby Talk in Six Languages. In *The Ethnography of Communication*, [Special Issue], ed. John Gumperz and Dell Hymes. *American Anthropologist* 66:103–14.

———. 1983. Sports Announcer Talk: Syntactic aspects of Register Variation. *Language in Society* 12:153–72.

Fillmore, Charles. 1971. Towards a Theory of Deixis. The PCCLLU Papers (Department of Linguistics, University of Hawaii), pp. 3–4, 219–41.

———. 1975. mimeo. Santa Cruz Lectures on Deixis, 1971. Indiana University Linguistics Club.

Firth, Raymond. 1936. *We the Tikopia*. London: Allen and Unwin.

———. 1939. *Principles of Polynesian Economy*. London: Routledge & Kegan Paul.

———. 1940. The Work of the Gods in Tikopia. London: Percy, Lund, Humphries.

202   *Bibliography*

——. 1970. Postures and Gestures of Respect. In *Echanges et Communications; melanges offerts a Claude Levi-Strauss a l'occasion de son boeme anniversaire*, ed. J. Pouillon and Pierre Maranda, pp. 188–209. Mouton: The Hague

——. 1972. Verbal and Bodily Rituals of Greeting and Parting. In *The Interpretation of Ritual*, ed. J. S. LaFontaine, pp. 59–78. London: Tavistock Press.

Fischer, John. 1969. Honorific Speech and Social Structure: A Comparison of Japanese and Ponapean. *Journal of the Polynesian Society* 78(3):417–22.

——. 1974. The Role of the Traditional Chiefs on Ponape in the American Period. In *Political Development in Micronesia*, ed. D. Hughes and S. Lingenfelter, pp. 166–77.

Fischer, John, with the assistance of Ann M. Fischer. 1957. The Eastern Carolines. *Behavior Science Monographs*. New Haven: HRAF Files.

Fischer, John, Saul Riesenberg, and Marjorie Whiting, eds. and trans. 1977. *The Book of Luelen*. Pacific History Series no. 8. Canberra: Australian National University Press.

Fishman, Pamela. 1982. Interaction: The Work Women Do. In *Language, Gender, and Society*, ed. Barrie Thorne, Cheris Kramarae, and Nancy Henley, pp. 89–101. Rowley, MA: Newbury House.

Foucault, Michel. 1972. *The Archaeology of Knowledge*. New York: Pantheon Books.

——. 1979. *Discipline and Punish: The Birth of the Prison*. Trans. Alan Sheridan. New York: Vintage Press.

——. 1980a. *Power/Knowledge: Selected Interviews and Other Writings 1972–1977*, ed. Colin Gordon. New York: Pantheon Books.

——. 1980b. *The History of Sexuality, Vol. 1: An Introduction*, trans. Robert Hurley. New York: Vintage Books.

Fried, Morton. 1967. *The Evolution of Political Society*. New York: Random House.

Friedman, Jonathan. 1975. Tribes, States and Transformations. In *Marxist Analyses and Social Anthropology*, ed. Maurice Bloch, pp. 161–202. New York: Wiley.

Friedrich, Paul. 1972. Social Context and Semantic Feature: The Russian Pronominal Usage. In *Directions in Sociolinguistics*, ed. John Gumperz, and Dell Hymes, pp. 270–300. New York: Holt, Rinehart and Winston.

Gal, Susan. 1991. Between Speech and Silence. In *Gender at the Crossroads of Knowledge*, ed. M. DiLeonardo, pp. 175–203. Berkeley: University of California Press.

——. 1992. Language, Gender, and Power: An Anthropological View. In Locating Power: Proceedings of the Second Berkeley Women and Language Conference, ed. Kira Hall, Mary Bucholz, and Birch Moonwomon, pp. 153–61.

Garfinkel, Harold. 1967. *Studies in Ethnomethodology*. Englewood Cliffs, NJ: Prentice Hall.

Garvin, Paul, and S. Riesenberg. 1952. Respect Behavior on Ponape: An Ethnolinguistic Study. *American Anthropologist* 54(2):201–20.

Gailey, Christine. 1987. *Kinship to Kingship*. Austin: University of Texas Press.

Geertz, Clifford. 1960. *The Religion of Java*. New York: Free Press.

——. 1973. *The Interpretation of Cultures*. New York: Basic Books.

Geraghty, Paul. 1994. Linguistic Evidence for the Tongan Empire. In *Language Contact and Change in the Austronesian World*, ed. Tom Dutton and Darrell T. Tryon, pp. 233–49. New York: Mouton de Gruyter.

Gerber, Eleanor. 1985. *Rage and Obligation: Samoan Emotion in Conflict*. Berkeley: University of California Press

Gewertz, Deborah, and Frederick Errington. 1991. *Twisted Histories, Altered Contexts*. Cambridge: Cambridge University Press.

Giddens, Anthony. 1984. *The Constitution of Society*. Berkeley: University of California Press.

Gilmore, David, ed. 1987. *Honor and Shame and the Unity of the Mediterranean*. Washington, DC: American Anthropological Association.

Givon, Talmy. 1986. Prototypes: Between Plato and Wittgenstein. In *Noun Classes and Categorization*, ed. Craig Collette, pp. 77–102. Philadelphia: Benjamins.

Goffman, Erving. 1956. The Nature of Deference and Demeanor. *American Anthropologist* 58:473–502.

———. 1964. The Neglected Situation. *American Anthropologist* 66(6):33–36.

———. 1967. *Interaction Ritual: Essays on Face-to-Face Behavior*. Garden City, NY: Doubleday.

———. 1974. *Frame Analysis*. Boston: Northeastern University Press.

Goldman, Irving. 1970. *Ancient Polynesian Society*. Chicago: Chicago University Press.

Goodenough, Ward. 1957. Oceania and the Problem of Controls in the Study of Cultural and Human Evolution. *Journal of the Polynesian Society* 66:146–55.

Goodwin, Charles. 1981. *Conversational Organization: Interaction between Speakers and Hearers*. New York: Academic Press.

Goodwin, Marjorie. 1990. *He-Said-She-Said: Talk as Social Organization among Black Children*. Bloomington: Indiana University Press.

Goody, Esther. 1972. "Greeting," "Begging," and the Presentation of Respect. In *The Interpretation of Ritual*, ed. J. S. LaFontaine, pp. 39–72. London: Tavistock.

———. 1978. Towards a Theory of Questions. In *Questions and Politeness*, ed. Esther Goody, pp. 17–43. Cambridge: Cambridge University Press

Gumperz, John. 1982. *Discourse Strategies*. Cambridge: Cambridge University Press.

Gumperz, John, and Dell Hymes, eds. 1972. *Directions in Sociolinguistics: The Ethnography of Communication*. New York: Basil Blackwell.

Hambruch, Paul. 1936. *Ergebnisse der Sudsee Expedition, 1908–1910*. In *Ponape*, ed. Georg Thilenius, vols. 2, 3.

Hanks, William F. 1990. *Referential Practice*. Chicago: University of Chicago Press.

———. 1996. *Language and Communicative Practices*. Boulder, CO: Westview Press.

Hanlon, David. 1988. *Upon a Stone Altar*. Honolulu: University of Hawaii Press.

Hanson, F. Allan. 1982. Female Pollution in Polynesia. *Journal of the Polynesian Society* 91:335–381.

Harraway, Donna. 1991. *Simians, Cyborgs, and Women*. New York: Routledge.

Harre, Rom, ed. 1986. *The Social Construction of Emotions*. New York: Blackwell.

Harrison, Sheldon P. 1988. A Plausible History for Micronesian Possessive Classifiers. *Oceanic Linguistics* 27(1–2).

Haviland, John. 1978. Guugu-Yimidhir Brother in law Language. *Language in Society* 8:365–93.

———. 1979. How to Talk to Your Brother-in-Law in Guugu Yimidhirr. In *Languages and their Speakers*, ed. Timothy Shopen, pp. 161–240. Cambridge: Winthrop.

Heine, Bernd. 1986. *The Rise of Grammatical Categories, Cognition and Language Change in Africa*. Bloomington, IN: Indiana University Press, African Studies Program.

Heritage, John. 1984. *Garfinkel and Ethnomethodology*. Cambridge: Polity Press.

Herzfeld, Michael. 1987. *Anthropology through the Looking-Glass*. Cambridge: Cambridge University Press.

Hijirada, K., and H-M Sohn. 1986. Cross-Cultural Patterns of Honorifics and Sociolinguistic Sensitivity to Honorific Variables: Evidence from English, Japanese, and Korean. *Papers in Linguistics* 19(3):365–401.

Hill, Jane. 1987. Women's Speech in Modern Mexicano. In *Language, Gender, and Sex in Comparative Perspective*, ed. Susan Philips, Susan Steele, and Christine Tanz, pp. 121–62. Cambridge: Cambridge University Press.

———. 1992. "Today there is no respect": Nostalgia, "Respect" and Oppositional Discourse in Mexicano (Nahuatl) Language Ideology. *Pragmatics* 2(3):263–80.

Hill, Jane, and Hill, Kenneth. 1978. Honorific Usage in Modern Nahuatl. *Language* 54(1): 123–55.

Hill, Jane, and Judith Irvine. 1992. *Responsibility and Evidence in Oral Discourse.* Cambridge: Cambridge University Press.

Holmes, Lowell D. 1967. The Function of Kava in Modern Samoan Culture. In *Ethnopharmacologic Search for Psychoactive Drugs*, ed. D. H. Efron, pp. 107–18. Washington, DC: U.S. Department of Health Education and Welfare.

Hoem, Ingjerd. 1993. Space & Morality in Tokelau. *Pragmatics* 3.2:137–53.

Howard, Alan, and John Kirkpatrick. 1989. Social Organization. In *Developments in Polynesian Ethnology*, ed. Alan Howard and Robert Borofsky, pp. 47–94. Honolulu: University of Hawaii Press.

Hudson, R. A. 1980. *Sociolinguistics.* Cambridge: Cambridge University Press.

Hughes, Daniel. 1982. Continuity of Indigenous Ponapean Social Structure and Stratification. *Oceania* 53:1.

Hwang, J-R. 1990. "Deference" versus "Politeness" in Korean Speech. *International Journal of the Sociology of Language* 82:41–55.

Hymes, Dell. 1962. The Ethnography of Speaking. In *Anthropology and Human Behavior*, ed. T. Gladwin and W. Sturtevant, pp. 15–53. Washington, DC: Anthropological Society of Washington.

———. 1974. *Foundations in Sociolinguistics.* Cambridge: Cambridge University Press.

Ide, Sachiko. 1989. Formal Forms and Discernment: Two Neglected Aspects of Universals of Linguistic Politeness. *Multilingua* 8(2/3):223–48.

Irvine, Judith. 1974. Strategies of Status Manipulation in the Wolof Greeting. In *Explorations in the Ethnography of Speaking*, ed. Richard Bauman and Joel Sherzer, pp. 167–91. Cambridge: Cambridge University Press.

———. 1985. Status and Style in Language. *Annual Review of Anthropology* 14:557–81.

———. 1989. When Talk Isn't Cheap: Language and Political Economy. *American Ethnologist* 16:248–67.

———. 1992. Ideologies of Honorific Language. *Pragmatics* 2(3):251–62.

Ito, Karen. 1985. Affective Bonds: Hawaiian Interrelationships of Self. In *Person, Self and Experience: Exploring Pacific Ethnopsychologies*, ed. White, Geoffrey and John Kirkpatrick, pp. 91–115. Berkeley: University of California Press.

Jefferson, Gail. 1972. Side Sequences. In *Studies in Social Interaction*, ed. David Sudnow, pp. 294–338. New York: Free Press.

———. 1979. A Technique for Inviting Laughter and Its Subsequent Acceptance. In *Everyday Language: Studies in Ethnomethodology*, ed. David Sudnow, pp. 79–96. New York: Irvington.

———. 1987. Exposed and Embedded Corrections. In *Talk and Social Organization*, ed. G. Button and J. Lee, pp. 86–100. Clevedon, England: Multilingual Matters.

Johnson, Alan, and Timothy Earle. 1987. *The Evolution of Human Societies: From Foraging Group to Agrarian State.* Stanford, CA: Stanford University Press.

Johnson, Mark. 1987. *The Body in the Mind: The Bodily Basis of Meaning, Imagination, and Reason.* Chicago: Chicago University Press.

Keeler, Ward. 1984. *Javanese: A Cultural Approach.* Athens, Ohio: Ohio University Press.

Keenan, Elinor Ochs. 1974. Norm-Makers, Norm-Breakers: Uses of Speech by Men and Women in a Malagasy Community. In *Explorations in the Ethnography of Speaking*, ed. Richard Bauman and Joel Sherzer, pp. 125–43. New York: Cambridge University Press.

Keesing, Roger. 1978. *Elota's Story: The Life and Times of a Solomon Islands Big Man.* New York: St. Martin's Press.

Kihleng, Kimberly. 1996. Women in Exchange: Negotiated Relations, Practice, and the Constitution of Female Power in Processes of Cultural Reproduction and Change in Pohnpei, Micronesia (Ph.D. diss., University of Hawaii) (UMI No. 9700526).

Kirch, Patrick V. 1984. *The Evolution of Polynesian Chiefdoms*. Cambridge: Cambridge University Press.

Kirkpatrick, John, and Geoffrey M. White. 1985. Exploring Ethnopsychologies. In *Person, Self, and Experience: Exploring Pacific Ethnopsychologies*, ed. Geoffrey M. White and John Kirkpatrick, pp. 11–23. Berkeley: University of California Press.

Kondo, Dorinne K. 1990. *Crafting Selves: Power, Gender, and Discourses of Identity in a Japanese Workplace*. Chicago: University of Chicago Press.

Labov, William. 1972. *Sociolinguistic Patterns*. Oxford: Basil Blackwell.

Lakoff, George. 1973. Hedges: A Study in Meaning Criteria and the Logic of Fuzzy Concepts. *Journal of Philosophical Logic* 2:458–508.

———. 1987. *Women, Fire, and Dangerous Things*. Chicago: University of Chicago Press.

Lakoff, George, and Mark Johnson. 1980. *Metaphors We Live By*. Chicago: University of Chicago Press.

Lakoff, Robin. 1973a. Language and Women's Place. *Language in Society* 2:45–80.

———. 1973b. The Logic of Politeness; or Minding Your p's and q's. Papers from the Ninth Regional Meeting of the Chicago Linguistic Society, pp. 292–305.

———. 1975. *Language and Women's Place*. New York: Harper Colophon Books.

———. 1977. Women's Language. *Language Style* 10(4):222–47.

Lave, Jean, and Wenger, Etienne. 1989. Situated Learning: Legitimate Peripheral Participation (Report No. IRL 89–0013). Palo Alto, CA: Institute for Research on Learning.

Leech, G. N. 1983. *Principles of Pragmatics*. London: Longman.

Leiber, Michael. 1984. Strange Feast: Negotiating Identity on Ponape. *Journal of the Polynesian Society* 93:25–38.

Levinson, Stephen. 1982. Caste Rank and Verbal Interaction in Western Tamilnadu. In *Caste Ideology and Interaction*, ed. D. McGilvray, pp. 98–203. Cambridge: Cambridge University Press.

———. 1983. *Pragmatics*. Cambridge: Cambridge University Press.

———. 1988. Putting Linguistics on a Proper Footing. In *Erving Goffman: Exploring the Interactional Order*, ed. Paul Drew and Anthony Wootton, pp. 75–84.. Boston: Northeastern University Press.

Levy, Robert. 1984. Emotion, Knowing, and Culture. In *Culture Theory. Essays on Mind, Self, and Emotion*, ed. R. Shweder and R. LeVine, pp. 214–37. Cambridge: Cambridge University Press.

Lindstrom, Lamont. 1981. Big Man: A Short Terminological History. *American Anthropologist* 83:900–903.

Lucy, John. 1992. *Language Diversity and Thought*. Cambridge: Cambridge University Press.

Lukes, Steven. 1974. *Power: A Radical View*. London: Macmillan.

Lutz, Catherine. 1985. Ethnopsychology Compared to What? Explaining Behavior and Consciousness Among the Ifaluk. In *Person, Self and Experience: Exploring Pacific Ethnopsychologies*, ed. Geoffrey White and John Kirkpatrick, pp. 121–145. Berkeley: University of California.

———. 1988. *Unnatural Emotions*. Chicago: University of Chicago Press.

Lyon, M. L., and J. M. Barbalet. 1994. Society's body: Emotion and the "Somatization" of Social Theory. In *Embodiment and Experience: The Existential Ground of Culture And Self*, ed. Thomas Csordas, pp. 48–66. Cambridge: Cambridge University Press

Lyons, John. 1968. *Introduction to Theoretical Linguistics*. Cambridge: Cambridge University Press.

————. 1977. *Semantics I & II*. Cambridge: Cambridge University Press.

Marshall, Mac. 1979. *Weekend Warriors: Alcohol in a Micronesian Culture*. Palo Alto, CA: Mayfield.

Marcus, George. 1984. Three Perspectives on Role Distance in Conversations between Tongan Nobles and Their "People." In *Dangerous Words*, ed. Don Brenneis and Fred Myers, pp. 243–66. Prospect Heights, IL: Waveland Press.

Matsumoto, Y. 1989. Politeness and Conversational Universals—Observations from Japanese. *Multilingua* 8(2/3):207–21

Mauricio, Rufino. 1993. Ideological Bases for Power and Leadership on Pohnpei, Micronesia: Perspectives from Archaeology and Oral History (Ph.D. diss., University of Oregon) (UMI No. 9402036).

McGarry, William, S. J. ms. West from Katau.

Milner, George B. 1961. The Samoan Vocabulary of Respect. *Journal of the Royal Anthropological Institute* 91:296–317.

Modjeska, Nicholas. 1982. Production and Inequality. In *Inequality in New Guinea Highlands Societies*, ed. Andrew Strathern, pp. 50–108. Cambridge: Cambridge University Press.

Moerman, Michael. 1988. *Talking Culture*. Philadelphia: University of Pennsylvania Press.

Moore, Henrietta. 1986. *Space, Text, and Gender*. Cambridge: Cambridge University Press.

————. 1988. *Feminism and Anthropology*. Minneapolis: University of Minnesota Press.

O'Barr, William M., and Bowman K. Atkins. 1980. "Women's Language" or "Powerless Language"? In *Women and Language in Literature and Society*, ed. Sally McConnell-Ginet, Ruth Borker, and Nelly Furman, pp. 93–110. New York: Praeger

Ochs, Elinor. 1979. Transcription as Theory. In *Developmental Pragmatics*, ed. Elinor Ochs and Bambi Schieffelin, pp. 43–72. New York: Academic Press.

————. 1987. The Impact of Stratification and Socialization on Men's and Women's Speech in Western Samoa. In *Language, Gender, and Sex in Comparative Perspective*, ed. Susan Philips, Susan Steele and Christine Tanz, pp. 50–70. Cambridge: Cambridge University Press.

————. 1988. *Culture and Language Development: Language Acquisition and Language Socialization in a Samoan Village*. Cambridge: Cambridge University Press.

————. 1992. Indexing Gender. In *Rethinking Context: Language as an Interactive Process*, ed. Alessandro Duranti and Charles Goodwin, pp. 335–58. Cambridge: Cambridge University Press.

O'Connell, James F. 1972. *A Residence of Eleven Years in New Holland and the Caroline Islands*. Reprint of 1836 editioin, ed. Saul H Riesenberg. Pacific History Series No. 4. Canberra: Australian National University Press.

Oliver, Douglas L. 1951. *The Pacific Islands*. Cambridge: Harvard University Press.

Ortner, Sherry. 1974. Is Female to Male as Nature Is to Culture? In *Woman, Culture, and Society*, ed. Michelle Rosaldo and Louise Lamphere, pp. 67–88. Stanford: Stanford University Press.

————. 1981. Gender and Sexuality in Hierarchical Societies: The Case of Polynesia and Some Comparative Implications. In *Sexual Meanings: The Cultural Construction of Gender and Sexuality*, ed. Sherry Ortner and Harriet Whitehead, pp. 1–27. Cambridge: Cambridge University Press.

Ortner, Sherry, and Harriet Whitehead. 1981. *Sexual Meanings: The Cultural Construction of Gender and Sexuality*. Cambridge: Cambridge University Press.

Pawley, Andrew, and Malcolm Ross. 1993. Austronesian Historical Linguistics and Culture History. *Annual Review of Anthropology* 22:425–59.

Peirce, Charles S. 1940. *Philosophical Writings*, ed. Justice Buchler. New York: Dover.

Peristiany, J. G., ed. 1966. *Honour and Shame: The Values of Mediterranean Society.* Chicago: University of Chicago Press.

Peristiany, J. G., and Julian Pitt-Rivers. 1992. *Honor and Grace in Anthropology.* Cambridge: Cambridge University Press.

Petersen, Glenn. 1977. *Ponapean Agriculture and Economy.* Ann Arbor: Xerox University Microfilms.

———. 1982. *One Man Cannot Rule a Thousand.* Ann Arbor: University of Michigan Press.

———. 1986. Redistribution in a Micronesian Commercial Economy. *Oceania* 57(2):83–98.

———. 1993. Kanengamah and the Politics of Concealment. *American Anthropologist* 95:334– 52.

Philips, Susan. 1980. Sex Differences and Language. *Annual Revew of Anthropology* 9:523–44.

———. 1987. The Interaction of Social and Biological Processes in Women's and Men's Speech. In *Language, Gender, and Sex in Comparative Perspective*, ed. Susan Philips, Susan Steele, and Christine Tanz, pp. 1–14. Cambridge: Cambridge University Press.

Philips, Susan, and Anne Reynolds. 1987. The Interaction of Variable Syntax and Discourse Structure in Women's and Men's Speech. In *Language, Gender, and Sex in Comparative Perspective*, ed. Susan Philips, Susan Steele, and Christine Tanz, pp. 71–94. Cambridge: Cambridge University Press.

Pinsker, Eve. 1997. Traditional Leaders Today in the Federated States of Micronesia. In *Chiefs Today: Traditional Pacific Leadership and the Postcolonial State*, ed. Geoffrey M. White and Lamont Lindstrom, pp. 150–82. Stanford, CA: Stanford University Press.

Pitt-Rivers, Julian. 1966. Honour and Social Status. In *Honour and Shame: The Values of Mediterranean Society*, ed. J. G. Peristiany, pp. 19–77. Chicago: Chicago University Press.

———. 1968. Honor. In *International Encyclopedia of the Social Sciences*, ed. David Sills, vol. 6, pp. 503–11. N.P.: Macmillan, Free Press.

———. 1977. *The Fate of Shechem, or the Politics of Sex: Essays in the Anthropology of the Mediterranean.* Cambridge: Cambridge University Press.

Pomerantz, Anita. 1978. Complement Responses: Notes on the Cooperation of Multiple Constraints. In *Studies in the Organization of Conversational Interaction*, ed. Jim Schenkein, pp. 79–112. New York: Academic Press.

———. 1984. Agreeing and Disagreeing with Assessments: Some Features of Preferred/Dispreferred Turn Shapes. In *Structures of Social Action*, ed. John Atkinson and John Heritage, pp. 57–101. Cambridge: Cambridge University Press.

Quinn, Naomi. 1987. Convergent Evidence for a Cultural Model of American Marriage. In *Cultural Models in Language and Thought*, ed. Naomi Quinn and Dorothy Holland, pp. 173–94. Cambridge: Cambridge University Press.

Reddy, Michael. 1979. The Conduit Metaphor. In *Metaphor and Thought*, ed. A. Ortony, pp. 284–324. Cambridge: Cambridge University Press.

Rehg, Kenneth (with the assistance of Damian Sohl). 1981. *Ponapean Reference Grammar.* Honolulu: University Press of Hawaii.

Rehg, Kenneth L., and Damian G. Sohl. 1979. *Ponapean–English Dictionary.* Honolulu: The University Press of Hawaii.

Rehg, Kenneth L. ms. The Linguistic Evidence for Prehistoric Contact Between Western Polynesia and Pohnpei.

Riesenberg, Saul. 1948. Magic and Medicine on Ponape. Southwestern Journal of Anthropology 4(4):406–29.

———. 1968. *The Native Polity of Ponape.* Smithsonian Contributions to Anthropology, vol. 10. Washington, DC: Smithsonian Institution Press.

Rosaldo, Michelle. 1982. The Things We Do with Words: Illongot Speech Acts and Speech Act Theory in Philosophy. *Language in Society* 11:203–37.

Rosaldo, Michelle Z. 1983. The Shame of Headhunters and the Autonomy of Self. *Ethos* 11(3):135–51.

Rosaldo, Michelle, and Louise Lamphere, eds. 1974. *Women, Culture, and Society.* Stanford: Stanford University Press.

Rosch, Eleanor. 1975. Cognitive Reference Points. *Cognitive Psychology* 7:532–47.

Rumsey, Alan. 1996. The Personification of Social Totalities in Pacific Oratory. Paper delivered at the American Anthropological Association Meetings.

Sacks, Harvey. 1974. An Analysis of a Joke's Telling in Conversation. In *Explorations in the Ethnography of Speaking*, ed. Richard Bauman and Joel Sherzer, pp. 337–53. Cambridge: Cambridge University Press.

Sacks, Harvey, Emanuel Schegloff, and Gail Jefferson. 1974. A Simplest Systematics for the Organization of Turn-Taking for Conversation. *Language* 50:696–735.

Sahlins, Marshal. 1958. *Social Stratification in Polynesia.* Seattle: University of Washington Press.

———. 1963. Poor Man, Rich Man, Big Man, Chief: Political Types in Melanesia and Polynesia. *Comparative Studies in Society and History* 5(3):285–303.

———. 1985. Other Times Other Customs: The Anthropology of History. *American Anthropologist* 85:517–44.

Sapir, Edward. 1929. The Status of Linguistics as a Science. *Language* V:209. Reprinted in D. B. Mandelbaum, ed. 1949. *Selected Works of Edward Sapir in Language, Culture, and Personality*, pp. 160–68. Berkeley: University of California Press.

Schegloff, Emanuel. 1968. Sequencing in Conversational Openings. *American Anthropologist* 70:1075–95.

———. 1984. On Some Questions and Ambiguities in Conversation. In *Structures of Social Action: Studies in Conversation Analysis*, ed. J. M. Atkinson and John Heritage, pp. 28–52. Cambridge: Cambridge University Press.

Schegloff, Emanuel, Gail Jefferson, and Harvey Sacks. 1977. The Preference for Self-Correction in the Organization of Repair in Conversation. *Language* 53:361–82.

Schegloff, Emanuel, and Harvey Sacks. 1973. Opening Up Closings. *Semiotica* 8:289–327.

Schenkein, Jim. 1978. *Studies in the Organization of Conversation Interaction.* New York: Academic Press.

Schieffelin, Bambi. 1990. *The Give and Take of Everyday Life.* Cambridge: Cambridge University Press.

Searle, John. 1969. *Speech Acts.* Cambridge: Cambridge University Press.

Service, Elman. 1962. *Primitive Social Organization.* New York: Random House.

Sherzer, Joel. 1983. *Kuna Ways of Speaking: An Ethnographic Perspective.* Austin, TX: University of Texas Press.

Shibamoto, Janet. 1987. The Womanly Woman: Manipulation of Stereotypical and Non-stereotypical Features of Japanese Female Speech. In *Language, Gender, and Sex in Comparative Perspective*, ed. Susan Philips, Susan Steele, and Christine Tanz, pp. 26–49. Cambridge: Cambridge University Press.

Shimizu, Akitoshi. 1982. Chiefdom and the Spatial Classification of the Life-World: Everyday Life, Subsistence and the Political System on Ponape. In *Islanders and Their Outside World*, ed. M. Aoyagi, pp. 153–215. St. Paul's (Rikkyo) University, Tokyo.

———. 1987a. Chieftainships in Micronesia. *Man and Culture in Oceania* 3 [Special Issue]:239–52.

———. 1987b. Feasting as Socio-Political Process of Chieftainship on Ponape, Eastern Carolines. In *Cultural Uniformity and Diversity in Micronesia*, ed. Iwao Ushijima and Ken-ichi Sudo. Osaka: Senri Ethnological Studies 21, pp. 129–76.

Shore, Bradd. 1989. Mana and Tapu. In *Developments in Polynesian Ethnology*, ed. Alan Howard and R. Borofsky, pp. 137–73. Honolulu: University of Hawaii Press.

Silverstein, Michael. 1981. *The Limits of Awareness*. Working Papers in Sociolinguistics. No. 84. Austin: Southwestern Educational Library.

———. 1987. The Three Faces of "Function": Preliminaries to a Psychology of Language. In *Social and Functional Approaches to Language and Thought*, ed. Maya Hickman, pp. 17–38. New York: Academic Press.

Stewart, Frank. 1994. *Honor*. Chicago: University of Chicago Press.

Strathern, Andrew, ed. 1982. *Inequality in New Guinea Highlands Societies*. Cambridge: Cambridge University Press.

Strathern, Marilyn. 1981. Self-Interest and the Social Good: Some Implications of Hagen Gender Imagery. In *Sexual Meanings: The Cultural Construction of Gender and Sexuality*, ed. Sherri Ortner and Harriet Whitehead, pp. 166–91. Cambridge: Cambridge University Press.

Sweetser, Eve. 1990. *From Etymology to Pragmatics*. Cambridge: Cambridge University Press.

———. 1992. English Metaphors for Language: Motivations, Conventions, and Creativity. *Poetics Today*, pp. 1–15.

Tannen, Deborah. 1990. *You Just Don't Understand*. New York: Ballantine Books.

———. 1994. The Sex-Class-Linked Framing of Talk at Work. In *Cultural Performances*, ed. Mary Bucholtz, A. C. Liang, Laurel Sutton, and Caitlin Hines, pp. 712–88. Berkeley, CA: Berkeley Women and Language Group.

Toren, Christina. 1990. *Making Sense of Hierarchy*. London School of Economics Monographs on Social Anthropology No. 61. London: The Athlone Press.

Trudgill, Peter. 1972. Sex, Covert Prestige, and Linguistic Change in the Urban British English of Norwich. *Language in Society* 1:179–95.

Tsing, Anna, and Silvia Yanagisako. 1983. Feminism and Kinship Theory. *Current Anthropology* 24(4):511–16.

Urban, Greg. 1991. *A Discourse-Centered Approach to Culture*. Austin, TX: University of Texas Press.

Vygotsky, Lev. 1962. *Thought and Language*. Cambridge: MIT Press.

———. 1978. *Mind in Society*. Cambridge, MA: Harvard University Press.

Ward, Martha. 1989. *Nest in the Wind*. Prospects Heights, Illinois: Waveland Press.

Watson-Gegeo, Karen, and Geoffrey M. White. 1990. *Disentangling: Conflict Discourse in Pacific Societies*. Stanford, CA: Stanford University Press.

Weiner, Annette. 1984. From Words to Objects to Magic: "Hard Words" and the Boundaries of Social Interaction. In *Dangerous Words: Language and Politics in the Pacific*, ed. Don Brenneis and Fred Myers, pp. 161–91. New York: New York University Press.

———. 1992. *Inalienable Possessions*. Berkeley: University of California Press.

Wetzel, Patricia. 1993. The Language of Vertical Relationships and Linguistic Analysis. *Multilingua* 12(4):387–406.

White Geoffrey. 1985. Premises and Purposes in a Solomon Islands Ethnopsychology. In *Person, Self and Experience: Exploring Pacific Ethnopsychologies*, ed. Geoffrey White and John Kirkpatrick. Berkeley: University of California Press, pp. 328–66.

White, Geoffrey, and John Kirkpatrick, eds. 1985. *Person, Self and Experience: Exploring Pacific Ethnopsychologies*. Berkeley: University of California Press.

Wikan, Unni. 1984. Shame and Honour: A Contestable Pair. *Man* (n.s.) 19:635–52.

Wilson, William. 1982. *Proto-Polynesian Possessive Marking*. Pacific Linguistics Series B no. 85. Research School of Pacific Studies.

Wittgenstein, Ludwig. 1958. *Philosophical Investigations*. Oxford: Blackwell.

Wolfowitz, Clare. 1991. *Language Style and Social Space*. Chicago: University of Illinois Press.

Zimmerman, Don H., and Candace West. 1975. Sex Roles, Interruptions, and Silences in Conversations. In *Language and Sex: Difference and Dominance*, ed. Barrie Thorne and Nancy Henley, pp. 130–51. Rowley, MA: Newbury House.

Index

Abbreviations, 35
Abu-Lughod, Lila, 178–79, 181, 191–92
Activity theory, 8
Affect, 48
  and honor, 179, 181–84
  and subordination, 193–94
Agency, 3, 9, 12, 41, 86–87
Agha, Asif, 13, 40, 42, 47–48
Argument, 77
Aspect, 30
Austin, John, 7, 15, 33, 44
Australia, 13, 43, 47, 55, 66
Avoidance, 55–56

Bakhtin, Mikhail, 52
Bascom, William, 28, 67, 189
Bean, Susan, 51
Bernart, Luelen, 24
Body posture, 37, 181
Boundaries, 112
Bourdieu, Pierre, 3, 8–9, 12, 34, 178–79,
  189, 191
Brenneis, Donald, 10, 13
Brison, Karen, 157
Brown, Penelope, 40, 41, 50, 87, 121n7
Brown, Roger, 50, 51

Chiefdom, 20–25
Chiefs, 11–12, 19–26, 29, 40, 42, 44, 48–
  50
  and protective spirits, 24
  and status raising, 96
  See also paramount chief; secondary
    chief
Chieftesses, 11–12, 20–26, 29, 85–86
  See also paramount chieftess
Christian ideology, 25, 29–30
Christian, F. W., 89
Clan, 19, 21, 126
  founding, 168
Classfiers, 30–31, 100–121
  differences between common and status-
    marked, 106–7
  semantic relationship with nouns, 103–4
Common speech, 10, 45
  possessive classifiers in, 100–107
Commoners, 11, 22
Comrie, Bernard, 42, 43, 56
Concept of person, 29, 125, 180
Context, 5, 8–9, 14, 43, 56, 58, 65
  and status-marked speech, 195
  recontextualization, 140
Control and non-control, 101, 105

Conversation, 7, 32–33
    analysis, 3, 7, 32–33
Craig, Collette, 102, 105
Culture, 9–10, 15
    and gender, 125–27

Davis, John, 179–80
Deference, 13, 25, 40, 42
Deixis. *See* indexicality
Directives, 55, 64, 127, 133
Discourse, 3
    and power, 127
Distance, social, 50, 61, 65
Dixon, Robert, 47
Dunn, Cynthia, 13, 38
Duranti, Alessandro, 8, 15, 28, 34, 41, 43,
        48, 51, 66, 67, 70, 88, 100, 138, 154,
        156

Earle, Timothy, 20, 22
Eating, 6, 14, 45
    and possession, 116–20
Egalitarianism, 13
Embodiment, 6, 37, 81
    of knowledge 157, 161
Errington, Joseph, 37, 39–41, 48, 49, 100,
        103
Ervin-Tripp, Susan, 40, 131, 141
Ethnography of communication, 3, 8, 32,
        33
Exaltive status-marking, 44, 46, 63, 69
    classifiers in, 118–20
Exchange relations
    of honor 187–88
Exclusive constructions, 5, 83–86

Falgout, Suzanne, 156–57, 177
Feasthouse. *See* nahs
Feasting practices, 6, 11, 120
    feasting and depletion, 193
    feasting and honor, 189–93
Fieldwork, 33–34
    See also methodology
Figi, 88
Firth, Raymond, 20, 22, 25, 28, 67
Fischer, John, 19, 55, 87, 120, 158, 168
Food, 45
    and honorifics, 13
    and possessive classifiers, 196
    high status portions, 192

presentation of, 6
redistribution of, 190
sharing, 12–14
Ford, M., 50
Foucault, Michel, 11–12, 181
Fried, Morton, 22
Friederich, Paul, 181

Gal, Susan, 123, 125, 137
Garfinkel, Harold, 32–33, 44
Garvin, Paul, 21, 43–44, 55, 73
Geertz, Clifford, 9, 37–38, 48
Gender, 3, 6, 10–11, 15, 19
    and conceptions of reality, 137
    and discourse, 123–25
    and hierarchy, 195
    and language, 123, 138
    concepts of, 125–27
    roles in Oceania, 126
Geraghty, Paul, 28
Giddens, Anthony, 9, 153
Gilman, Albert, 50
Goffman, Erving, 25, 32–33, 40, 41, 44,
        50, 77
Goldman, Irving, 189
Goodwin, Marjorie, 124–25
Greetings, 37

Hanks, William, 9, 25, 51
Hanson, Allan, 126
Harrison, Sheldon, 101–2, 111
Haviland, John, 13, 47, 51, 55, 66
Hawaii, 23, 24, 126
Heine, Bernd, 115
Heritage, John, 7–8, 32–33, 36, 47
Herzfeld, Michael, 179, 191, 194
Hierarchy, 12–13, 51
Hill, Jane, 39, 40, 44, 124
Hill, Kenneth, 39, 44
Homology, 6, 178–79, 193
Honor, 6, 11, 15, 178
    and anthropology, 179–80, 191
    feasts, 178
    importance of, 183
    and sentiment, 181–85
    and stratification, 179–80
    and women and men, 191–93, 196–97
Honorific lexicon, 12, 45, 47–49
    nouns, 45, 48, 64
    verbs, 69

Honorifics, 6, 7, 10, 11, 37–68
    classification of, 42–45
    differences in, 196
    domains of, 46
    and politeness, 40–42
    subjects of, 82, 84, 87–88
Hudson, R. A., 39, 50
Humiliation, 6
Humiliative status-marking, 3, 44, 46, 69, 73
Humility, 84

Ide, Sachiko, 40, 41
Inclusive constructions, 5, 31, 68, 83
Indexicality, 9, 10, 42
Information, 13
    conservation of, 156–57, 166
    management and status, 166–73
Irvine, Judith, 37–38, 41–43, 66
Ito, Karen, 180

Javanese, 10, 13, 37–38, 41, 43, 49, 51
Johnson, Alan, 22
Johnson, Mark, 36, 115, 156, 161

Kava. *See* sakau
Keenan, Elinor Ochs, 124, 191
Kirch, Patrick, 19–20, 28, 67, 126
Kirkpatrick, John, 29, 125–26, 180
Knowledge, 11–13, 15, 45
    conservation of, 170
    local ideas of, 155–58, 172
    and power, 11, 196
    theory of, 13
    as a verb, 159

Labov, William, 123
Lakoff, George, 36, 99, 115, 156, 161
Lakoff, Robin, 41, 124
Lamphere, Louise, 10–11
Language
    history of, 18, 19
    socialization, 9
    structures, 30–32
    as a tool, 8–9, 153, 156
Leech, G. N, 41
Leont'ev, A. N., 8
Levinson, Stephen, 9, 10, 13, 40–41, 43, 50–51, 56, 87, 121n7
Loanwords, 32

Luria, A., 8
Lutz, Catherine, 125, 180–1

Mana
    and knowledge, 157
    manaman, 12–14, 23–25, 55, 126
Matrilineality, 11, 19, 21, 23
Matsumoto, Y., 41
Mauricio, Rufino, 20–21, 23, 24–26, 133, 147, 168, 173
Meaning, 8–10
Metacommunication, 13, 45, 156, 177
Metaphor, 3, 12, 47–49, 99–100
    and knowledge, 161–62
    in possessive constructions, 115–20
Methodology, 14, 32–35
Micronesia, 18–20, 28
Milner, George, 55
Modesty, 29, 155–56
Modjeska, Nicholas, 14
Movement, 72
Myers, Fred, 10, 13

Nahs, 14, 23, 25–28, 44, 59, 88–90
Non-verbal, 5–6, 14, 25, 68, 69
Nouns
    honorific 45, 48

Oceania, 14, 18–19, 22, 24
Ochs, Elinor, 9, 34, 48, 70, 100, 123–24, 163
Oral history, 18, 20, 2, 26, 168
    and conservation of knowledge, 158, 167
    and honor, 188
Oratory, 5, 7, 13, 15, 54, 73, 79, 197
    of chiefs, 175
    of chieftesses, 145–53
    and embodied knowledge, 173–76
    of youth, 73–74, 78–79, 85

Paramount chief, 6, 13, 20–25, 28, 45, 70, 131–34
    See also chiefs
Paramount chieftess, 11, 20–25, 128, 132, 145, 192
    See also chieftesses
Passive construction, 87, 120
Petersen, Glenn, 21, 28–29, 59, 67, 157, 190
Philips, Susan, 39, 122, 124

Pitt-Rivers, Julian, 179–81
Politeness, 40–42
Polynesia, 18–20, 28, 39, 126
Polysemy, 47–49
Population, 18
Possessive constructions, 12, 14, 23, 31,
        45–46, 99–121
    in common speech, 100–107
    in exaltive speech, 110–12
    in humiliative speech, 107–10
Power, 3–5, 11–13, 50–52, 61, 195
Power sharing, 6, 12, 177
Pragmatics, 5, 40, 66
Prestige, 15, 123, 150
    competitions, 194
    and feasting, 189, 191
Pronouns, 10, 31, 45, 50–56
Proverbs, 134–5

Quinn, Naomi, 115

Rank structure, 20–22
Reality, role of language in, 153
Register, 10, 41, 55
Rehg, Kenneth, 18, 19, 30, 32, 43, 44, 48,
        73, 75, 102, 105, 110–11, 121n7, 142,
        174
Resistance, 134
Reynolds, Anne, 124
Riesenberg, Saul, 21, 29, 35, 43–44, 51,
        55, 73, 126, 155, 158, 167–68
Rosaldo, Michelle, 8, 10–11, 41, 44, 179,
        194
Rumsey, Alan, 66n

Sahlins, Marshal, 13, 22, 24, 51, 126
Sakau, 14, 20–21, 26, 28–30, 59–63
    and language, 176
Samoa, 19, 24, 28, 38, 42–43, 48, 51, 55,
        70, 88, 124, 138
Schieffelin, Bambi, 124
Searle, John, 7, 15, 33, 44
Seating arrangement, 70
Secondary chief, 91–97
    See also chiefs
Sentiment, 181–85
Shaming, 55, 166–67
Shore, Bradd, 55
Sight and status-marking, 158, 160
Silverstein, Michael, 34, 39, 44, 156

Social action, 7, 8
Sohpeidi, 135
Solidarity, 5, 12, 14, 50–56, 61, 65, 195–96
    and power, 50
Space, 5, 12–14, 23, 25, 45, 69, 87, 89–90
    arrangement of, 127–37
    distribution of, 127, 137
    and language, 90–91, 97, 197
    in Pacific societies, 138
    and possessive constructions, 101
    and rank, 25–28
Speech act, 7–8, 44
Stewart, Frank, 180
Subordination, 6, 179
    attitude toward, 182, 197

Teasing, 141
Terms of address, 6, 38–9, 123
    See also titles
Titles, 14, 21
    and food share, 117
    See also terms of address
Tonga, 48, 126
Topic, 5, 12
Transcription procedures, 34–35
Transitive verbs, 30, 47, 72–73, 77
Tribute, 145
Trudgill, Peter, 123
Truth, 37, 156–67
Tsing, Anna, 122

Urban, Greg, 51

Verbs
    and constitution of spatial hierarchy, 87,
        93–97
    humiliative vs. exaltive, 79–83
    of location and movement, 45–46, 47–
        49, 68–73, 94–97
Vygotsky, Lev, 8, 153, 156

Ward, Martha, 21, 125
Watson-Gegeo, Karen, 10, 23, 29, 156
Weiner, Annette, 24, 157
Wetzel, Patricia, 11, 13
White, Geoffrey, 10, 29, 125, 180
Wittgenstein, Ludwig, 8, 181

Yanagisako, Sylvia, 115